THE SILVER CITY

ION IDRIESS

ETT IMPRINT

Exile Bay

This 12th edition published by ETT Imprint, Exile Bay 2022.

for
Geoffrey Arthur Thompson
who brought his family to Broken Hill
by road

First published by Angus & Robertson Publishers 1956.
Reprinted 1956, 1964, 1966, 1967, 1969, 1973, 1976, 1985.
First electronic edition published by ETT Imprint 2017.
First published by ETT Imprint in 2020. Reprinted 2021.

ISBN 978-1-922384-82-9 (pbk)
ISBN 978-1-922384-83-6 (ebk)

Cover design by Tom Thompson

PREFACE

This book is not a tale of derring-do, of glamour girls, of detectives, or of scowling gunmen. The hero here is a sombre black hill frowning above a wilderness of mulga and saltbush. The heroine is Mother Earth, harsh indeed she is, yet can be exceedingly beautiful at times, moody, too. Hero and heroine dwell west of the Darling, a sunburnt, sombre land. It is of this land, part of our Land, that I 'write, though only as a wanderer peering here and there as through a mirage, so usual to that strange land.

But after all, we are all peering through a mirage, just wandering through life. What have I glimpsed through my short little day? From the candle to the neon light. From the horse to past the sound barrier. From the muzzle-loading gun to, alas, the hydrogen bomb. Far more happily, from the forceps to painless dentistry, from the nearly certain death of typhoid and pneumonia to the mercy of penicillin and the antibiotics. From the packhorse mailman to wireless, radar, television, electronics – such things appear in our "modern" life with comet-like speed, but we only see, hear, know of them as through a mirage. And thus you must read this book, for to portray what that harsh, strange country west of the Darling has given Australia would need hundreds of books from hundreds of writers.

Ion L. Idriess

I ON IDRIESS

'Jack' Idriess was born in 1891 and served in the 5th Light Horse in the First World War. He returned to Australia to write The Desert Column, which was published following his huge success with Prospecting for Gold. He went on to write 56 books and was largely responsible for popularising Australian writing at a time when local publishing was still not considered viable. A small wiry mild-mannered man, Idriess was a wanderer and adventurer, with a vast pride in Australia, past, present and future.

ETT IMPRINT has been publishing Idriess for over 25 years, including:

Flynn of the Inland
The Desert Column
The Red Chief
Nemarluk
Horrie the Wog Dog
Prospecting for Gold
Drums of Mer
Madman's Island
The Yellow Joss
Forty Fathoms Deep
Lasseter's Last Ride
The Cattle King (audio)
Sniping
Shoot to Kill
Guerrilla Tactics
The Wild White Man of Badu
Gold Dust and Ashes
Headhunters of the Coral Sea

AUTHOR'S NOTE

The second last chapter of this book, advocating the flooding of, and control of, the Menindee chain of lakes to produce for Australia "another Mildura", was written long before the present (1956) disastrous floods, of which the Murray River flood alone has been aptly described by the South Australian premier, Mr Playford, as "the flood of a thousand years".

Much of the country written of in this book, a country in which water has so often been proved of far more value than gold, is now a mighty lake; indeed, a great area of the Far West is now an inland sea. As for the "chain of lakes" country, it is now water from Menindee to the Murray and beyond, and in flood-engulfed towns, people are battling in a desperate effort to save their town and homes. In the same way, in two States hundreds of men and women have toiled throughout this long, heart-breaking period of the Great Floods. Even at far away Mannum, the wee township where William Randell launched his *Mary Ann* on her great voyage, flood-waters at this moment (21st August 1956) are swirling through the main street.

The tragedy of this great "flood of a thousand years" has proved that the Menindee lakes scheme is as practical as it is simple. It will be a far greater tragedy, a recurring national tragedy, if we do not learn how to control our river systems and how to make use of this wasted sea. For our continent, in the main, is a dry continent. The dry times will inevitably come again. In many States stock will perish of hunger and thirst where now lie seas of fresh water.

Pause, and, if only for a moment, try to imagine the unimaginable volume of fresh water that has rushed away to sea during these last few years alone. Then imagine the broken hearts that would not break, the homes we should save, the jobs we should keep, the individual and national wealth we should retain – imagine what we could do with that water in drought times.

Flood and irrigation control of our river systems, the conservation, control, and use of flood-waters – these are of far more importance to Australia than the making of many atomic bombs.

21st August 1956

I L. I.

CONTENTS

1. LET'S SEE THIS WORLD!

Three score years ago – it seems but a week or two back – I started out to see the world. There was I, about knee-high to a wallaby, in high adventure toddling along beside a railway line. What kindly fortune impressed on my mind that those definite, never-ending rails must lead somewhere, goodness only knows. For to have walked out otherwise into the Great Unknown could well have meant my becoming an angel – why not? – long before my time. There could have been no loneliness to the innocent adventurer who even then hearkened to the encouraging whispering of the sunlit bush, the gay abandon of the birds, the haunting breath delicately wind-borne from mountain, creek, and valley. These have proved siren voices to less fortunate adventurers. Timber and shrubbery then came right up to the back yards of the little mountain township of Tenterfield. Now those humble homes, those dark, low-built stores have grown into a prosperous town, the forest vanished to the open, grassy paddocks of developed closer settlement.

I must have kept on keeping on, according to stern accounts by old hands in later years, oblivious of a frantic mother and father away behind, of police and black-trackers, of saddling up of horses, townspeople organizing, messengers hurrying out to stations and outside mining camps. Alack-a-day, I've never stirred up such interest since.

They found me quite a few miles down the line, the sun fast going down. I must by then have been feeling awed by the gathering quietness, uneasily lonely among the lengthening shadows. I'm sure the black crows were there. And thus ended my first serious walkabout.

That railway line, reaching Tenterfield only about five years previously, led all the way back to Sydney, nearly five hundred miles away. Strange that wandering footsteps have ever led me back through the succeeding years. In the days of that walkabout the hansom cab was the fashionable means of transport in the capital cities. Many a maid received her first kiss, so I've heard whispered, even her breathless proposal, sheltered by the discreetly closed doors of the good old "jig-jog, jig-jog" cab – "After the Ball was O-ver"! I doubt whether our rip-snorting taxies are as dangerous today. Back in those days, too, many a sailing ship came to what has swiftly developed into one of the greatest cities of the world.

What is our Destiny to be, that our little nation has developed so mightily since the days of the hansom cab? It seems only yesterday that I rode in one, in about my second pair of long pants, entrusted to escort a sweet young thing home from the ball. It was about three months before I was game to ask her for a kiss. An hour or two is often enough these days. Time flies.

About five years before I trudged away on that first walkabout one of our greatest Australians, Sir Henry Parkes, had made his clarion call for Federation, to unite each separated, sparsely populated, struggling colony into the one Commonwealth of Australia, united in one, one for all. He made his speech in a grimy little hall, so the Ancestor tells me, before a "few score bushies" in little Tenterfield township away up in the windswept New England hills. He must have seen the Vision Splendid.

Tenterfield has "growed up" since then. Where was once a dusty road with a drover jogging along in his weather-beaten turn-out stretches a main highway with Juggernauts speeding to and from cities and busy towns. But still I can remember the screech of the mountain parrot, the mothers pegging the washing out on the line, the horsemen riding down by the gully, and "gold at Drake".

However, presently I was on the move again. Dad luckily got a job at Lismore – jobs were scarce in those days. He loaded the bulkiest of our few possessions on a bullock-wagon going to the Lawrence for stores and set off to secure his new job, making the rough trip down the rivers in a heavily loaded sulky.

How often I've watched the bullocks toiling where now a glimmer of steel and nickel roars by. The Ancestor tells me it was just after the big bank smashes that we made Lismore, in nice time to be marooned by the Big Flood of the day. Big things were really doing in the world in those days. The Ancestor insists that they were still talking about the world-shaking news of Stanley reaching the White Nile – some years after the event – and in awed tones discussing the fearsome doings of Jack the Ripper. Sheep had only recently been brought into the Lismore district; the local paper referred to them as "interesting animals". But indignant letters now and then hit the headlines about "those wretched sheep" grazing on the Lismore-Casino road, causing horses to "shy and bolt with their riders on Her Majesty's highroads" – nice goings-on indeed! There was a notorious bull loose, too, "terrifying the roads", "threatening" passing sulkies to the danger of women and children, "sticking up" pedestrian-ladies also! Dear, dear me! That bull must have had the time of his life. I wonder if some of the local bad boys had purposely turned the menace loose?

A through coach to Murwillumbah via Brunswick Heads had just started running, to a riotous flourish of trumpets. In this dashing era commercial travellers could now reach the Tweed and be back in a week. That was travel for you! Things were beginning to move with a vengeance, little wonder that young bloods like me felt impelled to move and see the world. When recently I remarked to the Ancestor that we could do that Tweed trip today by car in something over a couple of hours in comfort, in minutes by plane if need be, he merely snorted, "Yes, and not see one mile of the country! And probably break your necks into the bargain!"

But then I suppose other Ancestors in other times have snorted similarly to their progeny. It must have been a breath-taking day in the Prehistoric Era when the first adventurer, all tensed up to do or die, leapt upon some animal and found himself, clinging for grim life, travelling at breakneck speed. Oh, what a thrill! Who was the first horseman in the world? However such is progress.

There were no cars in the days of my childhood, and only bush roads, often unbridged, between the little townships. The population of all the continent was a bare three million. Many of us know the Lismore of today, a modern young city, one of the brightest and most prosperous in New South Wales. Fine streets, excellent shops, impressive cars in massed array on the busier days, the centre of a well-cleared, fabulously rich dairying and mixed-farming district.

Well, in my day of only yesteryear it was a struggling little township, sometimes with the household water-tank nearly dry; sturdily holding its own after the really mighty struggles of its pioneer mums and dads. My memories are of a dusty main street, little low-built shops, mostly gloomy inside, shirt-sleeved townsmen, demure matrons in bonnets and long, quaint dresses, shopping baskets over their arm. Bullock-wagons creaking along, probably loaded with giant logs, slouch-hatted, brown-armed horsemen in open-necked shirts, belts, and moleskins, the flash ones wearing polished leggings and long spurs that jingled as they dismounted and strode into the pub for a "quencher". Sinewy timber-cutters would be there, too – and sometimes, if you stood near these men, you could actually smell their environment, the faint, cloying scent of freshly cut timber. For they worked in and truly cut out the heart of the Big Scrub, that magnificent jungle forest, untouched since the dawn of time, that now saturated these surgeons with its spilt juices and saps, its scented chips and sawdust, the life-blood of countless trees. Noisy raft-men moved amongst the townsfolk, too, on a market day, and bearded selectors, tough cane-cutters in the cane season, an occasional mounted trooper, and strolling blackfellows with their gins, piccaninnies, and dogs. The sulkies and buggies, of course, the springcarts and drays. But we saw these busy happenings only on an occasional Saturday morning when we jogged along in the sulky "to town".

A quiet day in Woodlark Street, Lismore, 1890.

There were big fish in the river, too. Often Mum and I caught one for breakfast, the dew all fresh on the grass. It was a great day when I'd see a little steamer coming up river, or a schooner slowly gliding along. Our house was about three miles out of town, built up on a rise overlooking the not always peaceful Richmond. A little house indeed, but it seemed the world to me with its magic castle, those little attic windows right up on top. I used to climb up there and watch away down river those wonderful watermen with their long poles so surely jumping from log to log as they fastened each to its place in the raft, just like the long-legged little birds hopping from leaf to leaf right across the water-lily leaves. I used to watch the big deep punts, too, as they came slowly in to the bank to load cane during the season and, above all, I could see the goings-on away in the blacks' camp; What a thrill at night when old Topsy would come raging out of town from the lock-up! So soon as the shouts and shrieks came ringing through the night I'd scamper up to the attic window and watch the whirling firesticks as Topsy fought the camp

All around us was the dense wall of the Big Scrub, as yet only partly cleared in patches. Alas, I used to thrill to the echoes of the axes biting into that mighty forest, day after day, month after month to the shuddering crashes as giants came toppling over to bring smaller trees crumpling in their man-made paths of destruction. It was at eventide that the greatest crashes came thundering, a tornado of falling trees. Similarly, years later on the Atherton Tableland in North Queensland, I watched the clearing of the wonderful scrub lands there. Men would toil all day for "the run" pick three giants as "key" trees to bring down hundreds, estimate the way they could be made to fall, partly cut a deep scarf into them from that direction, then scarf lesser trees. In both jungles it was an inextricable tangle of vegetation, mazes of lawyer-cane creeping along the earth to climb far up and entangle the branches, lianas like huge cables looping from tree to tree. Towards sunset the men would cut into the largest giant opposite the first scarf, with great skill and wariness, for a miscalculation, a mischance, a change of wind could sway the trees to a fall in the wrong direction which could and at times did mean a terrible death amongst that crashing maelstrom of timber. At the last moment they would jump down and run for it. High up, invisible in that canopy of branches, the giant's million leaves were trembling, shivering. Imperceptibly that mighty crown was slowly, so slowly moving over, softly moaning. Faster now, faster. Then came a rapidly increasing sighing, a violent swishing, then she was coming as lianas high up tautened and throbbed like hawser ropes when a furious tide sways a steamer out from the wharf. Other tops were bending now under tug of lianas and pressure of branches, then with a shuddering screech the mighty weight was coming over, bending with it the other two giants with an increasing roar as they brought the lesser timber with them in a writhing mass of splintering, shrieking trees, frantically swaying branches tossing skyward, broken limbs and trunks all coming thundering to earth with rumbling echoes far through the scrub. In a good "run", perhaps a full acre of densely growing timber would be brought crashing thus in one fall. All food for the firestick.

For years it went on, all along the northern rivers, all along that magnificent coast right to the Queensland border. In later years I've often wondered how many millions of magnificent timber we felled thus and sent up in smoke. But it was only the cedar and pine and a very few other varieties that were valued in those days. All the rest had to go so that the settlers could plant their sugarcane, and later grass to be turned into the milk and butter and other farm products that have built those fine towns.

It was the beginning of the end for the entrancing bird life that helped to make a fairyland of my earlier childhood days. I can still hear the calls of the secretive birds that lived only in the cool, gloomy depths of the Big Scrub and inevitably vanished as their home vanished. The whip-bird's was just like the muffled crack of a bullocky's whip somewhere in the timber, and I can still see the flashing colours of the rifle-bird, the satin bower-bird of many beauties, and many other lovely ones that were lost with the ruin of their scrub.

As a toddler I attended the little school at Boorie Creek, and memory here is partly indebted to an old-timer, S. M. Garrard of Lismore, who has previously "caned my ankles" for several slips of memory. The tiny school was then but recently built at Boorie Creek, dense scrub towering all around. Teacher, kindly lady, used to come jogging along the road in a sulky drawn by a cunning old pony to collect the toddlers from the scattered farms. Each of us was only the size of one and threepence, but when we were packed in like sardines the old pony insisted on plodding laboriously along as if he were hauling a loaded bullock-wagon.

School-teachers in those days in the bush districts had to be battlers ready for all manner of emergencies. And our teacher was no exception. Numerous snakes used to come crawling in from the scrub to attend school, to the glory of the elder boys who would swagger as heroes whenever they found and killed a "big black 'un"! Arrived at school, Teacher used to unload her precious cargo, depositing us toddlers in safety in the clearing, with strict instructions not to move. Then, arming herself with a waddy, she grimly prepared to clear the school. The elder boys would be gleefully waiting, boastfully swinging their sticks. They would scout all around the school, then crawl underneath it, poking their sticks into the dark places, then finally tramp inside and make sure the place was clear of wrigglers before we toddlers were allowed inside. The Ancestor intrudes here, removes that awful old pipe from the weather-beaten visage, and proceeds to write my book.

"If you're scribbling about the days when you were knee-high to a bandicoot," he kindly remarks, "put in a word for those battling school-teachers. That one that had all you young bushrangers to put up with was a fine young woman. I can see her now tramping around the cutting armed with her waddy, determined to do or die, her little company cautiously toddling behind. There were lots like her away out in the lonely bush places doing great work. There came times when they had to put up with floods, bushfires, falling trees, bolting horses, accidents, and occasionally sulky blacks. Their job quite often called for courage and gumption at a moment's notice. You can't say too much about those lonely teachers in their tiny schools."

"Yes, Dad," I meekly replied.

Reflectively he raises a gnarled paw to scratch where hair once grew.

"Do you remember the church meeting at the little school," he chuckles, "the time the Sky Pilot came out to civilize us?"

"Can't say I do, Dad."

Schooner and raft at Lismore in the early nineties.

The family turn-out on a wedding morn in the early nineties, Tenterfield

"Lord bless my soul!" he growls disgustedly. "What memories you young fellows have! Why, I remember the very number of wrigglers they killed! It was nine, three were big black crawlers. Don't you remember the congregation coming from all up and down river by buggy and sulky and horseback, with the goggle-eyed blackfellows and their gins at the scrub edge yabbering and laughing and criticizing the show? Don't you remember the bonnets and furbelows those women wore? How frightened they were to show more than their ankles when stepping down from the buggies – with the goggle-eyed boys from the bush watching for one to slip? Don't you remember the bravos killing the nine wrigglers before the congregation could tramp into school for Church? The girls giggling and shamming to cling together as the young fellows rooted out the wrigglers, and the shrieks when that big young timber-cutter threw the carpet snake in among them?"

"I can't quite place the incident, Dad."

"Lord bless my soul!" And the Ancestor disgustedly paws the pate again. "Don't you remember them trying to sing hymns with the blacks all crowded at the door – those black heathen shrieking with laughter as the whites they knew so well tried to sing – it did sound a mournful caterwauling! Don't you remember when one of the elders wrathfully ordered them away and old Topsy turned on him and abused him and just about brought the roof down? She knew *too* much!"

"I'm not letting out any secrets in my book, Dad," I replied gently. "I'm too young."

The Ancestor gazed at me reflectively, obviously thinking he could say a lot.

As the Big Scrub fell all along those northern rivers and was burnt off the land was being planted with sugar-cane – which meant a livening up in the district during each cane-cutting season when strange, sturdy men seemed to be roaming everywhere. Those were cheery days, for the strangers always had a passing joke for the little boy sitting on a log on the hill slope watching their swinging cane-knives hour after hour.

Perhaps I dreamt of the time when I, too, would be cutting cane along the Clarence and far away in North Queensland. Which is why, perhaps, in those years to come whenever I saw a small boy gazing at us as we toiled I'd always wave to him.

The men used to load the cane upon the wooden sledges, and how the horses used to strain as they hauled the heavy load down the slope to the river! Here the big punts were moored, a long plank running out from the bank to the punt gunwale. Enormous loads those men used to carry on their shoulders; their straining arms could just meet round the load as they hurried at a Chinee jog-trot out along that swaying plank over the water to the punt to heave the load down off their shoulder. I'd watch breathless, expecting a man to slip and fall overboard with each load. Such a splash when it *did* happen! But the thrill came seldom.

The punts used to nose into the oddest corners of river and creek. Then, bowed deep in the water under their great loads of cane, slowly they would be towed downstream to Broadwater Mill.

That was the period of development before the dairying and mixed farming that has made the river districts so prosperous. First the early pioneers and the cedar, then the pine and sugarcane, then the cane, mixed farming, and dairying period.

From the slush lamp to the candle, the candle to the hurricane lamp, the lamp to that fabulous gaslight, from gas to electricity. From the tent, then the slab hut, to the weatherboard house, to the pretty modern bungalow, from the travelling hawker to the huge modern emporium. How our country has developed from the packhorse of yesterday!

Seven years ago the last full-blooded aboriginal in the Lismore district died there in her sleep, at ninety years. What amazing changes she had seen in *her* time! A woman, as was the last of the Tasmanian blacks. Thus with the primitives as with us it seems to be the gentler sex who last the longest. Oft times they need a big heart to carry on, anyway.

I just remember that when I was a toddler there were still quite a number of the "old folk" in the district. At the bottom of our paddock dwelt a rather notable camp of them, on the junction of Boorie and Leycester creeks. Well-known "old folk", these were. The boss of them all was the redoubtable Topsy, a born fighter with a reputation all along the river. Topsy was only a handful, but when full of rum – especially river-brewed – she was a fighting fury of claws and teeth. Sometimes she "got fresh" in town and put on a show to the delight of the townsfolk and exasperation of the local police. When Topsy was in form it took a couple of hefty young policemen all their time to lumber her, she could screech and claw and kick and bite like a wildcat. Just to show her contempt of civilization she would throw off her one and only garment in the main street as with a howling tirade she defied all and sundry.

Topsy was blessed with a very quiet, hard-working aboriginal husband, Charlie Brown. He was a good carpenter, a tradesman, rare indeed among aborigines in those days. When Topsy was cooling her heels in the lock-up Charlie would trudge into town and bail her out for five bob. Topsy in outraged triumph, with her thin chest puffed out, would then stride regally down the main street and back to the camp where she would order all and sundry to wait on her. But at length

Charlie grew sick and tired of constantly bailing her out, called it a day, and allowed her to languish in durance vile – which by no means cooled Topsy's temper.

On such occasions when they let her out she couldn't run back to the camp fast enough. Mother used to lock, bar, and bolt all the doors and windows if Dad was away; in our lonely little home she was terrified of the blacks. Topsy would come bolting into camp, seize a fighting waddy and hammer into Charlie like a mad thing. In an instant the whole camp would be in an uproar – yelling men, shrieking women, wailing children, howling dogs.

In the morning the gins from the creek would watch Dad drive away to town. Then, headed by Topsy, they would come prowling up to the little house and browbeat poor Mum until she handed them nearly all the tucker in the kitchen. Mum was terrified they might kidnap precious me, and later that sweet little sister.

Topsy had a famous nephew named Monty. This proud prodigy possessed an extraordinary mouth, armed with a perfect double set of teeth. Needless to say the sophisticated Monty commercialized this heaven-sent addition to his anatomy. Anyone who wished to view it had to pop sixpence into the capacious jaws to coax them to yawn open for examination. To gaze into those grinning jaws was to stare into the mouth of a human shark. Like the last woman of his tribe Monty lived to a ripe old age. One of the very last of the full-blooded men, he went to the Happy Hunting Grounds several years before Topsy.

But it is the Big Scrub, the mighty logs and the rafts that hold memory most. The straining teams hauling those great logs from somewhere deep within the labyrinths of the Big Scrub, the crack of the whip, the teamster's shouts drawing ever nearer, louder, until the swaying necks of the leaders appear from the scrub edge. Then the long haul down the cleared slope past our little house right down to the river's bank. Then the manoeuvring, the casting off of the team, the skids sloping from the wagon top down towards the bank, the levering, the poling of the great log from the wagon down to and over the bank, and the mighty splash.

Red cedar, that most wonderful of all woods, was still being won here and there, but the hungry years of the axe had almost eaten it out. The vast majority of logs were of magnificent pine; I can still see those truly beautiful logs, hundreds of years of time must have been absorbed in their growing. Of all the untold wealth of wonderful timbers in the Big Scrub just there practically all that was saved was cedar and pine. I used to watch great rafts of it slowly floating downstream. I remember often listening breathlessly to talk of "cedar pirates", but perhaps in my time when there was a little trouble on the river it would be with the pine. There was often talk of fights amongst rival gangs, particularly of one great fight that was discussed all along the river for weeks. The rafts got mixed up or broke away in a fresh; some swore the ropes were deliberately broken. The fights of rival gangs often enlivened the river.

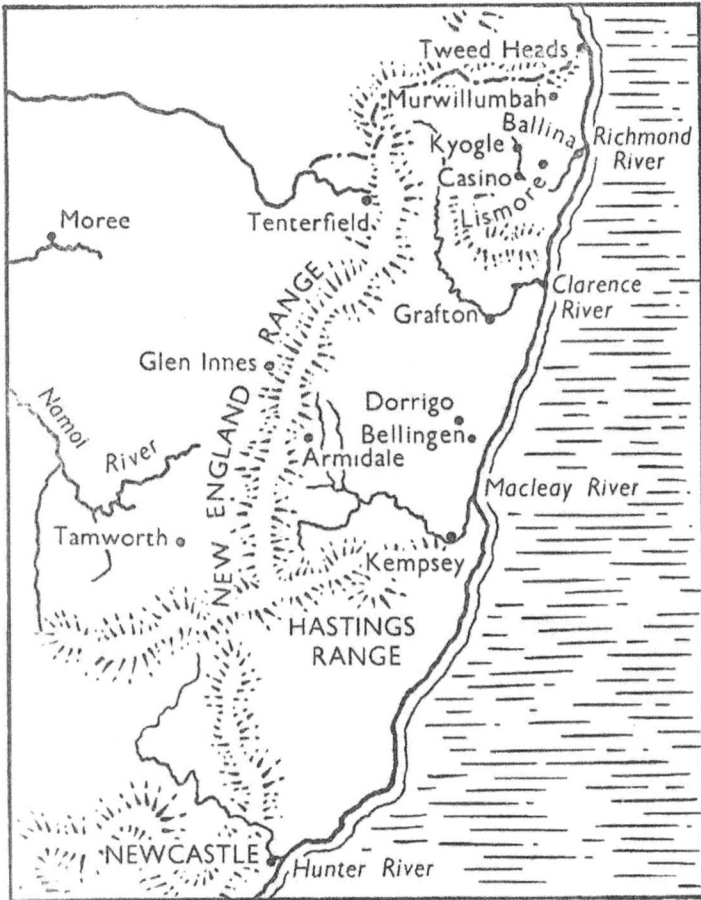

MAP 1. Part of the North Coast of New South Wales

2. THE GREAT TRIP

Dad's job, throughout life, involved considerable travelling. Six months of the year he was away on "outside" jobs, visits to isolated mining camps, backblocks townships, lonely selections, timber camps – from whichever centre he was stationed he was constantly travelling to out-of-the-way corners of "back o' beyond". And just before the family left Lismore he took me on my first big walkabout – a never-forgotten thrill for me, and a tearful occasion for poor Mum, who was certain her angel son would be "killed by the blacks", "drowned while crossing those terrible rivers", "burnt to death in a bushfire", "killed under a falling tree", "bitten by a poisonous snake", "lost in the terrible scrub", "poisoned through eating wild fruit", "killed by a bolting horse", "shot dead by an accidental gunshot", "gored by a wild bull", "crushed under a timber-wagon", "poisoned by ticks" (once I was, and have not forgotten it even after all these years) and fall a victim to all the other menaces she felt sure were lurking in the Great Bush for her wonder child.

Poor Mum! How little she knew, as all the world then little knew, of a war waiting in the womb of Time, a war such as humanity never even imagined, the war to end wars! And Mum's little angel survived four years of it, in the front line, too, when not in the casualty ward.

"The Devil looks after his own!" as the Ancestor casually remarked.

However, on one still-remembered morning we set off in the sulky, loaded, to the old pony's disgust, with tent and swags, well-filled tucker-box, billycan, quart-pot, pannikins, and all the changes of dry clothes, boots, blankets, Goanna salve, Painkiller, salts, liniments, ointments, and bandages that tearful Mum insisted must be taken, so sure was she her darling son would need them. The Ancestor in latter years chuckled over that bulky burden to our load. Cunning old dog, he meekly roped those bundles on. We'd only gone a few miles beyond Lismore when he gave practically the lot to a selector's wife.

"If you tell Mum when we get back home," he cautioned me amiably as we drove off, "I'll skin you alive! And use your skin for bait for a fish."

Thus we started on the wonder trip – a very small trip in these times, from Lismore to Tweed Heads along macadamized highways at fifty and sixty miles an hour, but very different in those days of the horse and bush roads and timber-cutters' tracks. Thirty miles a day was good going. In those times large areas of Big Scrub were still standing, only a very few years before it had stretched from the Richmond River right to the

Queensland border. Now there were many clearings, particularly along the Richmond and Clarence and Tweed. The settlers were busy planting sugar-cane or grasses in those places cleared, the grasses already beginning to turn areas of the country into the wonderful dairying lands to be. Slowly they were building up herds. Jogging along day by day, I would gaze at the men toiling at burning-off. These were the numerous scattered places cut out of the Big Scrub, the land not yet cleared, the timber felled but not yet burnt off. In such places was the newly erected hut of slabs split by axe, maul, and wedge, then trimmed by the adze of the selector, with a roof of sheets of seasoned bark or shingles. The clearing of this farm-to-be was a mass of fallen timber, great piles of trees toppled over one another in inextricable confusion. It seemed impossible that it could ever be burnt off. But a little farther on we would jog past a clearing with smoke from some scores of fires rising lazily. Here the lopped branches had nearly all been burnt in great bonfires, the mighty trunks slowly burning, great piles of charcoal and ashes littering acres of ground. The selector, very often with his wife helping, would be carrying big armfuls of branches to stack round other logs and start other fires. Slowly, surely, each year seeing yet a little more done, the scrub would be felled and burnt off, and the ground planted.

In the first clearing, still among the half-burnt logs, the selector's wife, swinging a hoe, would be planting corn and pumpkins to help keep the pot boiling. The youngsters would be doing their bit, too, of course, the elder boys and girls serious at their work, already having learnt that to eat they must grow things.

I can remember corn being planted amongst the half-burnt logs with the aid of a pointed stick. The woman, and youngsters, too, would jab the stick into the ground, press upon and wiggle it a bit, bend and drop a grain of corn into the hole, then stamp it "shut" with the foot, move on, and jab the stick down again. Long, hard toil, bringing pumpkins and corn, sorghum, melons for jam and eating, and the muzzle-loading gun adding wild duck, scrub turkey, wallaby, bandicoot, parrot pie, cockatoo, and galah to the menu, have helped start many and many an Australian selection.

Even after all these years when I travel past a waving field of corn in some beautifully cultivated paddock memory flashes back to that other corn sturdily growing amongst the burnt-out logs and stumps, to the cornflour bread and cakes, the delicious smell, the taste to a hungry boy of the russet golden grains of a freshly roasted young corn-cob, and of that cob, boiled, too, or freshly pulled, eaten raw, the young grains juicily tender and sweet. I can see the selectors' wives now – Mum, too –

grinding the corn into flour. Yes, cornflour bread, roast bandicoot, and boiled pumpkin – many and many a man and woman have toiled hard on such fare. It would not be until years later, when such a selection had developed and grown a few fruit-trees, that a mother could give luxury living to her ever-growing family – rhubarb pie and dumplings, preserved quinces from the quince-tree down by the tank, and on Sundays melon or jam tart, with home-made jams from the fig- and plum-trees. A selection was well developed indeed, and years and years of toil by man and woman had gone into it, when it could show corned beef with cabbage and carrots, and perhaps a pasty for Sunday's dinner, with dried apple and pear from the apple box in the storeroom.

Occasionally, as the pony jogged along, the sharp screech of a cross-cut saw would whine through the timber. Dad would pull into the bush track to have a yarn with and get direction from the sawyers. And didn't such toilers appreciate a yarn with a stranger! Especially hard work was pit-sawing, a method by which two men, using skill, elbow grease, and the long double-handled cross-cut saw could saw a big log into numerous boards and planks of handy length, width, and thickness. Selectors and farmers in out-of-the-way districts used such boards for their houses as they got on their feet. The nearer to the scattered little towns the more board houses, while the towns themselves, of course, were built of board, iron, and stone. It is difficult these days to realize what it meant to a woman, the luxury of a board house after the little slab hut.

At those times when we jogged along through open bush country my eyes were ever searching the roadside trees for birds' nests. And some parts of the roadside seemed alive with the unattainable prizes that I had no time to climb for. Alas, the boys of my day were fiends on bird's-egg collecting. Birds in bewildering variety made happy that sunlit bushland, the matey kinds in screeching, whirring flocks. There was lovely timber throughout these forest areas also and, like the scrub, they were going under to the axe and firestick. The time would eventually come when I should see open grasslands and gaunt cemeteries of dead trees where these heavily forested lands had been.

One evening we were camped on a creek with the old pony grazing near by. Away across on a flat a misty light appeared, vanished, appeared again, vanished, then rose up and glided away, only to "sit down" again. Soon it rose up, vanished yet again. In the evening silence that elusive glow fascinated me. It was not the twinkle of a campfire but a dim, steady glow that floated about and vanished and also settled on the ground by itself.

"What do you think it is?" murmured Dad.

"I don't know," I whispered, doubly awed now by the loneliness of the bush.

"It is only a cocky ringbarking by the light of a hurricane lamp," chuckled Dad. "Many of the poor devils work night and day. They have to, until they get their little selection going."

I knew then, of course, for as a young fiend with a tomahawk I had already ringbarked trees. As that settler walked round the tree the light would be blotted out, then appear again. He would "ring" those trees within radius of the light, then pick up the lamp and walk to other trees, and as he did so I would see the light floating knee-high amongst the timber. That nocturnal toiler, with steady swiftness, was walking round tree after tree, with light blows of the axe wrenching down the bark a few inches all round it, which would mean the death of the tree in a year or so. There was no sound of axe, not only because of distance but because the knack of ringbarking is to save strength, only light blows into the bark being necessary. This, with many other things, I was to learn in the years swiftly coming when I, too, would be ringbarking from just after sunrise to sunset at what was then a he-man's wage – of £1 a week.

But the nocturnal worker was carving out his own living from the good earth that also can be a taskmaster, hewing his own home from the virgin bush, now in company with the owls, the mournful curlew, the now wide-awake possum, and the snuffling, inquisitive bandicoot.

How many millions and millions of trees have been ringbarked to die! Then later Nature would send a violent windstorm and down would fall thousands of dead trees, at last ready for the firestick. Except for trees still standing, and stumps, that ground would then be ready for the planting of grass or crops. That was how it went in theory, but in practice it took years of laborious work. A hot summer would be chosen, making the timber dry and hot, then a warm wind awaited. Under such conditions a swift running fire disposed of the bulk of the fallen timber. But always there were left many half-burnt logs, practically all the stumps, countless half-burnt limbs and branches. Week by week these branches would be stacked against the logs and stumps and gradually burnt off when hot weather and wind were favourable. Such burning-off went on day and night under favourable conditions. It could take years to clear off a large paddock. The labour involved both for man and wife in thus taking up virgin bush and developing a selection would today certainly be called slavery. Up before dawn, wearily plodding back to the hut at sundown to eat what tucker there was, then the whole family tumbling into their bunks dead beat, asleep even before the possums could climb the bark roof.

Yes, when visiting the fine big country towns today and admiring the cars of the young fellows in town from the beautifully developed farms and stations I often wonder if the cheery young bloods realize how desperately hard their grandfathers and grandmothers, their fathers and mothers toiled.

Now and then, while plodding along some bush track that had been developed into a "road" from a bullock-wagon track, the Ancestor would pull up for a yarn with a cocky or his shy, bare-footed son driving three or four packhorses loaded with kegs, probably with a bulging old corn-sack hooked on each side also. From holes cut in the bag protruded heads of agitated fowls, on the way to market at some little township. There was home-churned butter in those kegs, generally churned out by the sweat of the selector's wife, and the few shillings received for it would mean a great deal to the family. The horses were trudging the dreamy miles through the bush to ship the kegs to Sydney from the nearest little port. I was deeply interested in those occasional packhorses, their loading and saddlery, their quiet, steady-eyed drivers. Strange that years and years later I had so much to do with far larger packhorse and mule teams two thousand miles to the extreme north, two thousand miles and more to the north-west!

Even butter-making was very hard work in those days, harnessed with anxiety, too, should the weather turn warm or thundery. I remember Mum used to "settle" the milk in a large flat dish in the coolest part of the house, with a wet cloth over it to keep down the temperature. Very anxious was she in the morning to see whether her precious milk had separated. She'd skim the cream off, then whip it into butter in a small dish with a big spoon. The final stage was always exhausting work.

Most of the settlers who were going in for dairying then made or bought "modern" cream separators, turning a wheel by hand, and the Ancestor tells me that the little towns had steam separators to which the nearby dairymen carted their milk. These steam separators were the forerunner of the magnificent creameries of the big, prosperous coastal and river towns of today, to which trains and big lorries pull in with their great loads of milk. And yet it is not so long since the packhorses with their kegs of home-made butter were ambling through the bush to ship their humble wealth to Sydney.

Day after day we meandered through forest lands, ever and anon coming to a patch of the Big Scrub, which folk of other lands would call jungle. Up towards Kyogle we were well into the Big Scrub again, the sulky creeping along wagon tracks walled in by the great trees, often with the regal staghorns and elkhorns growing high up on the towering trunks among bowers of bird's-nest ferns. The staghorns were prized by many a little home "in town", to grow upon their front-veranda posts. Just occasionally we would glimpse a pretty orchid high on a beech-tree among climbing clematis; the few orchids seemed to favour the beech-tree. Giant vines and creepers often twined and twisted into massive living ropes reaching far up into the branches that blotted out the sun. Here there was no sign of sky except at midday, showing far up there amongst the topmost branches directly above the track as a creek of delicate blue high overhead. While here below, just a few feet in amongst those mighty trunks that always whispered of life to me, was cool gloom and a brooding silence that seemed the breath of countless living trees domed by their impenetrable foliage. Here and there a saw-pit yawned beside a gigantic cedar stump, long flitches of sapwood lying about where early cedar-cutters had cast them aside from the saw. Only by walking through part of the Big Scrub could one realize the grandeur of such a maze of tree life. I used to wonder how those men had first found their way in the gloom, how they had cut a track through the apparently impenetrable undergrowth, then got their bullock-wagons up here and back across a hundred creeks, densely wooded, then, heavily loaded, right away down to the coast. No feed for bullocks in the Scrub, either; impossible for grass to grow amongst this vast mat of roots, each single one struggling for food for its tree. But such a job was all in the day's work to those pioneer bullockies. Numbers of them were pathfinders on a heroic scale. For instance, even in the district, I wonder how many folk know that Sandy McLennan and Alex Freeman opened up the bullock-wagon track in carting wool from the Armidale tableland to Grafton on the Clarence, to be shipped to Sydney. The trip used to take six months. Next time you are spinning down that well-graded, macadamized mountain road at sixty miles an hour try to visualize what those mountains were like in the days of their timbered forests and jungle, their unbridged creeks and absence of habitation. Many an Australian road today has thus first been carved out by bullocky pathfinders.

What a fascinatingly strange story is Life, the story of all things living! A small boy here, listening to, gazing at the life of this mighty Scrub, in parts already fallen to the axe and firestick, a boy in the loneliness here fascinated by the life in trees as he has been ever since, how could he know that in the staggering years to come, in a great World War, far across the seas, he would handle a rifle the stock of which had come from these very trees! For most of the rifle stocks for the British Army came from patches of this Scrub which survived, so doubtless Australian rifle stocks came from these timbers also. A lot of the timber used in bombers and aeroplanes in the Second World War came from the remnants of these scrubs, too. So that not only Australian men and horses, but Australian timbers have given their lives in these wretched wars.

However, in those days flying-machines and poison gas and wars to end wars were only visions in the minds of inventors and dreamers. It was in these scrubs that again I gazed upon the giant fig whose weirdness of enormous buttresses and maze of twisted aerial roots never ceased to interest me, as indeed they did years later in the jungles of North Queensland. How cruel it was, I thought, as Dad explained that a tiny fig seed dropped by a little bird could fall upon a lovely tree and feast upon its life-blood sap and grow and strengthen into downward clutching arms like the choking tentacles of an octopus, gripping tighter and tighter as they stretched round and down the body of the tree, arms ever multiplying, ever gathering strength, squeezing and growing as they slowly choked, gradually smothered the victim until at last only a shell of its trunk remained. Then this pathetic skeleton finally vanished into the now mighty bulk of the triumphant fig.

Occasionally Dad would pull up the always willing old pony and murmur, "Hearken!"

From somewhere within the scrub would sound the sharp, biting rasp of a cross-cut saw. We'd listen awhile, then Dad would pull in towards the sound and enjoy the usual yarn.

On one occasion we heard the sound and he mildly inquired, "Shall we go and have a yarn with the sawyers?"

"Yes," I replied in secret delight.

The Ancestor stepped down from the sulky and hitched the rein to a handy sapling, remarking, "Jump down – you're jolly slow for a young fellow."

"You go in and find him first." I nodded solemnly towards the trees.

He gazed at me a moment, scratching the first bald spot on the pate. Again came the rasp of the cross-cut saw.

"Don't you want to have a yarn with the man?"

"When you find him," I answered mildly.

The Ancestor unhitched the rein, climbed into the sulky, slapped the rein across the pony's back.

"Gee up, you lazy rascal!" he commanded. "And as for you, young feller-me-lad, next time you pull my leg you'll have another think coming!"

I laughed, the gloating, triumphant laugh of boyhood. For I knew the lovely, so secretive, so very clever lyre-bird. Many a time I had listened for him, tried to creep up on him, caught a glimpse of his beautiful tail as he sped through the gloom in the scrub facing our home – how terrified Mum would have been had she known I wandered in there! To me, the entrancing lyre-bird was the world's perfect mimic; many a time until I caught him out had he deceived me with the mew mew of my very own kitten. And he could wonderfully imitate the call of other birds, could imitate Mum rattling the forks and spoons also. Wherever the edge of the Scrub came down against a homestead the local lyre-birds there would imitate numerous sounds coming from house or yard. Dad might trick me lots of times, but he could not catch me out with a lyre-bird.

With lurch and roll over the slippery stones, we were crossing a tinkling creek before he next remarked, "H'm! I see you're growing mighty smart. Oh well, you've got to live and learn. And now I think we'll pull into that bullocky's camp for dinner", as through the trees came the distinct crack of a whip.

"How about it?" inquired the Ancestor.

"If you can find him," I answered mildly, but couldn't help grinning again.

"Oh, I see," grumbled the Ancestor. "So you know the whip-bird, too! Very well, smarty, we'll boil the billy by this creek."

Towards sunset that same afternoon the old pony was thinking it high time we looked out for a camp when we heard the tinkle of a bell.

"And now," quoth the Ancestor through his pipe, "I suppose you'd say that was *not* a bell!"

"Neither it is," I replied. "It's a bell-bird."

"H'm! Well, that's quite enough for today." He pulled the pony's willing head towards a green sward by a sparkle of water, an ideal camping place.

A Tenterfield threshing party in the nineties

3. WHERE THE BULLOCKS TOILED

When Dad had business at some timber camp deep in under the ranges I would gaze at the axemen so methodically swinging their axes, two together, swing for swing cutting the first scarf in a giant pine, so sure-footed upon their flimsy staging, probably ten feet above ground. Even in the gloom of the scrub how those blades used to flash, their cruel, biting song ringing so sharp and clear! Solemn-eyed I'd watch the straining bullocks hauling the great logs from somewhere deep within the tangled mazes of the foothills along the narrow lane cut through the dense timber to some distant forest place where rutted wheel-tracks would be called "the road". How patient those bullocks, their necks bowed under their heavy wooden yokes, how clever, too, particularly the leaders and polers, all answering every command of the alert-eyed, whiskered bullocky as casually he walked beside the team, long-handled whip over shoulder, the greenhide lash snaking along the ground yards behind him. To me, that handle seemed long as a fishing rod, the whip half as long as the team. It was just wonderful what he could do with that vicious whip, either by way of coax, threat, warning or deadly earnest. When the going was good he would drive all day with just an occasional call, occasional lazy crack of whip, occasional prod of whip-handle to a "Gee off, Baldy!" Probably Baldy is a bit of a rogue, liable to pole on his mates; should he think the teamster's eye is not for the moment upon him he won't pull, he merely walks along allowing the rest of the team to do his share. And just don't they know it! I was sure the poor dumb beasts used to resent a loafer amongst them, when added to their labour they felt the load drag and had to strain yet more into the yoke to take the weight their loafing mate was dodging! I firmly believed they were glad when they saw the long whip swing up with its lash unerringly descending upon the shirking one.

There was a rogue or two in every team, as there are among humans. But the bullocky knew every trick and way of every bullock, as well as its willingness and pulling capacity. That team was invariably his jealous pride. Thus, with an eye on the loafers, he kept them up to their job. A good driver could make a team of eighteen pull evenly from leaders to polers. He had to, for good team-work was essential. It was a picture to watch a bullocky and team with loaded wagon negotiating a hairpin bend, a fall of hundreds of feet beside one side of the wagon, a mountain-side rearing straight up beside the load on the other, team and wagon having to "turn on a threepenny bit" or go down in a plunging disaster of rolling wagon, writhing bullocks, and crashing trees. Or to see the wagon being brought out of the depths of the jungle between the walls of trees towering up within inches of the load. Or, out in the open forest, watch a heavily loaded team negotiating some Break-neck Hill, or laboriously but so surely winding in and out as they climbed up to negotiate some Devil's Gap, or with inches to spare safely creeping round some Devil's Elbow.

At times, in much later years, when watching a captain bringing his ship to a tricky wharf against wind, tide, and current, I've had a "flash-back" of a team negotiating an outback Devil's Elbow or Hellfire Gap of the old bullocky days.

Yes, when the wagon was easily rolling along, the blue-shirted bullocky in his moleskins walked casually along beside his team, long-handled whip over shoulder, with a "Whoa there, Roger! Gee orf there, Rocket!" to the leaders who swung to or away to the order. He would walk along the team with an occasional prod of the whip-handle to the ribs, each individual bullock answering to its own name and work in the team. His spotted heeler, tongue lolling out, came alertly along behind him, while behind the creaking wagon, loosely hitched there by a long rope, strolled his riding horse as if it couldn't care less. The old horse's job was to help muster the feeding team in the dewy hour of dawn. The spotted heeler earned his keep in heeling any rogue that sought to dodge the muster. Such a beast never had a hope. Like a blue streak the heeler would be after him; no matter how he twisted and turned, wheeled and horned at his tormentor that dog would wheel him and bring him plunging back to his mates, his green eye on him right back to the wagon, still watching him as the yoking-up for the day's toil began. The bullocky would calmly fasten on each heavy yoke, each pair of bullocks knowing exactly their place in the team, but my eyes were for the cunning dog that knew for a certainty which bullock was again edging to break away before it could be yoked up, knew how it would attempt the dash, and when. Marvellous the slithering swiftness with which the lean blue body shot after the breakaway, breath-taking how in a split second it had frozen to the ground as the frenzied hooves lashed out an inch over its head. A split second later and its red-hot teeth were at the bullock's "heel" again and the beast came bounding back in horn-tossing fury to his mates.

It seemed to me that each time, with devilish malignity, that spotted heeler would allow the bullock to break away, then be after him, exulting that he was now allowed to show his skill in wheeling and bringing back this half-ton of enraged flesh and muscle by those torturing snaps at the heel – surely the lumbering beast's Achilles heel.

The spotted heeler knew each one of those bullocks and everything about their little ways. The bullocks knew all about this sneaky, invincible enemy; I'm sure they watched him with hatred burning behind their patient eyes. The old horse knew the bullocks, too; the bullocky knew all of them, bullocks, dog, and horse. And they all knew him.

And they all knew the wagon, too. For though it was not a living thing it was with them always and always must be considered, for it affected every one of them, as did each differing load and track. Should it be a new wagon all would know immediately. For though wagons, like humans, are made on the same lines, yet each individual one is different, and produces differing reactions from those who come in contact with it.

Many a bullocky would give a "fancy" name to his favourites, such as "Dandy", "Bluebell", "Duke", and so on, according to some fancied resemblance in appearance or character. "Nelson", for instance, was a great favourite. The Ancestor used to chuckle over a yarn of his about a disillusioned teamster on the Casino side, whose wagon was hopelessly bogged despite all his skill, entreaties, whip, then expressively lurid language. At the height of his oratory a travelling parson came riding along and finally remonstrated.

'I'm sure such awful language will not help you – you should put your trust in Providence."

"Providence be damned!" roared the bullocky. "He's the worst bloody bullick in the team!"

To see a team start off was of intense interest to me; it seemed that the big wagon, anchored by its huge, ponderous logs, could never take the road, especially in soft soil; those few bullocks of flesh and blood and bone could never move that wooden mass. The bullocky would walk to the head of his team, face them, then with both hands to the whip-handle take it from his shoulder and slowly begin to swing it round and round high above him until the long greenhide lash was fairly whistling. Taking a deep breath, he would roar, "Come, Roger! Come, Strawberry! Nigger! Nugget! Roany! Bob! Baldy! Nelson! Tarpot! Pull, you sons of guns! Pull! *Gee-up!*" and the great whip would come down, cracking like a pistol shot, the bullocks would strain up into their heavy wooden yokes and keep straining as the chain tautened, shivered, jerked back then tautened again, a protesting creak from the wagon as every bullock strained more forward, then the whip cracked again and as the bullocks stepped out the huge wheels slowly moved to a groaning from the chained logs.

Brave, patient old bullocks. I used to gaze at those big liquid eyes, those poor dumb eyes, keenly feeling they wished so much to say something, as I've felt many a time since. The work those teams and drivers used to accomplish in winning logs from apparently inaccessible places were often little epics of foresight, ingenuity, skill, and patience of man and animal. Difficult to realize today that many an Australian road, and railway-line too, has originally followed the rut of the bullock-wagon.

I've lived through the last days of the horse and bullock, the camel, mule and donkey. Except where trains came slowly creeping out here and there all the transport work, the station work, the mail work, the timber work, the travelling work – except by sea – of the coming young nation was done by those animals. A mighty part, a great debt we owe them in the opening up of the continent. And in fighting for it, too. All bushmen, myself included, are sorry indeed to see them going – gone. Sorry, and yet glad. For the poor dumb brutes could not tell us of the untold pain and distress they so often suffered. Whenever now on my travels I see a bogged lorry I also see a phantom team, horses and bullocks, straining, plunging, breaking their hearts there at times at an impossible task under the whip. In a flash it is gone, and I am glad – glad the phantom teams have gone and that it is only a nerveless lorry there bogged in the mud.

During that first great trip, which may have sown the seed of years of wandering, to jog along a "road" to a town was an eagerly looked-for event. And each was different. One might be built on a Mitchell-grass plain, another by a river, another "just around the bend", another in a valley among the hills, another fresh-hewn from the living bush away up in the mountains. One might be a timber township with the bullock-teams and big logs, hum of the saw, crack of whip, pungent odour of sawdust. Another might be a mining township with fresh dumps and poppet heads and windlasses silhouetted on the skyline or "running along the gully", with holes everywhere, sunburnt men like ants swinging pick and shovel, tents and bark huts lining creek and gully and hillside. Yet another township on the river was a little port, with logs and farming produce being loaded from the river bank on to schooner or little steamer bound for hungry Sydney, with horse- and bullock-wagons pulling out of town loaded with supplies brought by those boats from Sydney for the district. Thus each town was different, and the activities there – the little shops and important post office and police station, and possibly the bank, to be gazed upon from outside with awe, the townsmen in their elastic-sides, the nabobs flaunting heavy gold watch-chain with dangling fob, sure to be wearing a large signet ring, the ringleted women peeping from shawl, or from under little dark bonnet with saucy feather, just a glance from dreamy eyes that saw so much – all this busy life, and the springcarts and wagons, a travel-stained shanghai, a dozen packhorses loaded with sugarcane going to a river or distant mill, the buggies and horsemen and other men's dogs, were of never-ending interest to a young adventurer on his first big walkabout.

Perhaps because I passed through there recently I remember the sunlit afternoon we jogged into Brunswick Heads. Sunlit, for I was all excitement to see that oft-discussed wonder – the sea! And its might was all sparkling under the sun, little curly wave-tops were toppling towards shore in the whitest of wriggling foam. And, joy of joys, a little steamer was anchored outside the bar and no less than *two* schooners! Men were rafting out from shore big cedar logs to the vessels; fascinated I gazed from a headland as the little figures away out there worked at hauling each big log aboard by winch.

The Ancestor swears he could not drag me away from that wonderful scene until sunset. He left me up there again, still watching, next morning while he went about his business. And I was up there again next day and watched the schooners sail – unforgettable sight – breaking sail, the white wings creeping up the masts; faintly I could hear the shouts, the rattle of gear, then the sails filled and they were away to Sydney Town, sunlight gleaming on their snow-white wings of romance.

How very, very different is prosperous Brunswick Heads of today! The former wild bushlands of its back country are now well-cleared farmlands – yes, right away back to Kyogle, though there are still patches of the Big Scrub there, to show Nature at its magnificent wildest. In those days men thought they would never clear the Big Scrub.

As we jogged north along the bush road leading out from Brunswick Dad promised me that in a day or two we'd be camping in a pretty little place called Murwillumbah. He thought maybe it was a blackfellow name. He thought, too, that Murwillumbah might someday grow into a town because it had such a good back country, but of course it was mostly all wild bush now. Still, it might grow up into a big town even in my time.

I thought of the Ancestor's prophecy a few months ago when I visited Murwillumbah. What a wonderful town now, with its rich, well-developed back country! I climbed a hill, and gazed out over lovely Murwillumbah, seeking to bring back the memory of that first big never-forgotten trip. Easy to understand how the young folk of the developed Australian districts of today utterly fail to comprehend the same districts of but yesteryear – of Grandad's day. What a miracle of development of a great continent so few have accomplished in such a few short years!

But the little old pony was jogging along a rutty bush road amongst the hills and dales leading to Tweed Heads. Another new town to see, another adventure, the boy all eyes as leisurely we jogged along into the north.

In later years that same boy was to go ever farther, much farther north, until, far away, he stood on Peak Point with his feet in the sea, standing on the extreme northernmost point in all Australia, gazing out towards Possession Island, where a Captain James Cook landed but the yesteryear before last and took possession, in the name of His Majesty King George, of the whole of the eastern seaboard of Australia. Less than two centuries, not a breath in Time. If Captain James Cook could but see his Australia now!

However, Tweed Heads was the end of this great walkabout. Dad told me that this was "the border". Across this Tweed River here was the Queensland border. He could not cross the border. When he had finished his business here he must turn back. Mum would be waiting, away back in the little home by the Richmond near Lismore.

"That is, if she's survived your absence all this long time," he chuckled.

I felt hostile to this border. I could but vaguely understand it, that it was some barrier forbidding us to pass farther. Mentally I decided that when I "growed up", then somehow or other I'd cross that border and travel right on into that mysterious Queensland.

The birds were calling sweetly all the long way back.

4. FROM THE TALL TIMBER TO THE SALTBUSH

Schooldays ended at Broken Hill, after some years at Tamworth. Happy years, even though old Nosey Bob, the school-teacher, with that big cane of his held us youngsters in awe. We liked him, though, and he was more kindly than we knew. Tamworth, with its wonderful back country, has grown into a young city, its modern shops and offices, fine streets and comfortable homes a marvel of development since the nights when our mums used to light the kerosene lamps in the little weatherboard homes, occasionally on muggy nights having to "shoo" out the moths and beetles with a towel, and maybe letting out a screech at a whopping big tarantula creeping up the bed curtains, his shadow gruesomely magnified by the lamplight. How Mum, and many another mum, used to shiver and gasp at such monstrosities, which brought cries of delight from the kids. Modern mums miss such a lot of fun – from the kids' point of view – what with fine mesh doors and windows, glassed-in verandas, electric lights, and all manner of modern gadgets. I could never imagine a snake under a washing machine in a modern home, but time and again I've seen Mum sprawling in a most undignified position with neck stretched to the ground, grasping a long stick and desperately jabbing at a wriggler that hissed back at her from under the wash-tub. In most country towns in those days the bush and bush things used to come right down to the outskirts of the town, quite often into the homes. In several homes we've lived in the possums and bandicoots and jackasses and sleepy old carpet snakes seemed to think they owned the place. I don't know what the poor beggars do now, with the bush in many places cleared so bare that even a diamond sparrow cannot find a place to roost.

At Tamworth we would often hear at night the wail of the curlew away down on the rich river flats. Alas, erosion has practically filled that river with sand now. By day, instead of the rattling movement of buggies and sulkies and carts along Peel Street, with wonderful horse-teams pulling in to the flour-mill to exchange wheat for flour, a drover's turn-out plodding along across the Common, horsemen in shirt-sleeves, moleskins and leggings – some would certainly be from Goonoo Goonoo – jogging along the dusty road towards town, there is now a vista of growing suburbs, lively bus services, a stream of sleek motor-cars and massive lorries heavily laden. The youngsters scoot along in their own brightly painted "cars", on scooters and on bikes over well-laid-out footpaths where we trundled our baby sisters in our home-made billy-carts along dusty roads or, with axles greased by sneaking Mum's prized dripping, held races at our peril down timbered hill slopes. The hills where we hunted wallabies right at the back of the town are now quite bare; Oxley's Look-out is a favourite tourist look-out, as is the Moonbi Look-out. The swagman is a shadow of the past, while young Lochinvar hums along to town at sixty – who said more? – miles an hour, garbed right royally. Gone is the spotted bandana handkerchief knotted carelessly yet so carefully round the sunburnt neck, gone are the tight-fitting, spotless moleskins, the polished leggings, the shiny, tinkling spurs. He still wears the old bush smile, though. And these days, especially if he's just received his wool or wheat cheque, he brings a roll a wallaby couldn't hop over.

Wide, modern streets, brilliantly lit shops at night, pretty homes bright with electric light. It was at Tamworth that I first saw that wonder, electric light, where before all "big" country towns were lit with gas. But few places had the light on as yet, the power station had only recently been opened, the first I believe to be erected in a country town.

Yes, prosperity in town, way up over the Moonbi Ranges, prosperity far and wide. A car flashes past at seventy with the radio going, aeroplanes speed through the sky where the eaglehawk once reigned supreme. And all in the few short years since old Nosey Bob gave me that "sixer" on that icy winter's morning! How proud I was that I held out the hand and took it and did not flinch, then walked sullenly back to the form with a hand that felt numb as a red-hot brick! But to puny individuals, as to nations, time marches on.

What a change was "the Hill" from the Richmond and the Big Scrub of the North Coast, the meandering rivers, luxurious plains and rolling mountains of New England! The mining town far in the western inland was then a place of deadening isolation. The climate, though good for most of the year, brought breathless summer with frequent dust-storms, occasionally raging violently for several days at a time. There was an acute lack of water, which had to be bought at a high price during droughts, and awful epidemics of typhoid and pneumonia. And for those toiling underground in the mines, especially in the oxidized zones, there was always the chance of lead-poisoning.

A very different picture today. The aridity remains in the district but not in the city; the summer is there as summers are everywhere, but gone are the terrible scourges of typhoid, pneumonia, and lead-poisoning; there is now plenty of water; isolation has given way to the Flying Doctor, the motor-car, to road and train and aerial transport; the kerosene lamp has dimmed before the brilliance of electric light; the meat-safe has lost its place to the refrigerator, the wash-tub to the washing machine. How our mothers used to toil over those wretched tubs in that frightful heat!

Thus, not only along the rich areas of the coastal lands, but seven hundred miles inland in arid areas progress is startling in but a few short years. Though here, west of the Darling, it was minerals that brought this transformation.

It was about 1900 that the family left Tamworth for Sydney, then went on to Melbourne, then to Adelaide, then up through South Australia to Cockburn, then across the border to Broken Hill, from a New England town in New South Wales. Thus, to get to a far-western town in New South Wales we had to travel just on 1700 miles through three States, a great adventure for a schoolboy, but days and nights of long, arduous travel for an anxious Mum with a family and a very scanty store of sovereigns to help her there. Now you can reach the Hill in an hour or two by plane from Sydney, Melbourne or Adelaide, by car from all directions, by comfortable train from Sydney or Adelaide, while the now tree-girded city is a lively place of modern hospitals and stores and schools, parks and gardens, of cool modern bungalows and houses that practically defy heat, sand and dust.

And motor-cars have come, let alone picture-shows and radio and the forty-hour week. And the permanent wave, come to think of it. Preparatory to the few-and-far-between dances when every woman dreamed of being belle of the ball, our mums had to do their own hair with curling tongs. So far as I remember the technique, Mum held this iron instrument in a candle flame until it was hot. Then, grabbing a hank of hair in one hand, she gripped it in the jaws of the hot tongs and twisted the handle round, holding it there with set, tense face until it had "taken", and that hank of hair screwed up in a curl. She carried on similarly with all the other hanks – a tedious, solemn job. She also cut up and twisted innumerable strips of newspaper, about six inches long. Through each curl she poked one of these pieces of paper, then tied the paper in a knot. She had, I understand, to retire to bed most carefully. In my very innocent days I have had a peep at a lady arrayed thus in bed; you could barely see her face, her head was just a mass of spiky ends of newspaper spills, looking like nothing on earth to me.

But then, next night you should have seen that glowing lady! In her shimmering silks, her beautiful ringleted hair, bewitching smile, sparkling eyes – we used to gape in awe at the entrancing stranger stepping from the bedroom out into a page of romance. And our Lady of Yesteryear could put it across the bouquet-carrying cavaliers just as effectively as the "modern miss" with all her modern aids, believe me – as doubtless she did in Cleopatra's day.

Yes, we had none of these modern helpers in those days on the Barrier. Nor had we hope in a future. The pessimistic idea was that the Hill was yet another mining town, with a possible further life of ten years. A dreadful place to live in, but the money was good if there was no strike on. Living conditions were hard indeed. Almost everyone lived in what were really shacks, with the idea of saving as much as possible to make a start elsewhere immediately the mines were worked out. Flies and dust and isolation, the deadening feeling that no one else in the world knew or cared whether we lived or died out there, typhoid, pneumonia, dysentery and lead-poisoning had to be put up with; so did the dirty brown water, so frightfully expensive, that in drought time came rumbling up in water trains even from South Australia. When I think of air-conditioning and painless dentistry and hearken back to the memory of those days – what a wonderful story is in the medical, transport, electric, chemical and technical discoveries that have done away with such an ocean of pain and death, that have eased so greatly the heart-breaking slavery of the mother's work, that have banished time and distance and isolation, making life livable in the wildest and most arid places all within the last few, swift years.

It is not so many years ago that numerous bush women baked their bread in a camp oven or home-made kerosene tin oven, or an oven cleverly dug out of an ant-hill. They hung the billy over the fire from a hook twisted by hand from fencing wire, one end gripping the billy handle, the other hooked into a link of the chain hanging down over the fire. And in years but a little further back many a mother felt quite "classy" when first she gained possession of a tea-pot, probably from some wandering Indian hawker. The chain was one of those handy ideas the settlers simply had to pick up. A pole would be let in well up and across the chimney, if an iron bar or rod could not be found. As soon as the old man could lay his hands on a length of unwanted chain he cut it into several handy lengths. The inevitable piece of fencing wire was twisted as a loose ring round the pole, and a wire hook connected this with the end link of the dangling chain. Thus Mum could push the chain along the bar to any position over the fire she wished. She made other fencing-wire hooks for the billies; she could hook them into links of the chain high or low over the fire to get any degree of heat she desired. When she was lucky enough to get four or five short chain-lengths she was on velvet. For then she could have the billy boiling, the 'roo-tail soup or the stew simmering, and have a spare billy near the boil for the kids all at the same time. Kids often needed hot water for something or other. Mum could hook on a kerosene-tin "bucket" for extra water if she wanted to, also to boil corned beef, or wild duck or turkey or pumpkin. At the same time she could have the damper or brownie baking in the camp oven, or in the coals and ashes raked out to the side of the stone, mud, or ant-bed hearth. Yes, a couple of short lengths of chain were very handy to the outback wife. Hooked sticks were used where there was no chain, but they were primitive compared to chain and fencing-wire hooks.

Water was in short supply in the early days of settlement at Broken Hill. During droughts it had to be carried from Adelaide, at first by camel and later by special water trains.

Many and many a feed I've enjoyed, or maybe wolfed, cooked under such conditions – cosy conditions, too, in wet or cold weather. Many and many a swagman has sighed in deep relief on reaching such a sanctuary with the sun sinking in storm-clouds, to be invited inside to devour a meal of corned beef and pumpkin, then by the firelight unroll his wet swag, dry his sodden clothes, stare into the friendly fire while listening to the howling rain outside. Yes, full-bellied and warm and sheltered he would sleep this night, rolled up in his dried blankets by the hearth, his hobnailed boots drying there, not too near the coals lest they roast while he slumbers.

It is miserable to have to pull on clammy wet boots after the night's rain. I know.

Broken Hill, of course, was a developed town. It was natural that folk should think the mines would cut out, for such is the fate of most mining fields the world over. But how mistaken in this case! They gave the field possibly ten years of life in 1900. During the fifty-five years since then the Hill has produced great wealth, and today there is no thought of the mines cutting out. Many estimate the life ahead to be at least fifty years. Some years ago the companies announced the life of the field as indeterminate, anything from twenty-five to fifty years, perhaps longer. For with modern drills boring down to great depths along the Line of Lode the drillers cannot reach bottom in depth of ore, while the Line itself has been found to extend for another mile. It was believed to be nearly three miles in surface length, remarkable even by world standards. It is now proved to be fully four miles. It is unknown how far in length this mighty ore body extends underground, while over the length of four miles it shows no sign of lessening in size or richness.

What a different feeling of content and security the folks at the Hill would have had when I was a lad at school there, if they had only known that the mines, far from petering out within a very few years, were really the greatest silver-lead-zinc ore body the world has known!

Far less could they realize that a goodly portion of the fantastic wealth away underground, harnessed by the labour and brains of men, was to build our great steel industries and bring about the discovery of amazing processes in the separation of minerals now utilized all over the mining world, was to make towns and ports, was to be a mighty aid to Australia throughout the world's greatest wars, was to build railways and ships, was to help the man on the land, and altogether to prove a mighty factor in the development of Australia. But then, we cannot see into the future. And, though some have the gift of peering a little way ahead, none of us can see underground.

Meanwhile we lads, fast growing up at school, like our teachers having no idea of the rich contribution this four miles of isolated aridity was to make to the prosperity of coming Australia, spent our precious hours of freedom watching the camel-teams come in from out of the mirage, walking long miles out on to the saltbush plains in search of the lovely Sturt's desert pea, climbing the rocky hills for the scarlet quandongs so our mums could make quandong jam, learning to swim in the Company's dams – which, alas, took toll of young life – tramping hot miles out to the dry creeks rabbit-hunting and for loads of precious firewood, often watching Cobb and Co's coaches come rolling in from Menindee and Wilcannia and White Cliffs. For those were the days when Cobb and Co. was King of the Roads.

The drivers, known far and wide, were of great interest to us boys. Often the coaches carried interesting passengers, too, and quite often – treasure. Small parcels of gold, sometimes many thousands of pounds' worth of precious opals. Always we longed for a coach to be bailed up, for then there would be great excitement. Alas for our entertainment, this happened but seldom.

The Junction Silver Mining Company, Broken Hill, 1888.

5. EXPERIENCE TEACHES

During our precious holidays the Ancestor would pile me in the sulky and away we'd go to where business might take him, to station or camel camp or outlying mining field, maybe south veering west to the silver camps at Thackaringa, its gnome-like outcrops of grey and pink rock jutting up from the plain above scraggy clumps of mulga always attracting me.

"If this God-forsaken desert was in a civilized country like Wales," observed the Ancestor on occasion towards the queer rock masses, "we'd know that only ogres, elves, trolls, gnomes and spotted fantods could exist in such outlandish places. Of course," he added, "we wouldn't grow such country in Wales."

"So then you wouldn't have the silver," I replied.

"Lord bless my soul!" he chuckled. "Fancy a young Australian learning to think for himself! Your schoolmaster *will* be pleased – if he's not too surprised," he added.

"There are no elves or gnomes in Australia," I remarked definitely.

"Indeed! And how do you know?"

"Because I haven't seen any."

"Lord bless my soul! Gee up, you lazy rascal!" he called to the pony. "But look here, young man, just because you haven't yet seen a Little Man of the Glen, or a cheeky gnome peeping out from under a sheet of bark –"

"But there *are* fantods in Australia!" I interrupted firmly.

"Oh, there are, are there? And where?"

"Around German Charley's shanty."

"By George!" exclaimed the Ancestor. "And what do *you* know about German Charley's shanty?"

"It's the place where men go to blow their cheques and get the horrors."

"Well, well, well!" mused the Ancestor. "How the younger generation do pick up things! Smarter than fowls! So you have learnt that there really are fantods. Well, let it be a lesson to you. When you grow up never go near a shanty, or you'll be seeing fantods, too."

"They're mostly pink elephants," I explained sagely, "though it's sometimes caterpillars big as crocodiles they see clawing after them – with eyes big as buggy lamps!"

"H'm! You haven't been learning all this at school."

"No, the teamsters tell us about them."

"Oh, do they? Well, I hope they tell you to keep away from the shanties – or you'll be seeing those fantods sure enough!"

"Have you ever seen one, Dad?" I innocently inquired.

The Ancestor's weather-beaten visage grimaced indignantly, but he thought better of it, shook the reins, and called, "Gee up, you lazy rascal! A young fellow of your age should know quite well there are no such things as fantods."

"Then how about your Welsh pixies?"

"Oh, they're different." And with a somewhat thoughtful expression the Ancestor changed the subject, leaving me grinning impishly inside, though innocent of face.

For but a week before the Ancestor had strayed home late – very late. He did so just occasionally, I suppose when he was fed up. When bed-time came Mum had been very worried. Not me, I well knew that whatever town we lived in for the time being the townsfolk soon remarked, "That old pony is human – he'll take Idriess home any time, whether in the bush or the town." Boy-like, I was quite certain the old pony would bring Dad home.

Mum had packed us off to bed. She sat in the kitchen alone, with the lamp and the moths and her worrying. It was a long time before I heard her jump up and hurry to the back veranda, then down the steps into the yard. When I heard the back gate click I knew the pony had brought Dad home.

I sat up in bed and listened, grinning at the Ancestor's protesting voice as Mum helped him up the back steps. She scolded him to bed. He was cheerfully inclined to sing "Men of Harlech".

"Oh, shut up that awful row!" whispered Mum fiercely. "You'll wake the children, you silly-looking brute! If ever there was a mess *you* are one! Go to sleep! Sit up and take your boots off first – if you can! And just wait until after breakfast in the morning!"

But the Ancestor blissfully replied with a don't-care snore.

When I heard Mum go quietly out into the back yard I sneaked out, too, though I knew exactly what she was going to do. Dad always looked after the old pony better than us, we youngsters used to complain. He would brush him down and feed him soon as he drove home at night, before he would come in for his own tea. Mum was doing it now. I peeped through a crack in the stable wall and saw her in the lamplight with brush and curry-comb, making a great fuss of the cunning old pony. Then she mixed him up his feed; greedily he insisted on stretching down his muzzle and snatching mouthfuls from her very hands as she mixed. She gave him a great big helping of chaff as she talked to him; she mixed a lot of bran mash in it, too, and gave him a bigger helping of corn than Dad ever did.

"Dad is going to cop it in the morning!" I said to myself as I sneaked back to bed.

And I was musing on this as we jogged on to the Pinnacles, which through the heat-haze were shimmering just like pyramids above the saltbush and mulga – while apparently the Ancestor was wondering just what I *did* know.

But away above a brigalow-tree a flycatcher was daintily hovering in the air, the note of his song so like the sharpening of a butcher's knife on a grindstone. And the sun shone on the bluebush, with here and there a big old-man saltbush towering above his fellows. "If this was in Wales," I thought, "Dad's quaint countrymen would swear that 'little people' lived deep in under those big thick clumps of old-man saltbush." I knew that here a boy was far more likely to dig out a saltbush snake, a nest of beetles; a sleeping lizard, or a pair of those swift, low-flying little ground parrots.

I lifted my eyes to the hills, hazy across the plain.

The silver-seekers, burnt almost black from the sun, earned their living the hard way. Over all these arid plains with their grey saltbush and bluebush, scattered clumps of mulga, of dead-finish and leopardwood, there was ever a frightening scarcity of water, not only for horse and camel but man, too. Civilized food was far away, living was of the roughest, and only hardy men could see it through. No wonder some grew crowsfeet round the eyes, for the distances on a clear day were only relieved by an occasional low hill or short, rocky range, so often reflecting heat. Northward stretched many of these low, sometimes fantastically shaped ranges, pleasant enough in winter, especially so after a good season, with their stunted trees and flowering shrubs and wildflowers making a blaze of colour in places, doubly fascinating in their often queer shapes and tantalizing scents. But in summer those sterile, almost waterless distances reflected a breathless heat. On such days the "Thud! Thud! Thud!" of a wallaby hopping leisurely down a rocky slope often sounded with startling clearness, and a stone knocked from its path and tinkling down from rock to rock could be clearly heard away down the gully. Even the hardy rock wallaby and the big rough old euro on a hot day used to lie sprawled in the shade of bush or rock awaiting coolness before venturing out to browse. Where we were jogging along over a saltbush plain in the silence under the vast dome of sky the flight of an eaglehawk, a crow, or a lone cockatoo winging strongly with set purpose to the shady gums of some distant dry creek would catch the eye.

Invariably that eye would watch until the lonesome bird dwindled into distance.

And yet soon after rains this sterility would be a paradise of wildflowers and noisy bird life, stalked over by the fine plain turkey, by the sedate emu so proud of her striped chicks scampering along behind, run and flown over by plover and flocks of topknot and bronzewing pigeons, screeching flocks of parrots and parakeets, white clouds of noisy cockatoos, pink clouds of galahs, brilliant clouds of budgerigars and diamond sparrows and spotted finches, leapt over by kangaroos that instinctively smell out where the sweet young grass is springing up. And everything would grow fat, stock and wild things and vegetation, too, as if this harsh Earth, now so bountiful, would atone to excess for the hard times. She spread the feast for all living things and actually flavoured it with salt, for up from her bosom comes the salt into the plant, to the goodly content of animal and man on the land.

Towards one hot sundown by the tall ridges of Kantappa, past Campbell's Creek, there was only the steady jogging of the pony's hooves. The Ancestor broke the brooding silence.

"Penny for your thoughts!"

"A thunderstorm is coming."

"Blow the man down! How observant we are becoming! I think we'd better rig camp before the storm breaks." And he turned the pony's head towards a gidgee forest.

In a matter of easy minutes the pony was turned out, the tent erected securely against the coming wind, the fire lit and the billy on, dry firewood gathered and thrown into the tent. The billy was just boiled and carried into the tent when the storm burst. What did we care!

"Snug as a bug in a rug," said the Ancestor as he unrolled the swag.

The storm was of the wild and woolly variety, but it blew itself out as we finished the sunset meal. Then came a brooding quietness, bringing the smell of steamy ground. But as the owls began to hoot I became aware of another smell, a somewhat unpleasant smell that gradually became more then more pronounced.

"What is that nasty smell?" I demanded presently.

"I smell nothing unusual," said the Ancestor, sniffing. And back went the old pipe to his lips. He was lying back on his blankets, arm under head, contentedly puffing up at the hurricane lamp strapped to the ridge-pole.

"If you bought a new pipe," I suggested, "you might be able to smell things."

The Ancestor removed the cherrywood from his mouth, his gaze benign.

"You leave those wise-cracks to your mother, young feller-me-lad. She can think up plenty."

"Well, what is the smell then?"

"Gidgee."

"You mean it's these trees that are smelling?"

"Yes, after rain, particularly if it's been humid, they often smell like this."

"Why did you camp here, then?"

"So that you would learn not to camp in a gidgee forest if the weather's damp."

"You could have told me about it."

"I've noticed that you learn better by experience, my lad." I considered this doubtfully.

"Oh well," I assured him, "you'll have to put up with this smell all night, just the same as me."

I don't believe he'd thought of that. He replied with some asperity. "That's the usual thanks Mum and Dad get when we try to teach you youngsters something. We've got to hammer it into you before you'll take any notice. I'll tell you something else, my smart young fellow. When the gidgee is in flower, it smells nearly as badly."

"You must have learnt that in the navy," I replied cheekily.

"When I was a lad in the navy," he retaliated, "they taught us things with a rope's end."

At which I snorted, but was distracted by the sight of two glowing green marbles staring towards us from the other side of the campfire.

The eyes vanished, but I knew they were still there. The campfire smoke was dreamily drifting up among the gidgee branches. A breath from the night sent the coals joyously fluttering into flame. The gidgee leaves coyly blushed a whitish-grey to the light, gently swaying to the kiss of the hot air as the smoke drifted up.

The eyes came again.

Although I felt it necessary to admonish the Ancestor for compelling me to spend a "nasty smelly night" merely because he wished to impress upon my memory an unpleasant habit of the gidgee-tree, I was much more interested in the life of trees than I permitted him to know. In the swiftly succeeding years, when as lads we used to roam the hills far and wide on our days off from work on the Big Mine, the animal, bird, reptile and vegetable life, and also the "mineral life", of the district was of unceasing interest to us. Particularly so to me, probably because the tree life here was so astoundingly different to that of the Big Scrub of the north coast or the luxuriant forests of New England. Here, except for occasional red-gums along the dry creeks, and for the river gums and flooded box and coolabah of the Darling, trees seldom grew more than fifty feet high. The scattered majority were fully grown dwarfs of thirty feet, the desperate energies of their gnarled roots ever seeking moisture deep down in the hot plains, wrestling with the rocky hillsides for every cranny that might hold soil or life-giving moisture. It was an aboriginal stockman who first showed us lads how the tough mallee had solved the problem of still clinging to life during a bad drought, in practically the same way as the lumbering camel – by storing water within itself. Man later developed the method of storing water in reservoirs in the earth – although desert aborigines, undertaking a long journey across sheer desert when prolonged drought has dried up most of the gnamma holes, carry water within themselves much as the camel does. Our aboriginal friend, in chuckling condescension, dug deep down to uncover the mallee roots, pointed out those which stored water, showed us how to chop them out, then cut through near the joint of each "compartment" and up-ended each length of a root into a billycan where the "reservoir" slowly drained out its water.

We could drink that water. Other trees similarly and in other ways stored water against the time when without it they would perish of thirst.

Thus various "reservoir" trees, shrubs, and bulbs – and some animals, like a certain desert frog – in saving themselves against thirst, have often saved the lives of primitive man, woman and child.

Our stockman friend with the perfect teeth also showed us "which way him leopardwood bin grow". He pointed out a thin, straggly clump of thorny bush. We had wondered why such unappetizing-looking vine took the trouble to grow thorns just to protect itself against grazing animals.

"Him bin grow up leopardwood tree," said the stockman.

"Yah!" we replied.

But it was a fact. From the middle of that scraggy, whiplike bush a centre stem grows up more strongly, developing eventually into the little trunk of the leopardwood tree, its spotted bark so reminiscent of a leopard-skin. Seeming to fit in so well with its habitat, it was a relief to the eye where it clothed the dark ridges all the way along the Barrier north to Bootra. Amongst it, just here and there up on the ridges, stood out vividly the shiny, dark-green leaves of the little quandong-tree, loaded with scarlet fruit in season, a prize sought eagerly by our sharp eyes.

It was this good-natured aboriginal, too, who gave us our first inkling of how trees and shrubs protect their precious "babies", their seeds and pods and bulbs, so that they may shield and protect their vital germ of life for years, even against the most terrible drought, the lashing of dry storm-winds raging with flying grit, against extremes of heat and cold and parched earth swept bare of mothering soil, in some instances seemingly defying Time itself, until at last cool rain, then kindly sun cause its shrivelled, almost iron-hard kernel to unfold and expand, bursting with life, to spring up into shrub and tree.

Of still greater interest to us at the time was another "secret" that we lads, wandering over those variegated hills, found out for ourselves – that different species of trees and shrubs and grasses grow on different soils, containing different minerals. It was natural that eager, observant youth should stumble upon this, to us, great discovery, for our young lives were all bound up in minerals.

It was while wallaby-shooting on Corunna run that we first noticed this, to be eagerly verified elsewhere on other expeditions. Wolfing lunch on some rocky hill, one of us remarked, "That seems funny! Look at all that mallee growing across there on the limestone! And just across on the schists that mulga scrub! Why, you could draw a line between the two different scrubs – just where the two belts of different rock meet!"

Of course it was so. Differing vegetation thrives on those soils which suit its "system" best. How strange it is that so often we do not see those things that are under our own noses! For, although we were earning our living by working exclusively among minerals, chemicals, and gases, it took us lads many years to realize that our own bodies are largely built up of these same things.

Part of this vast tract of strange country west of the Darling which intrigued us lads immensely was the black barrier rising parallel to the South Australian border, a forbidding wall shutting off the arid northern plains that vanished into distance and haze across the border. Away out there in sandy desolation lay the long chain of dead lakes coming down from the Corner Country, an area hundreds of miles in length where ages ago had sparkled the teeming waters of Sturt's Inland Sea. And about mid-way out there from the Barrier's western rampart, out over the dead creeks with their stunted gums, over the bluebush and canegrass flats, the dead-finish and needle-bush, sleeps Lake Callabonna. Surrounded by drear, windswept sand-dunes relieved only by scraggly samphire and drab mallow-bush, its salty encrustation stretches far away. But there was one bright spot of colour in the distant years when last I was there, far out in the centre a pool of brilliant blue outrivalling the bluest sky – probably the last pool of concentrated brine absorbing or reflecting colour from the brilliant sky so immeasurably high above. That glistening expanse is desolation in the extreme, the cemetery in which the last of the herds of Diprotodon sank to extinction in the drying morass.

This wall of ranges starting from Thackaringa and running straight north towards the Queensland border is formed by the Barrier, Coko, Mount Arrowsmith, Mount Browne, and the Whittabrenah and Grey ranges. Barren, dangerous country this, waterless across the sand-ridges and far away across the scorched plains. We boys only reached a point here and there, climbing up to some rugged pinnacle and gazing far out into the brilliant sunshine, wondering what lay far out there in the vanishing mirage. But in much later years I saw a lot of that strange country. In places the wall of the ranges is precipitous, cut by a thousand and one gorges and narrow valleys and high, rugged ridges. Along other escarpments the rocky spurs run gradually down into the sandy plain. Immeasurably old looks this weather-beaten buttress; the silence of a dead world seems to hover over it.

During the infrequent rains dirty water, as if spouting from Nature's sewers, hisses out from the thousands of rocky gullies to be immediately swallowed by the perishing sands or to spill out on the countless claypans or dreary dwarf-box swamps. Here and there from such places then comes a frantic croaking of frogs that have been cemented down in the sunburnt clay perhaps for two years or more; they claw their way madly up through the softening clay in hysterical search for sunlight and starlight, to find a mate and make love and live and move and sing throughout the few mad days and nights before the cynical sun drinks up the water and forces them to burrow down into darkness and immovability and silence again. What may be the "thoughts" of such a desert frog as it waits, cemented down in the sun-hardened clay, for a year or two or more?

Elsewhere along those hundreds of miles at the foot of the wall the precious water spills out into shallow depressions clothed in dense masses of wiry lignum growing higher than a man. It would be frightful to be lost in the lignum, to see only a few yards ahead and around and the merciless sky above, enclosed by those huge clumps of dull-green, dusty, wiry bush. A thirsty man fast losing control could imagine in the hot silence all manner of things crouching round him, awaiting him on the farther side of every bush. Such tragedies have happened.

In other places the water spills into shallow, meandering depressions covered with coarse, dense, suffocating canegrass. In yet other places it is immediately absorbed by low sandhills upon many of which grow stunted pines that sigh eerily to even a whisper of wind. Some ridges are golden, some red, some brown, some white. On moonlit nights the white ridges gleam just like snow – easy to imagine wolves peering from the black shadows under the pines.

But it seldom rains, and that long barrier of age-old rock reflects heat into a stillness and brooding quietness, except when the Dust Fiend comes howling with frenzied battalions of whirling sand and dust from the Dead Lakes country far out on the desolate plains. This storm rolling black or sometimes red as fire hurls itself straight against the immovable barrier and, beaten back there, eddies whining up through the gullies and gorges, screeches over the bare rock crests and hurries on in a howling fury to smother what it cannot blow down. A lone traveller caught thus must battle on, often for days, enveloped in dense clouds of dust and sand. Few indeed must travel across that country; foolhardy indeed is the man who attempts it unless he has a good sense of direction and, in summer, is comfortably loaded with water and food. The most nerve-racking thing, or so it has always seemed to me, is the frightening swiftness with which a bad sandstorm will blot out all tracks; even as you peer through sand-blinded eyes billions of grains of lively sand are already blotting out the fresh-made tracks of your own horses or camels, or, at the present day, of your car. There would be no chance of a new-chum finding his way back along his own tracks after a bad storm.

A queer country that, where the wall of border range faces the silence of the Dead Lakes plains. But then *all* the country west of the Darling, right to the difficult border lands, is a strange country, brooding over its mysteries, fascinating those who come under its spell.

Who could imagine that it held such fabulous secrets!

6. JUST JOGGING ALONG

It was still during the latter schooldays that the Ancestor and I would travel on other trips, sometimes west where the once roaring little town of Silverton was battling on, its kindly, stubborn citizens sure that "Silverton will come again".

A pity that Silverton had no Bret Harte.

"You've read of the treasure ships of the Don, my lad," remarked the Ancestor. "Well, then, enough silver has come lumbering up this dusty little street to load all the ships that ever sailed the Spanish Main."

"I don't believe it."

"Oh, you don't, don't you? And why not, by George!"

"Because the Spaniards conquered all the treasures of the Aztecs and the Incas. And the silver mines of Peru and Mexico."

"You may be right, smarty," agreed the Ancestor grudgingly. "Now I come to think of it, about the only things you seem interested in are minerals and yellow-footed wallabies and wagging it from school. But you are only half right. The actual amount of silver may have been greater, but in proportion to man-power, labour and time, it was less. For the Aztecs had a thousand years in which to amass their treasure, and millions of slaves to dig it for them. The Spaniards had a hundred years to take it from them. Whereas here, within the last very few years, a few hundred free men with their own labour have hewn a great wealth of silver from these iron-bound hills."

"And lost an ocean of sweat in doing it."

"Yet again, yes and no. For many of them won bullock-drays of silver slugs from the surface and a few feet below it, quick and lively. And if you still don't believe me then here we are at the Warden's Office. You can browse over the files and silver returns from the mines while I transact my business. And don't go sneaking away to yarn with those hard-bitten silver-gougers, or that blackfellow's dog either."

I didn't. But I saw the mail come in. And found a minah's nest in a wilga-tree.

Jogging north then to the primitively rough silver camp at Umberumberka, its inhabitants so willing to share their solid tucker and pannikin brew, then on through rugged country and along Apollyon Valley of many a silver romance with its scattered camps we came to the Paps, where our indignant old pony bought an argument with a savage bull camel and the Ancestor with a scowling, black-bearded Afghan.

As we drove away clear of trouble the Ancestor gradually worked off his temper, then affectionately slapped the pony with the reins and chuckled.

"Good on you! You silly old corn-chewer, I thought you were going to get the whole bally lot of us eaten up! Fancy a pocket handkerchief of old bones like you picking a fight with a bull camel! Why, he could have picked you up by the scruff of the neck and shaken the stuffing out of you!"

"I thought the Afghan was going to do the same to you," I murmured guardedly.

"Oh, you did! And what do you think I would have been doing to that heathen Pathan?"

Wisely I allowed the Ancestor to growl his wrath away as we jogged on to camp at Poolamacca, boiled the billy and rolled up in our blankets, dreamily listened to a concertina in the stilly night. How brightly the stars shone above! Sleep comes easily when it comes thus bathed in starlight.

Then the brown-red track to Purnamoota. And the sun shone brightly on the silver grass.

At Mount Robe, roughest and toughest and tallest of this abrupt little range, solemnly I sat on a box under a bough-shed while a cheery miner boiled the billy and cooked johnny-cakes in the ashes, his mate entertaining me by explaining samples of silver ores which they hoped would "make" at depth and thus make their fortunes. I wondered that the shilling tied securely in the bottom of my pocket should come out of a rock. The rocky mount under the fierce sun was scarred deeply by a rabbit warren of crosscuts and shafts seeking the elusive silver lode, dumps of broken stone bearing mute testimony to the Herculean labour of the silver-seekers. When next morning dawned in beauty and we jogged away on the long miles towards Yanco Glen the Ancestor murmured speculatively, "I hope you are learning something on each of these trips, young feller-me-lad! I hope that you are learning, too, that these poor chaps, each with a heart of gold, has rarely any gold in his pocket. You could not meet better men, perhaps, but they live hard – they live on hope! For each one who strikes it rich a thousand carry the swag away to look for a job."

And then, to emphasize his warning we pulled up at a miner's hut and found his sun-tanned wife seated on a box engrossed in the job of making boots. Up on the hillside her fourteen-year-old son was toiling at the windlass, hauling mullock for the father working below. At a shout they strolled down the track to the hut and boiled the billy. It was by no means the first time I had watched the making of home-made boots, or seen wash-tubs fashioned from a hollow log. The wife had been making boots for her children from tarpaulin, and rawhide. She cut out pieces of tarpaulin and fashioned them into the side of a boot. She had cut the soles to shape from greenhide, which had been thoroughly dried and scraped. Her awl was a sharpened nail. She sewed the soles and tarpaulin sides together with wallaby sinew – her husband had made her a needle by heating and hammering a nail out to shape on the forge. She had already made two pairs, and was busy on a third when we drove up in the sulky. She had made a good job of them, too.

Down by the waterhole was her wash-tub, neatly made from a hollow log with the ends boarded up with slab. The father had made a neat job of it; she told us the clothes came out nice and clean. The whole family mustered very few clothes indeed, but then I suppose it felt nice to have them always clean. I'd seen similar wash-tubs made by settlers for their wives years before this. Almost impossible these days to realize how difficult it was to obtain the most ordinary things away out in the unsettled bush of those years, let alone to understand the value of five shillings to those folk who had to live on the smell of an oiled rag before they got on their feet.

"Real nice people," remarked the Ancestor as we moved off, "but you see how hard they live – as you've seen the battling settlers away back along the coast. Well then, learn all you can at school, so that you won't have to slave as they do."

But the Ancestor's intuition had come too late. The battle with the rock-bound heart of Nature had already claimed me. Like these very men I was to bore into that elusive heart by the sweat of the brow. And I was to carry the swag away, too.

Also, many a time I was to heel and sole my boots with greenhide. In fact, on the North Queensland tin-fields I was to go without any for long periods. But much of the work there was in water.

Numerous such trips, including many taken later with mates when I was old enough to work in the Big Mine, must have stirred the roamer in me. Across the bluebush plains, across the red-gum creeks whose scanty waters lay hidden underground, jogging past a wild lemon-tree breathing its haunting perfume from masses of white flowers, on past the cotton-bush and the pretty wilga, ever jogging on towards some rocky little range that often would play fantastic tricks under the rippling vibrations of vast, cloudless sky, heat and haze.

Once a fantastic figure came floating upon us out of a mirage, a gigantic horse stretching out in enormous, noiseless strides up in the air, its monstrous hooves, frighteningly silent, threatening to pound straight down upon us, the floating rider with whiskers big and rough as an eaglehawk's nest, a fearsome figure; half giant dog, half giant wild man. To within a few hundred yards he came floating down upon us, then finally shrank and settled normally upon earth as Thackaringa Billy with his beloved dog sitting upon the saddle before him as usual. One of the numerous characters of the grey saltbush plains was Thackaringa Billy with his old horse and dog. That dog was known from south-west Queensland right across the Far West and across the South Australian border to Adelaide. He had made the trip many times with his god, Thackaringa Billy, droving the mobs through good seasons and bad, swimming flooded rivers, battling through droughts, surviving thirst and hunger, fatigue and fire, snakes and dingo-poison baits and hardship, growing rolling fat in the good times, putting up with it uncomplainingly when ribbed like a poor goanna, guarding his master day and night, through thick and thin.

No one dared lay a hand on Thackaringa Billy unless Thackaringa expressly told the dog this man was a friend and was allowed to do so. Even then the dog's eyes, smouldering with suspicion, never left the man while he dared touch Billy.

"Gives you a creepy feeling," I'd heard men complain, "from your heels up your spine. *Blow* shaking hands with Thackaringa! That devil of a dog would tear a man's throat out if ever he thought an enemy was going to lay a hand on his precious Thackaringa."

And the dog nearly did once.

Billy's dog was known in Broken Hill to lots of folk, for occasionally when on travelling stock jobs Billy had to come to town on business. Sometimes when he'd had a few drinks he'd love to show off his dog, coaxing dubious friends to touch him. A great joke of his was when a stranger talking to someone across the street would take off his hat and hold it. Thackaringa would merely say, "Go get that hat!" and the dog would immediately trot across the street, seize the hat, and bring it across to the laughing Thackaringa.

One day in town when Billy was yarning thus a visitor who had not seen him for years spotted him and came straight across. Now this man was of the jovial type who, on seeing a friend, likes to come up behind him and give him a rattling thump on the back just to make his presence felt. This man did so, and instantly red-hot fangs fastened in his heel. As he leapt up and around with a yell the dog flew straight at his throat. It was only by one of those miracles of good fortune that his throat was not torn out.

Thackaringa was very careful in town after that. But in the bush the dog had free rein. For the Far West stock-routes were "wild" those days, besides being very lonesome. And Thackaringa Billy's "run" from Queensland to Adelaide was more than a thousand miles of the lonesomest, while the shanties dotting this long line at strategic watering places sometimes housed very questionable guests. Queer things have happened at such places, incidents long since passed into bush mysteries. And Thackaringa, in common with other boss drovers, was not only a highly trusted man in charge of a valuable mob of stock, but on such trips was commonly supposed to carry money for the outfit's expenses.

But Thackaringa had supreme confidence in his doggy bodyguard when of necessity he had to camp near dangerous company. It was whispered that the dog had saved Thackaringa more than once. That dog would willingly have given its life for its master. But then Thackaringa without compunction would have shot the man who harmed his dog.

It was with delight then that I made friends with this famous dog, while the Ancestor and Thackaringa yarned and the old pony and Thackaringa's horse yawned and nudged each other in a matey sort of way. What boy wouldn't delight in making friends with such a dog! Of course, no thoughtful bushman would, for it was an unwritten law among the real old diehards that you must not make friends with another man's dog. But with a boy it was different, and the dog knew it as well as I did. Knew it as well as he knew that on a hot day with no stock duties to attend to he could leap up on to the knee-pads and ride before his master, could leap up on a packhorse and sit straight up and ride, thus resting his own feet until duty called. A dog that could drove and guard stock, that could not only look after its master but look after its master's horse, was precious indeed. When Thackaringa was making a call he would dismount and leave the reins trailing so the horse could quietly feed. The dog would see that nothing disturbed it. When Thackaringa wanted the horse he would whistle. The dog would quietly pick up the end of the bridle rein in its mouth, and sedately bring the horse along to the master.

That dog knew so many, many things. Of course a boy would make friends with such a dog.

It was years later – alas, how time flies for everyone! – that I heard how Thackaringa Billy had "gone over the range". He was taken off the train at Peterborough, all dressed up for his beloved bush, his stockwhip around him. He had left a mob of bullocks at Naryilco station in south-west Queensland, having brought them from Quinabye, and had travelled to Adelaide to complete arrangements for their sale. And now he was coming back to lift them, eager to cross the border and mount the old horse again.

But Thackaringa Billy had crossed his last border, swum his last river. And now he was going on his last ride. His horses and plant were sold at Tibooburra. If memory is correct, selector Jackson bought most.

The dog died.

Another well-known old character Dad introduced me to was a cranky, though to me kindly, old station cook, "Jack Without a Shirt". He gave away the only one he had to a passing swagman. Not the only rough diamond to do so, apparently, for I've met other Jacks without shirts in other States. Anyway old Jack Without a Shirt always had a huge hunk of brownie for me and a quart-pot full of tea with plenty of sugar in it whenever we passed that way.

Jack grew a big, bushy moustache; it was dark brown, but the most gingery one I'd yet seen where its "veranda" had been stained by trailing in countless pannikins of hot, strong tea. Lots of men had that gingery fringe to their moustache; some really used it as a strainer in those times when they were travelling and the waterholes drying up. That bushy moustache, deep in the pannikin lid, would strain away from their lips much of the mud and at times slimy things that often appeared in drying waterholes. "Beetle-strainers" , they called that big fringe moustache that came down over the top lip. But I did not like those tea-stained moustaches, and had made up my mind that mine would be one of those smartly trimmed ones – when I could get scissors – and I'd wax the ends with tallow as the flash stockmen did. (Actually, when at long last the adornment blossomed, I grew a "handlebar".)

One character Dad seemed to take a chuckling pleasure in introducing me to was Saltbush Ned; we met him by the Noonthorangee Range on a trip to Nuntherungie. He was "dressed", for he wore the bushman's red handkerchief loosely knotted round his sinewy neck. In blue shirt, carefully ironed moleskins, polished leggings and spurs and elastic-sides, he was going to town. His eyes were amazingly cobwebbed with crowsfeet burnt in by the glare of many suns, many hazy distances – keen, kindly eyes. Grizzled and grey, like so many of the old-timers, he had that lean, weather-beaten look, cheek-bones bronzed by the weathering of hard summers, sinewy figure eloquent of wiry strength. It was said of Saltbush Ned that he had swum nearly every Queensland river clinging to a bullock's tail, and never knew what it was to live in a house until he married. He was born in a tent, as were many of the old-timers. In his day, there was more than one mother who had had her baby in a tent or under a wagon or bough-shed, only the husband by her side, and for other company the cackle of a jackass or the "cark" of crow, probably the howl of a dingo by night.

But then, throughout the ages, babies have often been born under much harsher circumstances. I hope such things never happen again.

It was near a certain lonely shanty that Dad pulled up at sight of a greybeard staring dubiously at a fence. Fences were certainly few and far between, but he was glaring at this one as if he had never seen a fence before – lanky old chap, skinny as a poor goanna.

"Good day," called Dad.

"Day," replied the greybeard, his eyes never lifting from the fence, and kept muttering to himself.

"What's the trouble?" inquired Dad.

"This darned fence," answered the greybeard, frowning. "I reckon I'm the best blooming hopper ever browsed on *these* plains – but I can't jump *that* fence!"

Dad slapped the reins on the pony, leaving the greybeard still staring at the fence, still angrily muttering.

"Let that be a lesson to you," advised the Ancestor.

"What's the matter with him?"

"He's just about recovering after a spree, or else just developing the horrors. At present, he thinks he is a kangaroo, but can't jump the fence. I'll call in at the shanty and tell them they'd better go out after him and bring him in. Otherwise he might wander away and perish. Let that be a lesson to you, young fellow, or one of these days you might imagine *you* are a kangaroo!" And the Ancestor passed the time until we pulled into the shanty by giving me horrifying examples of men he'd seen in the horrors. In coming years I was to see for myself that he had not been drawing the long bow either.

However, the Ancestor's hair-raising examples became a little monotonous to a bored youth jogging along in a dusty sulky watching the little grey butterflies darting amongst the grey saltbush.

"Who put up the first fence in this country?" I inquired as he paused for another horrid example.

"H'm!" he mused. "Well then, who *did* build the first fence?"

"I don't know."

"Really! And so you just asked me the first question that came to mind to stop me warning you of the evils of drinking bad liquor? Oh well, you'll grow up and learn. And now, young smarty, I'll tell you who *did* put up the first fence west of the Darling. The three Maiden brothers. The boundary fence between Kinchega and Netley stations. In 1871. Below Menindee. Now how about *that!*"

"You appear to be well-informed, Dad."

"Lord bless my soul! He must have learnt that in a school book! You could tell me the date of the Battle of Hastings yet you couldn't tell me when the first fence was built upon the very land which now gives you your bread and butter! By George! And though you've camped at Maiden's Hotel in Menindee, you don't know that Maiden once owned the South Broken Hill Mine!"

"I didn't know that, but I did know that he and his mate Pretty found the Pinnacles."

"Oh, and so you're interested at last! Well, he did. He owned millions and millions, but – he didn't know it. He really owned the Central Mine also. That is, he had pegged the country out. He offered it for nothing to some wandering prospectors, but they turned it down, they were looking for copper at the time."

Rasp's Shaft, on the block pegged by Charles Rasp in 1883, was the first to be sunk on the "Broken Hill". After the rich silver deposits were found two years later, the "sea of mulga scrub'" was rapidly replaced by a thriving mining town.

"You're talking of the early days now."

"Lord bless my soul! The *early* days! Why, it was only *yesterday!* By George, how the young of the species do grow up! Very well then, to you I suppose it might seem the early days. Maiden and his father were working contract work on Mount Gipps station before Charlie Rasp developed a bee in his bonnet that the hill in the Broken Hill Paddock was a hill of tin. You appear to be quite interested now in the story of the fence. Books could be written about 'em, me lad, if you only knew how. Well then, young Sid Kidman, then but a few years older than you, was working there too as a station hand, slaving for twelve bob a week. But that far-sighted young fellow was also doing a little horse-dealing. And he didn't slave long in the one place, as you can tell by those fine butcher's shops of his back there in the Hill. Which is another story in the panel of a fence. Maiden's name crops up quite a lot in the early Silverton silver rushes, as I've heard you mention once or twice. And in the wildcat excitement of later rushes he really did peg what is now the South Broken Hill Mine. But of course then it was only a parched, scrub-clad hill; no one then dreamed of the wealth below. Neither did he, and thus a mighty fortune, rather fortunes, slipped through his hands – as happened to many others during those exciting years. But at the time he thought he did very well out of it, for he sold it for a thousand pounds to Jamieson and Keats, to the disgust of Charlie Chapple – Chapple Street is named after him – who just missed out in the race. It was this way. Maiden had returned to Menindee, disgusted with the Hill. Of course the place then was only the big old bluff standing up above a sea of mulga scrub, with a thick patch of bull-oaks near where the Junction Mine is now; the whole bally paddock didn't seem worth a bucketful of cold water: Soon afterwards the McCulloch-Jamieson crowd struck chlorides in Rasp's shaft. It was a race then for adjoining blocks. Maiden had pegged the South and Jamieson and Keats were in the saddle hell for leather with Charlie Chapple at their tail, a wild and woolly race to Maiden at Menindee, seventy tough miles away. Jamieson and Keats won the race. Maiden gladly accepted a thousand for his Block. Not long afterwards it was worth a million and a half."

"I'll bet Mr Maiden was mad!"

"Not very," answered Dad. "What was the use? It was all in the game those days. Anyway, how about the surveyors?"

"What surveyors?"

The Ancestor chuckled. "He's so cocksure he knows all about mining, yet he doesn't know about the surveyors! Well then, before Charlie Rasp pegged the Hill it was used as a look-out post by a party of surveyors, maybe for surveying Mount Gipps station. They piled up stones, a little trig station, fair on top of the outcrop from which they took sights on the surrounding country. It was an ideal look-out for surveyors as well as wandering bushmen. They worked there for some little time, then packed up their tent and rode away, well pleased to be finished with the heat and savagery and loneliness of that sun-scorched bluff. Well now, what do you think of the feelings of those couple-of-pounds-a-week men when they realized they had been sitting and working on top of a mere hundred million or so?"

But I could only whistle, "Phew!" to the Ancestor's chuckling content.

"So just remember, young feller-me-lad," he remarked, "it's not only in your head you need eyes – as I've warned you time and again when you slip out of camp at night without a light. One of these fine nights you'll find yourself squatting down over a tiger snake! And now, about this fence. So far as the Barrier is concerned, Harry Lord is said to have put up the first fence. I could tell you a volume in that little story of a fence my lad. But what do you think about it?"

"Seems to me, starting from Menindee to the Hill, you've mixed up a number of fences."

"Maybe so, maybe not," replied the Ancestor thoughtfully. "Life is a fence my lad, and there are many panels to it."

A Murrumbidgee Whaler was plodding along heavily in the distance. Slumbrous jogging of the pony's hooves, faint smell of dust. Red-capped robins looked neat and pretty as they busily discussed the events of the day in a bull-oak. Right beside the dusty track was a big mound of old dried sticks, the mouths of little burrows running through it. From nearly every burrow peeped a quaint little nose, tiny twitching ears, jet-black eyes, furry little head. This was the home and castle of a colony of the quaint little bush rats. I used to have great fun watching them building their castles, struggling with, tugging, pulling those building sticks along the ground from quite a long way away. Then the manful job of hoisting and levering them up into place. Energetic little workers they were. Alas, that imported pest the fox and the tame cat gone wild have since massacred them to extinction, as they have unaccountable numbers of our native birds.

"Who is this George you often speak about?" I inquired.

"George? What George?" replied the puzzled Ancestor.

"*I* don't know – I was asking you. This 'By George' you often mention when you're surprised."

"Lord bless my soul!" said the Ancestor in slow disgust. "He doesn't know who Saint George is! These barbarian Australians! Have you *never* heard of Saint George and the dragon?" he demanded.

"No. Not unless it's the funny old picture I've seen on a sovereign."

The Ancestor fairly gasped, lifting his eyes to the skies. Then, drawing a great, calm breath, he patiently explained, "Saint George is the patron saint of England, a knight great and true. When dangers threatened the castle he saddled up his charger, rode out with his trusty lance, and vanquished the enemy."

"What about that dragon, Dad?"

"Doesn't seem much use telling you," he growled. "You don't seem to have the gumption to understand. Very well, then. One day a mighty dragon came belching flame and smoke up over the hill and came prancing straight down for the castle. Saint George charged out upon the terrible enemy and, after a mighty fight, vanquished it."

"He must have had a bellyful of German Charley's rum that day!" I said admiringly.

The Ancestor held up the reins in a hopeless sort of way, then resignedly dropped his hands and gazed straight ahead.

"Anyway," I said in conciliatory tone, "I'll bet Saint David could beat Saint George holler! Haven't I heard you say that Saint David was the saint of Wales?"

"Yes."

"Well then, how did Saint David get along with Saint George?"

"Like a house afire!" replied the Ancestor cheerily. "Saint David gave Saint George a job – made him his horse-boy."

Though late afternoon, it was bright sunlight. Dreamily I noticed how individual each shadow was, each very long, and very dark, and very distinct upon the yellow grass below each tree.

And out of the corner of my eye as the sulky passed I saw a pretty little dun-coloured dotterel running swiftly, crouched to the earth. I knew she thought she was deceiving this big noise rumbling along; she had run to protect her precious home, to delude the coming danger to chase her. If so, in little short runs she would sham lameness and flatten to the ground. Then when danger was almost upon her she would run haltingly a little way again, and thus entice the danger farther and farther away from her precious babies.

As we passed by I wondered if they were hatched out yet, or if she . had even covered her inconspicuous eggs with a wisp of grass. Mother Earth is warm out there. The loving breast of the little dotterel is warm also.

A different character was German Charley. We pulled into his notorious shanty on the road to Tarrawingee; there was some trouble there over the clumsily timed shooting of a beast that carried another man's brand. Such accidents did happen now and again out in the mulga.

Old Charley, whose "fighting rum" was notoriously known far and wide as "snake-juice", was moderately sober and insisted on our staying "for a bite", while a bleary-eyed crony of his glared at us from above a walrus moustache. During that feed of hard tack washed down by black, milkless tea Charley did his best to entertain the boy guest by telling him tales of the "wild mens" he'd known in the wild silver rushes. He could tell a good yarn, too, though obviously finding difficulty in toning the language down to the youthful company.

"They vos vild boys," he said regretfully as we prepared to depart. "Good boys vos, too! Too — smart for those policemans!"

Dad, who was a "government man", tactfully said nothing, I thought to Charley's regret.

"Yes," sighed Charley, "and I have some smart mens through my hands, too! But Sid Kidman smarter of the lot!: he added admiringly.

As we drove away the Ancestor chuckled.

"What's funny?" I asked.

"Oh, Sid Kidman put it all across that old rascal in a deal once. Charley thought he was going to snare a simple bush lad, and what a surprise he got! There are few men in Australia who could take down Sid Kidman in a cattle deal, which German Charley found out to his sorrow when he locked horns with him." And the Ancestor chuckled in a pleased sort of way.

"Charley doesn't think much of the police," I said impishly.

"He used to think quite a lot of them – he *had* to!" replied the Ancestor grimly. "But for all that the old scallywag actually howled when Cullen died – the first policeman to die on the Barrier. 'The best mans on the Barrier is dead!' moaned Charley. And he meant it, too. Cullen was as spry as Charley was. For a long time it was a battle of wits between them. They both enjoyed it – even when Cullen proved the better man."

We jogged on over almost bare, rolling lands thickly covered with "hailstones" that were snow-white quartz pebbles. From a clump of acacias, pretty in their masses of spike-like flowers, diamond doves were calling. A range of sunlit hills rose in the distance. Up among those hot grey rocks, I knew, toil-stained men were doggedly working, each one spurred on by the faint, wild hope at his heart that some time, some day, a stroke of the pick would turn him into a "Silver King".

Yarns about old German Charley have passed into legend, as with the Eulo Queen across the Queensland border. As with Charlie Chapple, Harry Pell, "The Baron", "The Count", and some scores of Silver Kings who in the wild and woolly days had made and gone through fortune after fortune during the roaring days of Silverton, followed by the fabulous early years of the Silver City. Where there are wild men there must be wild women, and here "Goldie" and "Kate Killarney", with other sparkling sisters, were to the forefront in the limelight. And that limelight was always bright, luridly so when the Silver Kings came to town.

Books could be written on the "characters" who were still lively as crickets not only out in the mulga but in the Silver City itself when I was a lad.

7. WHERE THE DARLING FLOWS

One great trip of happy variety was south-east through the mulga and saltbush to Horse Lake station, jogging on past Box Tank to the Darling at Menindee. Every boy loves a river. But how much more entrancing the gleam of those long, cool, tree-shaded water stretches to a boy who has already learnt the value of a pannikin of muddy liquid! Sunset on those quiet pools, softly kissing the mirrored depths through the massive limbs of the old river gums was beautiful indeed. And, yes, there hurried a full dozen red-legged waterhens, running along the bank. I wondered what they sought, or whether they were the hunted. For the waterhen has to fight its own battle of life, like everything else. Presently starlight littered the placid water with diamonds. A rosy ripple glowed out across the stream as nightly I built the campfire big as I could. The trunks of big old coolabah and flooded box danced in pictures to the merry song of the blaze. Silently the water flowed by in that utter quietness of a Darling night.

Breathless excitement then as Dad's line stretched slowly out and – oh yes he's hooked a big one!

Whopper fish were the Darling cod, and how good they tasted, fresh-cooked in the frying-pan in the morning! With the chill of dawn giving way to a rosy glow as the sun rose out of the vast grey plains. The tang of cool water, flowering foliage, and moist river bank. Hilarious chattering and whistling, cooing and trilling of exuberant bird life, with lively beak busily combing wings and feathers for action, in a hurry to seek breakfast. Perhaps a honey-eater fluttering joyously up round that big bunch of mistletoe – the honey-eater that is the glorious singer of the far western bush. The billy boiling we reach for a pannikin, a hunk of damper, and fried Darling cod.

"There's not much of you," the Ancestor would remark gravely, "but by the quantity of fish you can put away you might grow brains. Here's hoping, for the family badly needs 'em."

But I'd be too intent on breakfast and the doings of that big old crane fishing down there by the water's edge to be bothered by the meanderings of a mere parent.

Jogging along the grey road by the river bank under clear sunlight to the squawking of birds, their first gluttonous hunger now eased, anxious for a spot of fighting or love-making, we were sometimes aware of a distant growing hum growing louder, then the busy thrashing of paddle-wheels. What a thrill as the Darling "Dreadnought" came sailing among the big old river gums with the water, now in rippling motion, fairly shouting in song! What a sight the heavily laden barge being towed astern, its tiers upon tiers of bales of wool towering away up among the leafy branches, that Golden Fleece from the back o' beyond on its long voyage to Melbourne, then longer voyage to the English mills. Lying half sprawled on his back upon a coil of rope, hat tilted forward over his eyes, a man in brown shirt was playing "Waltzing Matilda" on a concertina, his dancing fingers putting lively little trills into the old bush tune. The music sounded well with the song of the paddle-wheels and churning water as the vessel came into full view, now almost beside us. I gazed out from the sulky, eager to read the name on the bow; Dad would surely know the captain and yarn about him, for the river captains and the "strong men" among the bargemen were rich material for yarns all along the Darling, the Murrumbidgee, and the Murray. Those bustling, cheery river men had brought life to the rivers in more ways than one.

We jogged past a swaggie quietly sitting on a log by the river bank, smoking his pipe, fishing line in hand, unrolled swag spread beside him, billy on the boil. In a hollow limb away above him a dad and mum galah were busily feeding a noisy family. Dad and the swaggie waved – "Good day, mate!" – as we jogged past. I saw he had a good fire, a box log steadily burning. Box makes good coals; most of the timber in the far west burns away to a clean white ash. As soon as there were enough coals he'd scrape some aside and quietly bake a damper before moving on. I wondered who the stranger was, one of those "ships that pass in the night", I wondered where he had come from, where he was going, whether anyone loved him. Maybe intuition was faintly stirring that some day I also would be carrying the swag – just me, and Bluey, and the billycan, and the lonesome bush. And would fish on river banks, too. But would grumpily hate to have to bake a damper.

A homestead, the tops of the river gums rising behind it, as with every homestead along the river itself. Stretching away into hazy distance the flat country, either red or grey, relieved only by its few box-trees, fading into a misty distance of dull grey saltbush.

Exhilarating freshness in winter, breathless heat on summer days. And always the lazy squawk of the crow. Alas, if the seasons have been dry there is tragedy down in the steep muddy banks of the river, for bogged sheep lie there helpless, gazing pathetically round for the helping hand of the boundary rider while in terror of the eye-picking beak of the crow.

"That's the roof of a comfortable homestead across there, peeping above the old gum tops," said the Ancestor one morning.

"Yes."

"Well, only a few years ago, just after I landed on this barbarous country of yours, that homestead was a heavily patched tarpaulin roped over a bullock-dray. The family living-room was under the dray. Before that, the dray was a blackfellow's wurley. Well, the dray quickly grew into a bough-shed beside it and thus the family could move about in their growing home. The bough-shed grew into a bark hut, and believe me the family were comfy then, even though they had to make wild-duck eggs do instead of flour when the supply teams were twelve months on the road. The bark hut turned into a kitchen when they built their new homestead of mud and stone. My! Didn't they have a palatial home then, though there wasn't room to swing a cat in it! But their mum was real proud of that mud and stone hut and she kept the ant-bed floor swept real clean. Her husband made her brooms out of bush twigs. The old homestead grew again, and but two years back finally grew into that very nice place we passed just now.

"And so the homesteads, and the stations grew along this, and many another river, my lad, as the early settlers came trudging out into the new lands. But we do not see it as we jog along in this comfortable old sulky along this plain road, and admire a homestead that we pass just now and then. But in the days, only a few years back, when this dusty road was a bullock-track men, women and children trudged this so new, but so weary way, seeking a spot to say 'At last!' and outyoke the team, and start their homestead under the old dray. From South Australia and Victoria women have trudged a thousand miles and more before they reached 'At Last!' They have come, too, right from the coast of New South Wales, from Queensland also. Would you like to trudge a thousand miles barefoot into new country beside a bullock-dray, my lad?"

"Yes."

"Humph!" growled the Ancestor. "Then you're a better man than I thought you were. Oh well, you just think of those poor devils who trudged that thousand miles, often under a blazing sun, often in bitter cold and rain and mud without a bellyful to eat, before you make up your mind. Whenever you sight a fine new homestead just spare a thought to the old dray, and the horses, and the dog, and the man and woman and children slowly trudging along."

To a rhythmic, smart tattoo of hooves a squatter came dashing past in a dust-cloud, driving a spanking four-in-hand splendidly matched. The old pony cocks a quizzical ear at these beautifully groomed thoroughbreds pounding by in muscled strength, the swiftly turning wheel-spokes reflecting sunlight, the buggy the last thing in squattocracy, the harness a-gleam with nickel.

"That squatter didn't come trudging up here a thousand miles on bare feet beside a bullock-dray," I remarked.

"Of course he didn't, fathead," replied the Ancestor, "but his father did. That spry young lad was born in a mud hut – I know him. He is a product of the swift development of this barbarous but amazingly wonderful country of yours – plus some extraordinarily good luck in seasons and catching the tops of the markets. But that flash young buck's good luck will be nothing to the prosperity I feel sure will come to the man on the land by, say, about the time you have grown into a man. Would you like to be a squatter, my lad?"

"I'd rather be a swagman," I replied.

"Lord bless my soul!" said the Ancestor disgustedly. "Why?"

"Because then I could fish all day in the river."

"What nonsense! Why, the squatter could buy all the fish in the river!"

"Yes. But he couldn't catch them."

The reply to this was a disgusted snort, echoed by the screech of cockatoos and parrots, busy calling of greenies and minahs and diamond doves in happy conversation up among the honeyed blossoms of a scarlet-flowering gum. The warmth under that mighty dome of sky at midday, the cool shade of gnarled coolabah and flooded gum by water as we boiled the billy in that insect-humming, dreamy quietness of that two-hour siesta of the bush ...

Jogging along again, and a horseman appears, a good one, too, so easily handling a flighty blood mare. He sports a handlebar moustache, a beauty. Around his cabbage-tree hat is wound, as neatly as a 'Ghan would wind his turban, a large puggaree of spotless white with a neat plait over the crown of the hat, the two long tails flowing down the back of the neck, the ends teased into fringes dyed red and blue. The long muslin ends of the puggaree made for coolness and also protected the back of the neck from sunstroke. Seeming part of the animal itself, he nodded "Good day!" as his mare shied and pranced past the sulky, our poddy little pony glancing indifferently at the beautiful animal plunging by.

"That young fellow fancies himself," remarked the Ancestor as we jogged along. "Did you notice the beeswaxed mo and the pretty puggaree? A dandy, that lad."

"I've seen you wear a puggaree yourself," I replied.

"You seem to see quite a lot," remarked the Ancestor perkily, "more than is good for you at times. Anyway, *I* never wore a puggaree all frilled up at the ends with painted pansies on 'em!"

"A Sturt's desert pea would look better," I mused, "more like the country. Anyway, pansies would not suit you."

"And why not?" demanded the Ancestor.

"You're not handsome enough."

"Of all the cheek! Gee up, you lazy rascal!" called Dad to the pony.

Thus we would jog along into the lengthening shadows of sundown when the old pony would turn off of his own accord to some grassy patch under the trees. That pony certainly had a determined mind when he reckoned it was time to camp.

"Oh well, if he says so, then I suppose we'll have to camp," Dad would say resignedly.

There would be lively squabbling of birds as they, too, sought camping grounds, making the most of the last rays of sunset, screeching at one another of the mighty events of the day. Some would be tales of hairbreadth escape and of tragedy, I felt certain, for there were bound to be some among them who had lost wife or child or friend to the swooping hawk, slinking wildcat, cunning goanna, or treacherous snake. One day I had even seen one taken by a fish. The bird was an insect-eater, hovering almost upon the surface of the water when with a swirl a great black head arose with open jaws and gleaming teeth that snapped – and both bird and fish had vanished to the depths. And already more than once I had seen a bird break its neck when in frantic flight from pursuing hawk it misjudged speed and distance and crashed into a tree. I was always certain the birds discussed the day's adventures after they had come flying home to camp as sundown brought its coolness, gradually merging into the dreamy quietness of early evening. Cheery hum of the campfire. Slow dying down into coals. Then "Plop!" of a fish in depth of night.

Sleep.

One day we drove into tree-lined little Wilcannia – what an adventure to come to a township, so very rare away out there! A very small township, it is true, but surprisingly busy in the easy-going way of the Far West. All in shirt-sleeves, mostly in the white cotton shirt of the day, the bushmen generally in white moles and "'lastic-sides", the men who worked in distant rocky hills in hobnails, the townsmen alert for business in an easy-going fashion – cheery folk these. A Dreadnought loading wool by the river bank, a mob of cattle being swum across river at the Crossing, with Jack Burgess in charge, of course. Yes, and there, sitting hump-backed, cross-legged on a big old flood-washed log stranded high up on the river bank, smoking his pipe, contemplatively watching the swimming mob, was Snagging Jim in his cabbage-tree hat.

Snagging Jim, who had the cheek – or was it the reckless ignorance? – of contemplating opposition to Jack Burgess at this very Crossing he had developed himself. If any man knew the river Jack did. And right here he would cross any mob of cattle quickly and without loss, which means a lot to owner and drover where a big travelling mob is concerned. I can still remember the shrug of the boys when someone wondered "how long will Snagging Jim last".

Jack Burgess was noted as one of the finest bushmen of the Far West, which is saying a very great deal. Some of his remarkable feats of endurance, of path-finding, of mastery of horse and cattle, even then were discussed nightly by many a campfire. A small, sturdily built man, panther-quick on his feet, he was blessed with an astonishing strength and agility. It was believed that no flooded river could drown him unless he was struck on the head by a submerged log. With cold, alert eyes above a well-kept red beard he was always smart in personal appearance. Something elusively peculiar about those eyes – many bushmen swore he just *must* have "cat's eyes". It certainly would appear so, for already he had proved he could ride through dark night over rough country with the same astonishing speed as he could by day. And any man who has ridden through wild bush on a dark night will understand what that means. He possessed initiative and brains as well as his sinewy strength, and had already proved he could use all. In feats of bushmanship and endurance in the near future he was to accomplish what was believed impossible even by the toughest men in that tough country. Admired by all for his bushmanship, Jack was, it was tacitly agreed, "a dangerous man to cross". And against this powerful character, secretive as the owl when he liked, tough as the mallee root, Snagging Jim dared to contemplate opposition!

When strolling along that prettily tree-lined little street-hedged by its low, old-fashioned buildings, Dad took pleasure in pointing out to me "a pioneer". There were almost always half a dozen or so of the grizzled, sturdy old-timers in town. For Wilcannia is a town with a history, it was "going" years before silver and opals immortalized the district, and away out in the saltbush still lived and rode and drove some of the best-known pioneers west of the Darling.

"Couldn't kill 'em with an axe," the Ancestor would chuckle admiringly. "They're that tough they mix gunpowder in their dampers to put a kick in it. What they don't know about stock wouldn't blink the eye of a flea. They can still show the young fellows something, too, can show 'em plenty. And they were battling here, opening up the country, living on the smell of an oily rag long before Paddy Green found Thackaringa, before Johnnie Stokie discovered Umberumberka in 1876, before Joe Meech dropped exhausted and woke up on the Day Dream one miraculous morning in 1882."

"It was a great mine, Dad, wasn't it?"

"They took silver out of it by the dray-load my boy," answered Dad soberly, "slugs of horn silver and silver chlorides near big as a man. The cave of Ali Baba and his Forty Thieves was a pawnshop compared to the silver they found lying out in the mulga there. But I was talking about the men and women who first brought the horses and the cattle and the sheep to the Darling. You young fellows back on the Hill think only of minerals. You never think that if your bellies were not full of meat you could not even *look* for minerals!"

We stood and watched as a Cobb and Co. came rolling into town on the last dash, Jim Denison handling the ribbons, sweating horses with heaving flanks, the big coach rocking, flourish of driver to jingle of harness, musical creak of braces, then screech of braked wheels as the lumbering vehicle pulled up. Boisterous laughter from the thankful passengers, so ready to clamber down.

Frequently thus came a crowd of lively opal-gougers from White Cliffs to "wet their thirst" in Wilcannia town, fresh from their waterless camps. Their eyes always went first towards the river. Presently they would be pulling a battered tobacco tin from the pocket, opening it with loving care, and there, flashing in beauty upon a dark cloth bed, would be lovely little ring and pin and brooch stones already cut and shaped and polished. These were for sale, or for gifts to friends.

A camel mail was setting out to goodness knows where, and now, coming lumbering grudgingly away from the Dreadnought, mooched a long string of camels heading the way the coach had come, out into the blazing sunlight on the dry trip west to the Cliffs, some loaded heavily with cases and cases and cases and bags and bags and crates of stores, others lurching along with a cask of beer lashed to each side.

"That Yellow Amber will be well churned before it reaches the thirsty souls on the Cliffs," said the Ancestor, grinning.

"Why do men drink beer?" I inquired.

"Because they like it!" chuckled the Ancestor and changed the subject before I could think up something smart.

Always sunburnt stockmen were strolling in town or riding into it, in broad-brimmed hat, polished leggings, corduroys freshly washed "for town", belt with tobacco knife in tiny pouch, rolled-up shirt-sleeves, generally a "flash" spotted handkerchief loosely knotted round the neck.

If a mob of shearers also happened to be in town, then the boy who had arrived in the dusty sulky saw interest and excitement indeed.

The pub in those days meant not only bed and food and drink for the traveller, but the place where you heard all the news – not only of the township, but of the entire district and, in case of travelling stock, for instance, of far beyond. The publican received all the gossip of the boys in from the stations, of the drovers, of the travelling shearers, miners, teamsters, and travellers either overland or by river, and relayed the information to those particularly interested. Many people thus received news of one another and of events in the district in general, also from beyond the Queensland border right across the west and down into South Australia.

How all hands would have stared at a prophet had he told them a day was coming when such a thing as wireless would be invented!

On the return trip inland from the river back through the Dolo Hills we might camp a night at hospitable Weinteriga station, where surely I would find myself down at the cookhouse being regaled by the tales of the cook, who would certainly cut for me a mighty hunk of brownie, that luxury of bush days for lots of years to come. Just wouldn't I enjoy a hunk of brownie now!

A few days later we would be jogging along little rocky hills where I would ever be alert for the sight of a wallaby, particularly a yellow-footed one, on over the bluebush plain, all eyes for sight of a plain turkey. An afternoon would come when we would both be listening – the pony, too. Finally we would hearken yet again to the welcoming, mighty hum of the mills coming far away out over the plain – the song of the Silver City.

On other trips we travelled for days along the strange Mootwingee Range while I gazed at those fantastic rock masses, those narrow, gloomy, forbidding valleys, each of which to boyhood's fancy was a Khyber pass. The gigantic Rockholes, churned through a valley of sheer bare rock, must have been torn out by monstrous forces when the world was young indeed, fit setting in many places along that queer range for monsters from another age. Especially so in the deathly loneliness down in the Devil's Elbow, also in Cymbric Vale. At night, with the blaze of the campfire playing in weirdly twisting shapes on the tortured faces of those strange masses of rock, I was glad the Ancestor did not start dreamily yarning of the witches and fairies, the gnomes and hobgoblins, elves and giants and fantods of his own beloved Welsh hills. He had the happy knack of making a lad's hair stand on end with solemn stories of trolls and hobgoblins who delighted to cast a spell upon a boy and turn him into a toad, or into some pathetic, wriggly thing that they made slave for them – tales a boy could snort at if told at home or in daylight, but bloodcurdling when told out here in this desperate loneliness, this brooding night hemmed in by these grotesque shadows, these weird surroundings. He got very near it, though, by day, for the shape of some of these great rock masses we passed reminded him of famous old Welsh castles, and the enthusiastic yarns, the cut-throat border forays, the murders and ghosts, the yells and screeches, the black dungeons where fearsome rats gnawed the manacled prisoner, the walling up alive of unfortunate ones fairly made my hair stand on end. Warming to his subject, he'd tell then of stories of many a fair knight who won his spurs while privately I thought he'd richly earned the rope. Ned Kelly could not have held a candle to ninety-nine per cent of those bold barons. When I mentioned this to the Ancestor he nearly took a fit from righteous indignation.

But of more interest to me was the weird Mootwingee Gorge where the Ancestor showed me, deep in that rock-bound solitude, the strange blackfellows' carvings and paintings on the great rocks and ledges, explaining that our own ancestors had painted on rocks in the same way in the days when they wore bearskins and daubed themselves with woad, fought bears, and chased one another with clubs.

Subdued our voices sounded down there in the rock-bound solitude as the Ancestor held forth while I gazed absorbed at the strange designs. Later I was to see more variegated ones still thirty miles farther on at Sturt's Meadows, mysterious pictures these of hunters, of geometrical designs, of stars and wheels and barred circles, of animal, bird, and spirit tracks, of many things of the primitive bush and a vanished symbolism.

"Don't you despise the aborigines, my lad – but, all the same, never let one walk behind you, or you'll feel his club on the back of your crown. But don't think any the less of him for that – always remember that our own ancestors were very much the same."

But it was good to see proof that in these almost frighteningly primitive surroundings real men and women and children had lived their lives happily enough – and were doing so even then, as a matter of fact, for next day by a lovely rockhole we came upon a little camp of their descendants. It pleased me greatly that they had met Dad before, and obviously liked him.

One long trip, long for those days of the horse and trap though never long enough for me, was from the Hill to Menindee, then jogging along the Darling to turn off through the mulga via the Nineteen Mile Tank heading for the swarming camp of the troglodytes, the White Cliffs opal-fields. After a week on the road, as we cut the heavily trodden Wilcannia track, Dad nodded towards a cloud of rapidly approaching dust.

"The White Cliffs to Wilcannia mail-coach. I don't know what travellers and the mails would do without Cobb and Co.; their coaches are on the roads all over Australia now wherever they can pick up a load. They've got some dandy drivers up on the box, too. They have to be – half their horses are unbroken young colts."

"But the horses would bolt! How can they drive a coach safely if the horses are not broken in?"

"By the skill of the driver high up on the box seat, and because of the two well-trained polers. Always strong, very intelligent. They work with the driver, know his every command and sturdily help him keep the wild young horses in check. I'm surprised you don't know that! You've knocked about quite a lot by now. By Jove, they're coming at a rattling pace! Billy White – or is it Mick Ridge? – handling the ribbons by the look of it. They're using a spider, too."

"What's a spider?"

"That leading horse with his head thrust forward in the middle. You see, there are three horses in the lead. There are generally two, harnessed to the swingle-bars which work from the pole just ahead of the polers. When they need an extra horse they put him in the lead in a set of harness called a 'spider'. And here they are – well loaded, too."

And as we pulled aside the big coach seemed thundering upon us, horses going all out, the coach swaying and creaking, passing with a yell and hat-waving from passengers. High up on the box, the driver greeted us with a flourish of his whip.

"Loaded with opal-gougers going to do in their good money in Wilcannia," said the Ancestor as we jogged on into the swirl of dust. "When you're a man with your pocket full of sovereigns don't go and waste them, my lad."

"But they've worked hard for their money, Dad, they've earned it. Why shouldn't they spend it as they like?"

"Because money is far too hard to get," he replied decidedly.

"But if you got a lot of money suddenly – say out of a mine – wouldn't you like to have a good time?"

He hesitated over that one, then replied soberly, "I'm afraid such luck is not for me, my lad."

Poor Dad! Poor many a dad and mum of those days! It seems but yesterday when a shilling was really important, when ten shillings was a valuable sum of money. Indeed, ten shillings would buy two pairs of boots, good ones, and socks to go with them.

Dad yarned awhile with a couple of kangaroo-shooters who were just pulling off the road for the mulga. Boy-like, I admired the expertly plaited rawhide hat cord with the "Turk's head" round one man's hat, saw at a glance the calibre of the Winchesters at hand, wondered if the other would keep his Captain Kettle moustache so carefully waxed once he got out into the mulga. Their two-horse thoroughbrace loaded with gear, with a "So long! Gee up!" they left the road for the distant foothills. Those sure-footed horses, that jerky old thoroughbrace would need no road; it could cross steep gullies, bump over logs and rocks and stumps when the going was extra bad, and never need any new springs. Our old pony snorted a cloud of dust from his nostrils, shook himself until the harness rattled, then we were jogging along the road again.

Away out over the saltbush in the haze, two emus of gigantic proportions, stalking sedately one behind the other, appeared to be striding along on stilts. A family of kangaroos, giants too, hopping along to cross ahead of them seemed bounding in monstrous strides. I wondered why distance and heat and haze sometimes magnified things so.

As the miles jogged by the Ancestor told me entrancing yarns of fortunes won and lost, of parcels of beautiful gems haggled over by seller and buyer, of bitter quarrels over the jumping of claims, of dark deeds by night as the "ratters" stealthily climbed down shafts and robbed the miners' treasure so hardly won, tales of "Company's men" and independent miners, of furtive deals in snide (stolen opal), of hatred fought out in vicious deeds underground when a gouger found out he'd been robbed by a mate, of miraculous luck and hectic living where a man today could be broke but before tomorrow's sundown could bottom on a fortune. Tales, too, of the notorious Stumpy Push who tried to boss the township, and of the all-in fight when one day the miners came yelling and running together and drove the whole Push off the field for good.

I asked a question just now and then. But of the very tale I wished him to tell he said not a word. How I had been staring, longing for that very thing to happen while I watched the mail-coach approaching!

"Tell me about the hold-ups, Dad! About men in masks suddenly holding up the coach and taking the registered parcels of opals from the mail!"

"Now look here, young feller-me-lad," replied the parent impressively, "there are some questions that should *not* be asked, no matter in what country you may be. As you grow up learn that a quiet tongue is the safest tongue! It's a wise policy to keep your eyes and ears wide open – but your mouth shut. Gee up, you lazy old bag o' bones!" he called to the pony.

In time we jogged into White Cliffs, a clump of iron shanties like a mirage under the sun, low-built little stores and pubs that a tall man had to stoop to enter, an army of lean-tos and tents. Kindly women here, too, and lively youngsters, numbers of them now up on the hill busily scratching at the dumps as the windlass men hauled up and tipped the buckets of whitish opal dirt. Eagerly, so seriously the youngsters, aboriginal youngsters among them, too, scutched flat the soft lumps of stone, carefully breaking each lump in search of "colour", seeking any stray opal missed by the miners below. In time coming I was to work at this fascinating task myself – and how breath-taking when one found a "stone"! Surprising how many were missed, be the miner ever so careful down below. And it was the unwritten law on any opal-field I have been on that once the mullock has been tipped on the dump then the noodlers can keep what they may find. I have seen a stone worth over £100 found that way; such a stone would be worth five times that amount today, quite probably a lot more.

Those little bare hills were pockmarked with thousands upon thousands of holes and cuttings and "paddocks", veritable catacombs tipped with innumerable dumps and windlasses, swarming with toil-stained men like busy ants upon and vanishing within an ant-hill. And over township and claims and camps a thrilling atmosphere, a sturdy feeling of independent toil urged on by the beckoning hand of fortune round the corner.

Here, under the vast sky among these tiny, almost treeless hills that were but grey knobs above a drab plain of coarse grass and saltbush, far out here west of the Darling where there was not enough water to quench the thirst of a crow, was the motley township of White Cliffs, whose tiny hills were supplying the whole world with the loveliest opals ever known – though probably barely a hundred men of the hundreds of millions overseas even knew that such a place as White Cliffs existed.

A miner and his family at Thackaringa.

Frontier life in the far Central West of New South Wales.

8. THE "HEADLESS HORSEMAN"

We took the road back to Wilcannia, dust cloud after cloud now as we passed loaded teams toiling slowly towards those hills of the troglodytes with stores and supplies.

I loved camping at Wilcannia; it seemed always pretty and so interesting with its brown horsemen who might just have ridden in from – where? West of the Darling? Or east? From the Queensland border? Or north-west from northern South Australia and that mysterious Corner Country, out where the great stations lie?

The bushy-whiskered, turbaned 'Ghans, too, were to be met here, and ever and anon along some sun-parched track. I remember old Roda Singh, who went "looking for blood" when on the booze. I've seen his turbaned companions mercilessly lash him to stakes driven into the ground and let him broil under the sun, gnawed by flies and bitten by ants until the yelling, teeth-gnashing fury should subside. Roda was very proud of two whip-like strands of whisker that reached down to his waist. When going on trek he would wind these two strands right up to his chin round a polished stick of bone. Another old rogue was Azim Khan, and there was Cabal the Strong with the fierce eyes, who strode so majestically ahead of his team in his particularly voluminous trousers that on a windy day blew out like balloons. Abdul Kader was another; I can see him heading his heavy-laden team under the great arc of sky towards the pine-clad sandhills along the South Australian border, his caravan lurching steadily on its way to Mundowdna station. An occasional visitor to the Hill was Bejah Deverish from Marree, our 'Ghan hero. For he was the guide to the Calvert Expedition, was really – to us, anyway – the hero of that ill-fated expedition into the unknown west that in mystery then stretched away through Central Australia and nearly two thousand miles on through Western Australia to the Indian Ocean. Two good men lost their lives on that terrible trip, but Bejah came out of it with colours flying. He was one of the main men, too, who opened up the Birdsville Track, already famous to every man of the land in the Far West. Track after track throughout arid lands had Bejah Deverish opened up and thus greatly helped the pioneers who doggedly formed stations far out in the wastes where even wheeled teams could not go. He had saved the lives, too, of lost men who otherwise would have perished. Little wonder then that the tall, erect figure of the piercing-eyed Afghan clad in his many-folded turban, long garishly decorated jacket, long baggy white trousers, striding out of the mirage ahead of his tall camels, was a figure of romance to us boys.

Occasionally from the Darling Dad would jog along south over the saltbush plain to tiny Ivanhoe sweltering under its extreme isolation, heat, and mirage. Each trip was approved of by me, knowing security in sulky and the pony, cool water in the water-bag, tucker in the tucker-box, the certainty that Dad would know how far the next waterhole was on ahead; this utter loneliness under a brazen sky held no terrors for me. I did not realize in what frightening isolation the few men and women throughout that vast area lived – not until I visited Ivanhoe many years later in a sixty-mile-an-hour car, and saw a railway line coming through.

From Mossgiel we jogged on to Booligal on the Lachlan, camping one glorious sunset on the edge of a big swamp. Eagerly I threw together a few sticks and put the billy on, anxious to sneak a peep at the wild ducks before the last rays of sunset merged into whispering night. Abundance of sweet green grass was here after recent rains, the Ancestor arguing with the impatient pony that insisted on eating before the harness could be taken off. Night settled swiftly as hungrily we ate to a hearty croaking of frogs, from a dead stump came the hoarse cry of "More pork! Moore poork!" and the fire blazed warmly as night brought its chill. One ear to the cackling of ducks, the trumpet blasts of some pugnacious old-man swan away out on the swamp, I put away the tucker things, then unrolled the swags as Dad meditatively cut his plug tobacco, slowly rubbing it to size in the palm of a gnarled hand. Pulling off my boots I sat on the blankets gazing out over the dim sheet of water, hearkening to the mysterious night noises of the bush I already loved. With forefinger and thumb Dad solemnly plugged the tobacco into the smelly old bowl, reached for a firestick, placed the glowing end to the bowl, and puffed. Momentarily I glanced at the coal-illumined face, for the first time noticed there were deep lines chiselled in that face, distinct grey bristles jutting out from the ancestral chin. Serenely he laid the stick back within easy reach in the fire, puffed contentedly as again I listened out towards the swamp. A gentle rustle in the grass behind us told of an inquisitive little bilbie attracted by the firelight. I knew that presently I would see a pair of glowing green eyes or swimming red ones staring at us from out of the edge of darkness. The throaty cackle of waterhens rose piercingly from the reeds.

In the momentary silence the Ancestor's musing voice remarked, "Do you know the name of this swamp, my lad?"

"No."

"The Headless Horseman Swamp."

I glanced towards the Ancestor. He was not nearly the age then that I am now, but then I was a boy of nearly fourteen, passionately longing for that age so I could leave school and go venturing into the world. I reckoned I was nearly a man now and was not going to allow the Ancestor to put one over me if I could help it. But he was innocently puffing his pipe, gazing dreamily into the fire. The warm, cheery glow felt more cheery still.

After a pause I inquired, "Why do they call it that?"

"Because," he replied casually, "he has often been seen here – the Headless Horseman, I mean – particularly on moonlit nights."

I realized moonlight was coming, as involuntarily I glanced around. Yes, already there was growing the reflection of big old trees on the mirror of the swamp. The night seemed to have grown chilly. And deathly quiet.

Musically then came the tinkle of the pony's bell, a water-softened cackling of wild ducks. All was well. I glanced doubtfully at the Ancestor. Gazing into the .fire, he was scratching that grizzled chin thoughtfully, the grating noise eerily distinct.

"Have you ever seen him?" I asked, with what I hoped was a superior smile.

"No. But the drovers have told me, men I know well and believe." He paused, to reach for the firestick again, to puff, and lay the stick down again. "He comes suddenly, galloping on a black horse. A black cloak is wrapped all around him – but he has no head! He gallops through the camp like a phantom – and is gone!"

Again that deathly silence. His pipe was puffing well. I longed to jump up and throw more wood on the fire. Suddenly I remembered the little home in distant Broken Hill. How cosy it would be back there with Mum and the girls, Mum longing for her wandering boy to be home again, Mum little knowing how her pride and delight was longing to be home right now. The swamp was growing more moonlit every moment. And chillier!

The Ancestor chuckled, gazing into the fire.

"Of course," he murmured conversationally, "it is only a ruse of cattle-thieves, clever, *dangerous* cattle-thieves. When a mob of travelling cattle are to camp here the thieves know they are coming days beforehand by mulga wire. When the travelling mob settles down here for the night the thieves are planted near by. Then in the dead of night the 'headless' rider mounts his black horse, drapes the black cloak over head and shoulders and all around him, leaving only a wide slit for the eyes. It is cleverly done. He appears to be headless, frightfully hunched up, clinging like grim death to his black horse. He digs the spurs in, and with a startling crackle of hooves over dead sticks is coming at full gallop for the camp. The resting beasts are up on their hooves on the instant, then away in a maddened stampede. Little mobs are broken up by the timber, of course; the 'headless' man's mates are all around the camp and head these off and away. The drovers always lose some, for these fast-moving cattle-thieves know every inch of the swamp and the country for many miles around. And now what if we put the billy on and down a pannikin of tea and a slice of damper and cocky's joy before we turn in?"

I did not fall asleep for some time that night. Rolled up in the blanket, I presently became aware that Dad was sleeping with one eye open.

When for a longish time there came no tinkle of the bell he half rose on his elbow, listening, then sank back again when finally came the reassuring tinkle. I realized then he was anxious for the pony. But of what use would our humble pony be to a well-mounted gang of cattle-thieves? Interesting how danger or tension will enliven the human mind, for instantly I realized our pony was a sturdy, staunch pony; on many a hard track he had proved himself so. Such would be obvious to the trained eye. And horse- or cattle-thieves, no matter how well mounted, could find good use for such an animal where all horses were valuable. With a shock I wondered then what we should do without the pony, on a lonely track with travellers few and far between. Suddenly came the wonderful relief that at least here was plenty of water, and abundant wildfowl for food.

Lessons such as that often linger with us. In the years fast coming I was to think ahead and be cautious on distant tracks lest I lose my own precious horses.

I learnt that Dad had not been pulling my leg about the Headless Horseman, though I suspect this particular gang were operating some time earlier. Sooner or later that Headless Horseman would have stopped a bullet. The drovers of necessity were tough men. Such a scheme, carried out by determined characters over a suitable locality would prove successful a number of times under such isolated conditions of travel, distances, and border life. But the drovers' bush telegraph would warn them far and wide, and eventually the Headless Horseman would cause his last stampede. Years later, after crossing the Queensland border and riding along the Bulloo to head off towards Eromanga I came across another Headless Horseman, similarly operating in the wild country there of those days. Whether this was the same gang working in pastures new I never inquired; I was always pushing on in those eager years.

In those times along the State borders in this region, especially up towards the Corner Country, the operations of horse- and cattle-thieves were energetic and constant, for of course the horse was the chief method of transport, and was thus of considerable value, indeed of national value. The Corner Country is the farthest nor'-west of New South Wales, the meeting of the "corners" of New South Wales, Queensland, South Australia, and the Northern Territory. A huge area of country, largely semi-arid, very sparsely populated and watered, a desolation in drought-time but a garden in good seasons. An undeveloped country of isolation and distances, demanding good bushmanship from the battling station men, particularly so in travelling, whether with stock or "just travelling". A wonderfully strategic escape route for stolen stock from Queensland was "down through the Corner", south-west down the barely inhabited Cooper, Diamantina, or Georgina, then across the border along that harsh, stark track of a thousand romances, the Birdsville Track, through the corner of South Australia, skirting Lake Eyre across the maze of watercourses of Goyder's Lagoon, weaving in among the sand-ridges past the mulga claypans, then riding into the mirages towards Marree, headquarters of the camel-teams, and at last riding south, parallel to the jagged outlines of the Flinders Range, all the hot way to the markets near Adelaide. A closely parallel route led from anywhere round Longreach in central Queensland south-west down the Cooper, across the border at Innamincka of the Burke and Wills tragedy, on through the sandhill country to Marree. Legitimate mobs used these famous tracks, of course, but most of the Queensland cattle travelled east towards the meatworks and big town markets along the coast, or south-east towards ever-hungry Sydney. But every step stolen stock trod down along this isolated "back door of Queensland" led them farther and farther from the distant eastern coast with its organized law and order, eventually to be sold far away in the extreme south of another State. Not only so, but the stock-thieves could choose any one of three States – or Colonies, as they were before Federation – South Australia, New South Wales, or Victoria. Once a stolen mob had got a start on they took some catching up, even should the owners discover they were not travelling towards the eastern markets. Quite often, despite long distances, a mob would be sold and the rustlers widely scattered before the manager of a big property discovered his loss. In those days of isolation, of very few fences, great stations of thousands of square miles, and huge mobs wandering practically at will, there was no radio, no motor transport, and overland communication, except in settled telegraph areas, was by endurance of man and horse.

When Broken Hill got a boom on, first in 1887, a new, rich, and hungry market was opened up for daring night riders. West across the South Australian border were only a very few large stations, then a thousand and more miles of uninhabited wilderness almost to the

Western Australian coast. North for hundreds of miles into Queensland were great scattered stations and a few tiny isolated townships, while south to the Murray were but a few stations. To the east for three hundred miles or more only stations and a few townships. So that the rapidly growing, hungry Silver City lay in a sea of bush isolation, a dream market for horse- and cattle-thieves.

As well as the horses and cattle "lifted" from big north-west New South Wales stations there were those that came down a route from central Queensland running south to the border along the Warrego, skirting Bourke to travel along the Darling to Menindee, thence nor'-west to the Hill. Or, farther west, they moved down the Paroo and the Bulloo to the Border, skirting White Cliffs to strike the Darling near Wilcannia, thence to Menindee and the Hill. Again, there was the tough track among the Eurowie hills to the Hill.

Quiet, busy little Victoria, minding its own business while nestling along the south of New South Wales, every now and then enjoyed stolen New South Wales and even Queensland steak for breakfast and dinner, though of course quite unaware of the juicy fact. Several other routes were from Queensland, each through the isolated nor'-west of New South Wales. One came down the Paroo to cut across to the Darling and along that obliging river to Menindee, then south to the border of New South Wales and Victoria at Wentworth, along any one of half a dozen great anabranches of the Darling. Another route down the Warrego skirted Bourke and crossed the Darling, travelling straight south across the red country, passing Ivanhoe and Mossgiel down to the Lachlan right by the Murrumbidgee, thence on to Echuca on the Murray at the Victorian border. It was this route that passed by the Headless Horseman Swamp. A busy town indeed was Echuca in those days, Australia's great inland port. How very, very few Australians today know that such ports even existed! Echuca is still a prosperous town, but gone are the busy river trade, the noisy fleets of river steamers, that long, high-built warren of river wharves, the hectic life of the bargemen and boatmen.

Gone also are the horse-thieves and cattle-duffers. They certainly toiled long and strenuously and accepted heavy risks for their questionable gains – unlike their modern counterpart, the motor-car thieves of today.

Recently, not by plodding horse along the dry, dusty track, but at fifty miles an hour in a modern car, I passed by Blanchewater station near Mount Hopeless in the north-east corner of South Australia. This station, in my boyhood days owned by the Beltana Pastoral Company, used to be, so far as my knowledge goes, the greatest horse-breeding station in

Australia, probably in the world. Blanchewater enjoyed a hungry market for its horses, both here and in India. The horses, for light, medium and heavy transport, were bred from magnificent blood stock continually introduced. Tales of horse- and cattle-thieving in that Corner Country were legion. When I was a young fellow it was said that one gang of horse-thieves lived off Blanchewater station alone, and quite possibly it was so.

Over those great unfenced spaces waged a perpetual war, a constant battle of wits and physical endurance between the station-hands and the horse-thieves. One notorious gang, after successfully operating for some years, escaped being wiped out only by the dogged staunchness of their leader. He was caught at last, through an oversight by a member of the too-confident gang over a roan horse. In the flurry during the surprise arrest one member of the gang leapt on his horse and galloped into the bush, heading towards the Territory. He was never seen again. The others stood fast, nonchalantly going about their business, while their captive leader was threatened and cajoled, all to no purpose. In sullen mood he would either say nothing or reply with jeers. Finally he was offered £1000 – very big money those days – and his freedom if he would name the others of the gang.

"I'll see you all in hell before I'll squeal on my mates!" he growled.

"But you would be very foolish not to tell us their names. You are being offered £1000 – and your freedom!"

"Keep it!"

"But –"

"Look here! I'm a man yet, and I'll die one, or try to! You'll never get the names of my mates from me."

"You'd save yourself at least two years in jail."

"I'll do my two years – *more* if I have to!"

The gang warily carried on during their leader's enforced absence, banking his share of the profits until he could return to the mulga.

The eventual downfall of this gang was brought about by informers from "outside", men who seemingly drifted into the country and took jobs round about – with their eyes and ears open. Inducements were believed to have been heavy, for this well-organized gang were hardened experts and stuck together like glue, and an informer must be clever and prepared to take big risks, knowing a blunder would mean a bullet for him away out there somewhere in the mulga.

Yet there was a gang thereabouts who would always give a traveller a horse if he had "lost" one. He only had to go to the leader in desperation and say, "Hey, Tom, I've lost my horse!"

"Go on! That's hard luck."

"Yes, he's my best horse. I can't do without him. I daren't travel on."

"That's bad, but never mind. We'll fix you up with a horse – we've got plenty, you've got to get on with your job."

And he'd give the traveller a horse – but of course not as good as the one he had stolen from him.

But gone now is the army of Blanchewater horses, the splendid animals that used to roam in big mobs far and wide over a great area. A grand sight it was to see the fiery-eyed stallion of a mob pawing the earth, neighing his defiance from distended, blood-red nostrils. As we sped over the gibber plains towards Marree I missed, too, the camel-teams lumbering up out of the haze. Marree used to be a great headquarters, the largest Afghan camp in Australia. From there the long teams, heavy-laden, spider-webbed to all points of the compass to the scattered stations and mining camps. West of north into Central Australia, west into the queer lands that vanished into nowhere, north-east into south-west Queensland, east into north-west New South Wales, south down into South Australia. Difficult to imagine how the pioneers in the semi-arid areas could have done without the camel; old-timers have often assured me they could not have settled the far out lands without the 'Ghan and his "humpies". But the camel, too, has vanished with the pioneering years. Only a few dispirited old 'Ghans remained in Marree, including several I had known as a boy at the Hill. As we purred into the tiny old township an aeroplane flew clearly silhouetted against the sombre outline of the Flinders Range. What a great change the invention of the internal combustion engine has brought, not only to Australia but to all the world in less than a man's lifetime! What a breath-taking era the youth of today is born into! But perhaps the young fellow had better put the brake on a bit lest he run away with himself. However, in those days of Headless Horsemen the motor-car, the flying ship, wireless, the refrigerator, and many another "impossibility" were but thoughts in the minds of a few iron-willed men.

As the Ancestor and I jogged back into the Hill after each trip a breeze would bring us the hum of the great mills along the Line of Lode, ceaselessly pounding the ore day and night. That welcome breeze would die down and the mighty hum die away. But when we came within a mile of the town the roar of the mills would not be denied. Pounding, pounding, pounding, grinding, grinding, grinding, hour by hour, day and night, year by year their own song – what a great song it has proved to be! – pounding into the mighty chorus of Australia's destiny.

9. THE WHITE MAN COMES

It is interesting to see, though through the vanished years and only as in a mirage, how this fact has come to be.

The first note was struck by an indomitable man named Sturt. A grim note, for this then was a grim country. While exploring inland he discovered, on 18th January 1829, a big but then almost dry river dribbling through a far inland locality called Wurtamurtah by the wild aborigines. Eventually to be called Bourke, this sunlit bush region was three hundred miles north-east of a sombre, lonesome rock outcrop called by the local aborigines Willyama, many years later to be called the Broken Hill. Sturt rode some distance down this steep banked river, the first white man to muse upon its solitude, its solid, gnarled trees that had defied so many droughts and untold floods; he rode on to wonder at the heat haze shimmering over these vanishing plains in part covered with a strange, drab shrubbery which he shrugged away as worthless.

He left on record that there was no life there, that the stillness of death hovered over those hot red plains, those drear grey plains leading to he knew not where. He was mistaken. But in his wonderful journeys into this harsh new country the truly great explorer was dogged by terrible drought again and again, and this misled him.

Strangely enough, Sturt noted some slight evidence of minerals – as did Mitchell, the next explorer to strike the Darling. Mitchell followed the meandering river course down to a favourite aboriginal camp, which the kopi-painted tribesmen called Minandichee. Inscrutable Fate in this last continent was at last leading the white man to where would spring up a "Silver City". How little those first explorers dreamed of such a miracle, with sweat-streaked brows slowly riding through what appeared to them as a weary wilderness, barren and worthless.

And yet, each man mused on the possibility of minerals!

Watched by curious, fearful eyes within the deep-set sockets of primitive men, Mitchell camped under the big old trees at Minandichee, unaware that Willyama, look-out post of the aborigines, the black rock Willyama, now lay but eighty miles north-west of his camp.

What a wonder, what a fantastic dream it would have been to Mitchell, had he found it! He was keenly interested in minerals; many of the outstanding landmarks discovered on this trip were named after prominent geologists.

Sturt's next epic was the open-boat voyage down the Murrumbidgee, thence into the Murray, down through Victoria and South Australia to the lakes at the great river mouth, discovering the junction of the Darling with the Murray on the way.

Thus, although day by day drifting far away from that isolated black hill to the north, he was still bound to its destiny by some strange link of Fate, for those river waters that carried him and his gallant band for so many hundreds of adventurous miles were the very same that in the now fast-coming years were mightily to help the overlanders in the development of all the north-west by transport of their food and stores, and of their produce as gradually they settled in the country. They were also to help in the hectic development of Willyama, a Silver City undreamt of. But these events were not foreseen by any living man, not even as in a mirage.

It was in 1844 that Sturt made his last trip inland in search of the Inland Sea he so ardently believed in. From the Murray he travelled up the Darling and formed a base camp, as Mitchell had, under the old river gums at Minandichee, which later would be called by white men Menindee. Surely the slow, certain hand of Destiny had directed all this! Mounted, the party rode out into the great loneliness yet farther west among those dwarf trees, so strange to them, of drab mulga and gidgee and clumpy mallee, of bloodwood stunted yet lovely when flowering in glorious masses of cream and rose. They believed the dead-finish too miserable a shrub to call a tree, unaware of its pride and glory when unfolding to the vast blue sky its spiky, fuzzy, yellow balls of flowers. The spotted leopardwood caught their laggard interest as the dead-finish and needlewood repelled it. They despised the kochia bush, the cotton-grass, the mulga-grass, in foreboding crossed many a dead watercourse to gaze glumly at the black box of the dried-up swamps, hearkened to the sighing of the belah, uneasily turning in their blankets to the boom of the bittern by night, the hoarse croak of the mopoke. Far from their fellow men in this great loneliness, quietly they rode over the bluebush plains under a burning sunlight, travelling slowly north-west, on a windy day staring in amazement at countless brown roly-polies chasing one another across the plain, rolling over and over like enormous brown, flimsy balls, many as tall as a man, constantly being caught by an old-man saltbush only to jump or edge round it, urged by a spurt of wind and go hurriedly rolling on and on. As far as the eye could see were others hurrying, rolling, rolling on, battalions following battalions of them, limitless reinforcements coming piling on behind, hurrying on, rolling on, hurrying on. Never in their wildest dreams had they imagined plants behaving thus; they would sooner have believed the yarns of Sinbad the

Sailor than the truth of this before their wondering eyes. The simple fact, of course, is that roly-poly, a slender, very lightly built bush, grows in a rounded shape to the height of a boy or a man. Summer dries it to brown, a big rounded ball of feathery, wiry stalks. It dies, drying to a feathery lightness but keeping its shape. Then the first strong wind snaps it off from the withering stem and whisks it away, tumbling it over and over, often blowing it for many miles in a series of slow, then violently agitated rolls and leaps according to the varying velocity of the wind and the contours of the ground. On a gusty day, where the plain happens to be bare of trees and shrubbery, the nervous, hurrying battalions leaping and rolling and dancing along before the wind, with ever and anon the innumerable laggards putting on a wild spurt to catch up with the others scurrying ahead are a fantastic sight indeed, and so the early adventurers found it.

So, with the song of strange birds in their ears and distance spreading far away into the unknown before their inquiring eyes they toiled cautiously on, peered at by wild men and women and frightened children, by curious kangaroos and emus, by wallabies and dingoes, all seeing for the first time their deadly enemy the White Man, and those frighteningly monstrous animals – horses. It was the beginning of the end for many of these wild things, for in the swift years coming the strange new animals of the White Man were to eat them out of home and bush. Some eighty miles from the big river the travellers gazed at a grey, rocky, scrub-clad little range stretching like a forbidding barrier up out of the plain. This Sturt named the Barrier Range.

One morning he climbed up towards the summit of a rough, black, rocky hill. It was Willyama, strewn with a confusion of giant boulders as if part of the hill in some titanic struggle of Nature had been riven and broken. Sturt climbed steadily up, startling the rock wallabies, until, a lone figure silhouetted in the vastness, he shaded his eyes with his hand and gazed eagerly north, seeking any sign of his inland sea. Yes! There it was, stretching far away out into the haze.

Presently he became bitterly aware that he was gazing upon a dream sea. Many a time that mirage was to beckon him on – on – luring him to a gleaming expanse of water ever dissolving in haze away.

Disappointed, Sturt became interested in the sunburnt, heavy, unusual looking rocks at his feet. He broke some, examined pieces thoughtfully, and collected samples for analysis on return to civilization.

Had Sturt only known that he was standing upon a hill of silver!

He and his men rode on, to the tragedy of the Depot Glen. Had he not stumbled upon that wee, rock-bound glen it is extremely doubtful whether he and his men would ever have been heard of again. For its crystal-clear water pool was a gem of life in a dead land.

But, made prisoners there by the fearful drought, gradually weakening from scurvy, they sank into growing despondency at the hopelessness of it all as the days dragged into weeks and the weeks into scorching months. Sturt set his dispirited men to heavy work, hoping to pass the time away, anything to try to keep them in health and ease this hopeless brooding. Man-handling heavy rocks, laboriously they began building a big pyramid of stone up on a little red hill beside the glen, ever since known as Mount Poole. It was Poole's monument, for he died there. I have stood beside that great cairn and wondered at the mystery of Fate. For down below in the quiet glen lay hidden gold. Only in one little place, in one little patch, it is true, but alluvial gold for all that. And above all, the water there to work it.

If only Sturt, keen on minerals, had found that gold, had even thought of setting his men to work on the vague possibility of finding some! How different their plight, their surroundings would have appeared then! For the magic yellow specks would have brought eagerness and laughter and health; hopelessness and drought and death would have been forgotten. They would have been eager indeed to work, with talk and laughter and golden dreams round the campfire o' nights – very different to the silent, sombre forms just lying there staring up at the everlasting stars, waiting for the drought to break, or for themselves to perish one by one.

Tomorrow, if tomorrow ever came, they would be morosely toiling up the red hill again, carrying rocks under a blazing sun, with blistered hands and aching limbs building a monument to a dying comrade.

We leave them marooned there in the burning loneliness, Sturt breaking his heart for the chance to ride out into the mirages, seeking his phantom sea.

In ages gone it really had been there, an inland sea of fresh water girded by great forests, screamed over by flocks of wildfowl, its luxuriant plains roamed over by weird and mighty animals. But long since it had vanished. When Sturt at last did see remnants of its bed he called it "Desolation".

Yes, Time brings mighty changes. Both the vast aeons of Time, and the little breath of Time since I was a boy. Is there really such a thing as Time?

Sturt's specimens of rocks were never assayed; the samples "became lost" by some mischance, oversight, or sheer carelessness, and were never officially assayed.

Again and yet again Fate would seem deliberately to conspire to keep the great secret until her own good time. And how wonderfully that time was to merge for good into the destiny of Australia!

Upon his return to civilization, Sturt's diaries and careful maps, especially after his last trip, opened up visions of a vast expanse of unknown country to those land-seekers far south in South Australia and Victoria, south-east and east in New South Wales. And presently, converging on this long, "new" river, the Darling, came riding the first of the pioneers caring not for Sturt's forbidding account of that outlandish country. They would come and see for themselves, following in the tracks of the explorers, and explore yet farther – as others would presently come following in *their* tracks.

And thus it was that the Darling, and eventually west of the Darling, was gradually opened up by the run-hunters. But slowly, for it really was a strangely new and harsh country, of extreme isolation and terrible dryness, of hot distances which farther westward faded away into the totally unknown. This country was really "new" in this still new continent – new soil, new climate, new timber, drab and unusual shrubbery, doubtful-looking grasses, very different to the fresh, luscious grasses of bountifully watered Victoria and the eastern New South Wales lands. Thus these land-seeker explorers had to learn their way, not only in finding water and suitable land in unknown country, but learn the very earth from which their few head of precious stock might cling to life. And that hot, red earth, that grey, dry earth, those sun-baked gullies claimed the lives of numbers of them. And broke the hearts of women.

Good seasons came, bringing pleasant surprises. For the sere-looking shrubs, now called saltbush and bluebush and the other bushes and poor-looking grasses proved surprisingly nutritive and were greedily eaten by stock which grew rolling fat as this sombre land was transformed into a wildflower garden. Acres and acres of everlastings draped the harsh slopes with white of snow and yellow gold, of sky blue and scented russet. The recently watered flats blazed into vast carpets vivid with the big "ham-and-egg" daisy, acres of purple gilgai pea, lovely brown and yellow and purple swainsona. Birds in bewildering variety made merry this surprising land, wild game came in abundance while crucifers and goodenias made beautiful the dead-finish flats now blazing with the scarlet of Sturt's desert pea. The far scattered settlers gazed in an unbelieving joy as an even more resplendent miracle in this now pleasant land unfolded itself. The Dry Lakes!

Typical of this "new" country, these lakes are caused by a great number of creeks that carry water only in the rare heavy rains spilling out from the small rocky Barrier ranges on to the great open plains where their waters form the Box-tree and other swamps, the lagoons and gilgai holes and claypans, also by a number of the inland Queensland rivers such as the Paroo and Bulloo with their numerous tributaries flowing south and south-west to spill across the New South Wales border into the Corner Country and vanish. But during floods they flow much stronger and farther and spill out into numerous dry depressions, forming lakes for longer or shorter duration, according to size and depths. The Darling, too, with its great network of channels and surging anabranches spills out over a vast area of plain country, filling yet other lakes. During an occasional flood year these lakes run into hundreds of lakes, even forming a chain of lakes right across western New South Wales from the Queensland border to the Victorian, linking border to border with a chain of life indeed. As the waters recede into the river channels those depressions remain as shallow lakes. Comes the hot sun, and evaporation. Slowly, then faster, lake after lake begins to dry up, all but the very largest of them. But, where every lake has been, what an entrancing picture! A verdant mass of herbage and clover gay with wildflowers, merry with bird life, a bright green oasis of plenty stretching for miles away. No wonder those horny-handed, sunburnt run-hunters were entranced when they first gazed upon such a scene, this sun-scorched land transformed into a paradise.

Such an intriguing, such a deceiving land it can be!

I've never forgotten, though I saw it away back when I was a young fellow, Moncooney Lake on Annandale station. I rode up on top of a big sandhill at sunrise and gazed down on the lake. Where a few weeks ago had been a sheet of water stretching distantly away was now a "lake" of verdant green delicately tinged with rose, then the sheen of gold coating the smooth slopes of the surrounding sandhills as the glorious sunrise brightened from fire into gold. And then the lake was an emerald green, a fitting couch for angels. Now jewelled above the clover shone the pure white and golden yellow of lilies, while under the rapidly brightening dawn masses of blues and scarlets of countless flowering plants kissed their petals to the sun. Away out towards the centre a remaining patch of water gleamed like a diamond within its setting of intense green. And from here came faintly the call of waterfowl, among huge white flowers that were nesting pelican. Surely no babies of the wild could ever be born in a more beautiful paradise. Studded thickly over all the grass and flowers were many cattle so lazily fat as to be awaiting the growing warmth of the sun before they would deign to dine. At the distant edge of the lake, fair under the rising sun, lazily arose a blue coil of smoke. Then came little figures to sit by the campfire at the call of the cook. Up to their knees in herbage, with the sun's rays reflecting upon them from the sandhill slopes the stockmen's horses shone like blazing chestnuts. A lovely picture under a soft blue sky, and one in which man did not look out of place.

Easy to understand, then, that those among the early land-seekers who rode into the Country of the Lakes in such a season believed themselves in some strange paradise, watching in delight their foot-weary stock growing fat before their very eyes.

In my day – long after the overlanders of course, and by the time the country had become well stocked – as many as nine thousand head of prime fat cattle have been lifted from the Annandale lakes alone in one year.

Alas, there is a reverse side to the picture, as throughout life there so often is. To that same station and throughout all the Corner Country, south-west Queensland, even east of the Darling and all country west of the Darling, right across the north of South Australia, came a terrible drought, as has happened before, has happened since, and will again. The earth became a burning desolation, cattle dying of starvation everywhere over a vast area, while round many a waterhole that still held putrid water thousands of beasts slowly sank to an awful death, too weak to heave themselves from the bog. The only sound over all that stifling desolation the "Kark! Kark! Kark!" of gorged crows, by night the snap of the dingoes' fangs tearing into helpless beasts.

Two large mobs of Annandale cattle became marooned in the height of that drought. The only hope of saving them was to shift them to Birdsville, to a waterhole on the Diamantina, over a ninety-mile dry stage without a blade of grass. One mob just got through, excepting those that fell out exhausted, of course. The other mob started out for Coongie Lake by the Cooper at Innamincka. The drover had scouted the route a week previously to assure himself that a known waterhole on the way would hold out until the cattle could arrive. The beasts would fill themselves with the putrid water remaining there, then plod on again on the last dash. To reach that waterhole meant an eighty-mile dry stage with already weakened cattle. When the mob arrived the waterhole was dry; even the mud had caked up into blistering fragments. Evaporation under the stifling heat can be terrific out there.

That mob had to be abandoned. The drovers, with perishing horses under them, barely escaped with their own lives.

Thus, within fifteen years of Sturt's return, a few hardy ones took up large areas of country between the Darling and the Victorian and South Australian borders, the South Australian overlander drays and teams slowly toiling up north and north-east from Adelaide, six months on the track – a journey now done in comfort in a few hours by car – the Victorians crossing the Murray and plodding north through unfamiliar "dwarf" bush, the New South Wales horsemen coming from away east riding towards the setting sun with here and there their womenfolk with them. Some overlanders travelled a thousand long, slow miles before at last they found a wild bush tract they believed they could tame and call home. The women were brave, for day by day they were creeping ever farther out into the unknown, living on weevily flour and wild game shot from the old muzzle-loading gun – still in use when I was a boy – at times in need of a strip of rawhide to repair their boots, ever worried lest they find no water by sunset, in constant dread of the blacks, of slithering snakes, of accident and sickness to their menfolk, as day by day slowly they plodded farther and farther away from friends and civilization, growing yet more uneasy at the whispering loneliness of this vast and limitless bush. By night the wail of the curlew brought shivery recollection of the banshee of the far-away land they had left for ever; the howl of the dingo was the howl of the wolf. Far worse things were heard at times, for many a pioneer mother of ours has crouched in tent or hut or under the wagon with her baby clasped to her breast, shivering to the roar of corroboree from stamping feet and savage throats of wild men down by the ridge not a mile away.

Eventually the run-hunters reached and formed a base at Sturt's old camp of Minandichee on the Darling, and thus the pioneer township of Menindee arose, a historic river township still going strong today. By 1860 the big station men had pushed out west of the Darling and crossed the South Australian border until halted by the frightening country of the Dead Lakes. Beyond there, for nearly two thousand miles west right to the Indian Ocean, brooded the totally unknown.

Poking about here and there with the adventurers came the "claypan squatters", seeking a corner of good country or grass wherever waterhole or passing thunderstorm had brought up sweet herbage. Quaint boys these claypan squatters, generally dour men, born nomads all, hardy as the nomads are. This was a very small and passing phase of Australian settlement; these taciturn men sought not so much to settle definitely upon land as to roam independently on the fringe of settlement, shepherding their little mob of stock to a patch of good country, surlily striking camp and pushing on when pushed on by more numerous and permanent home-seekers. Unrecorded, bitter struggles were here and there fought out in the great loneliness between these differing individualists. Meanwhile another thin wave of settlers came slowly battling through the bush from the east in New South Wales, travelling westward on a more northerly course, striking the Darling north of Menindee, which led to the forming of picturesque little Wilcannia. Others again struck the Darling farther north still, and the town of Bourke grew up in the locality Sturt had discovered and named Fort Bourke back in 1835. Meanwhile Queensland men from their south-eastern coastal lands began creeping out to their far south-west, and eventually over the borders into the Corner Country.

Thus laboriously, gradually, a thin film of settlement reached the Darling. A few crossed it, creeping on into the harsh country eventually to be known as "West of the Darling". And there still a lonely black outcrop overlooked the silence, a primal rock of ages bathed in silver by the light of a million moons. Still the look-out post of primitive man and the eaglehawk, this Willyama rose massive above the saltbush plain, now only eighty miles nor'-west of a little settlement called Menindee. A sunburnt, forbidding outcrop of black rock brooding in a wilderness. What human could have dreamt what it was to mean to those three big States, to all Australia?

But now this Willyama of the aborigines had gained a new name, though known to very, very few, it is true. The towering buttress had attracted an occasional horseman among the ever restless land scouts who climbed it to gaze out over the country as Sturt had. So as a landmark it gradually gained, then held its name of "the Broken Hill".

"Out by the Broken Hill. Yes, there's a big dry creek lies about eight mile west of the Broken Hill."

Eventually that particular area of country was taken up in a great station called Mount Gipps. Considerably later a section of 50,000 acres of it was fenced in. That broken hill was in the centre. So the paddock was called "the Broken Hill paddock".

That far western country, so distant from roads, let alone settlement, could not have been occupied so quickly had it not been for the strategically spaced rivers, the Murray, the Darling, and the Murrumbidgee in particular. For from the settled south these rivers offered, except during drought time, easy transport inland for many hundreds of miles, out into the unknown back country. These were Nature's water roads through three States. This fact, of course, was but guessed at by the early coastal settlers, who for long had wondered at the riddle of the rivers. How far did their waters flow inland? From whence did their waters come? Sturt solved the major riddle by sailing in a whaleboat down the Murrumbidgee into the Murray and on right to the bar-locked mouth of Australia's greatest river at Lake Alexandrina on the South Australian coast near Adelaide. But it was not until 1852, when settlement had slowly spread inland from the coasts along the Murray that the long discussed possibility of transport by river to the inland settlers creeping towards the Darling was put to the test. William Randell of Mannurn, South Australia, launched his famous "steamer", the *Mary Ann*. She was as tiny as she and her crew were game. The blacksmith at the little bush township of Mannurn had built her boiler; she was a dinkum bushman craft. She puffed away on her great adventure upstream in August 1853. Actually her voyage was that of an inland Columbus, for the tiny "puffing Jenny" chugged her way a thousand miles upstream.

Unfortunately for her indomitable skipper, and quite unknown to him, a hefty rival was hurrying in his wake. She had come from the sea, then into the river mouth and over the great bar several days after Randell started upstream. This rival was the *Lady Augusta*, Captain Charles Cadell, RN. A paddle-wheel steamer built in Sydney, she was a modern ocean greyhound compared to the Tom Thumb *Mary Ann*. One night away upstream, while peacefully anchored, the astonished Randell and his crew hearkened to the soon unmistakable sounds of a sturdily approaching, noisy paddle-wheel. Of all that they might expect along that lonely, uncharted waterway, this was the very last thing. But as the stranger's lights began illuminating the big river gums Randell realized he was not dreaming. His crew sprang to get the *Mary Ann* under way as the *Lady Augusta* passed them in a blaze of light, contemptuously rolling them in her backwash.

The race was on. A stirring tussle, both crews toiling like galley slaves as the two vessels, chancing snags, taking all risks before their tiny bows, forged several nights and days up this big, twisting, timber-lined river. Excitement for widely spaced settlers who galloped to the river bank to cheer on the race, one vessel, then the other, forging into the lead!

To Randell's bitter chagrin the *Lady Augusta*, sensing a short cut, thrashed her way to the little settlement of Swan Hill some four hours ahead of the *Mary Ann*, the first vessel to be moored in cheering triumph to the big gums.

The settlers turned up from far and wide to join in the shivoo. The Murray had been navigated, as the monument at Swan Hill commemorates. "The first steamers on the Murray, the *Lady Augusta* (Captain Francis Cadell) and the *Mary Ann* (Captain Wm. R. Randell) arrived here from South Australia 17th September, 1853."

The *Mary Ann* carried on and eventually reached Echuca, which in aboriginal language means "the meeting of the waters" – that is, of the Goulburn and the Murray rivers.

Then followed a different kind of race, to build steamers for what promised to be, and eventually developed into, a great river trade. Within a few months a steamer had travelled upstream from Goolwa near the Murray mouth in South Australia 1468 miles to Albury, on the border of New South Wales and Victoria. Then Cadell steamed from the Murray inland along the Edward. In 1860 two steamers reached the township of Deniliquin in New South Wales along the Edward; then Randell, still in his beloved *Mary Ann*, turned from the Murray into the Murrumbidgee and reached Hay, far inland in New South Wales. Then it was Randell in the *Gemini* who steamed from Wentworth on the Murray north into the Darling, right up through western New South Wales past Bourke and into and along the Barwon to Walgett, almost to the Queensland border. What a game trip! How difficult today even to picture that far inland voyage! Then a busy little boat went nosing up the Murrumbidgee to Wagga Wagga, others along the Edward, the Wakool, and the Goulburn almost to Seymour.

By 1870 the Murray and the New South Wales western rivers had been navigated in those Tom Thumb vessels for 3600 miles. So our grandfathers were energetic lads indeed throughout this great, empty continent by sea, land, and river in the days when their beards were black.

Which brings us back to west of the Darling, with the overlanders in high glee at this river transport, because for those who had settled along the rivers the long wait for the wagon with stores was now done away with. Some settlers had had to wait even up to twelve months for the longed-for wagon to come. The swift and cheap transport by river seemed a miracle in comparison. Settlement outback from the rivers gained correspondingly, for the teams loaded at the river bank and had only the distance from river to station to crawl over. The development of river traffic all over that vast area was even more revolutionary to the old-timers than aeroplane transport has been to us.

It even meant a change in the stocking of the land. For now wool in bulk could be transported long distances quickly and cheaply. In the years coming the stations would gradually, then faster begin to change from cattle to sheep.

The far-sighted, energetic South Australians and Victorians well deserved the rich river trade that quickly grew, the big prize being the now developing wool trade of the increasingly prosperous Riverina east of the Darling. Echuca village became the second port in Victoria, second only to Melbourne – a port on an inland river!

And a truly great port it was in 1864, when Echuca was connected by rail to Melbourne, one hundred and fifty miles south. Soon there were fleets of "Dreadnoughts" trading along the Murray, Darling, Murrumbidgee, Edward, Wakool, and Goulburn, from Goolwa away down by the mouth in South Australia, to the far north right up to the Queensland border. Within a very few years 100,000 bales of wool a season, loaded on the big barges, were coming down these inland rivers to be unloaded on to the Melbourne train at Echuca. Big cargoes, too, of wheat and salt and timber and stock, and later of mineral ores, cargoes growing so rapidly that the ever busier railway from Echuca to Melbourne was in desperation at times to keep the line clear. Great service was done by those rivers in the opening up of our inland west. A blessing to the inland womenfolk were the river hawkers, each boat a complete river store loaded with anything from needles to furniture, the largest of them as fully stocked as a big store. Not only did they serve the river township and station homestead; this big old noisy paddle-wheel store would willingly pull up at the most humble camp on the river bank. It was a red-letter day for the lonely women and youngsters when a river hawker came noisily churning round the bend. The kids had seen it early, of course, and mum was already eagerly waiting on the bank long before the floating store tied up, with cheery greetings, to the handy gums. And mum and the kids, and probably dad, were aboard for an enchanting half-hour among the treasures displayed. The overlanders of but a few years before had never dreamt of such a luxury as this.

Thus progress again put yet more teams off the road. But the teams could not have carried the produce that so rapidly began to increase with the opening up of the river transport. Far away up through New South

Wales to near the Queensland border the Dreadnoughts were now chugging to Bourke – were doing so even in my day. To the lonely horseman it was a strange sight on a hazy day to see a distant steamer gliding over the plain.

How few of us know that Bourke, then a little bush town five hundred miles inland from Sydney, became widely known as "the Old Port" – the reason being that ever-increasing quantities of wool and station produce came slowly converging upon it by camel-team, wagon, and drover from east and west in New South Wales, from the north, north-east, and north-west from Queensland. Not so many years back, when I was a lad, the huge bulks of wharves along the river banks were still handling and receiving the cargoes ever rolling in. Yes, Time brings changes. That little inland township up towards the Queensland border developed into a busy port indeed.

BROKEN HILL No 18

10. THE WHITE QUARTZ RUSH AND THE SHEPHERDS

Thus in the Far West big stations and tiny settlements had been formed, now linked to distant civilization by "the River". The settlers, patient men and women carving out their homes, still lived hard, the majority content could they but hang on and keep the wolf from the door – while right under their noses, inconspicuous as the sere earth, the sombre rocks, the drab shrubbery over those sunlit distances, lay such wealth as even an Indian Rajah never dreamed of. Again and again, east and particularly west of the river, a lonely horseman with a life of toil before him ending in burial under a coolabah-tree, has ridden over vast wealth and never dreamt it was there.

Of the treasure houses awaiting under that sombre earth two were to prove the greatest of their kind in the world.

As the years glide by and the pages unfold in the development of the continent I have grown gradually more sure that it really was Destiny – that holding back, as of the earlier goldfields, of vast, quick wealth until the unfolding years would enable this last old-new country to take the greatest advantage of it. In this as in other ways the pattern of Australia's destiny has been slowly unfolding towards what is eventually destined to be, I really believe – the Greatest Nation.

Settlement accomplished, sparse though it was, and with river transport now linking inland activities to cities and the sea, the game was set to play. Fate played her first card cruelly.

Across the South Australian border in 1867, carried there by teamsters, it was said, came word that back in the outlandish Barrier country there gleamed "hills of quartz"!

"So the shepherds say, anyway."

A stampede, known as "the White Quartz Rush", came scurrying across the South Australian border from the little outpost townships creeping northward there. The stampeders found no gold, some found death from thirst. The others straggled back as best they could, bitterness in their hearts.

But it was the writing on the wall! An odd one among those who staggered back across the border on that tragic dry track to Peterborough was haunted by memory of those grim, dark-grey hills that stood up into the mirages above the saltbush plains. Those heavy, black and brown, sun-split rocks might not contain gold, but might they not contain copper?

To the stockmen battlers west of the Darling it seemed a madman's dream that mineral could lie out here in this sun-scorched wilderness. But away back east men had the gold fever, as also had their Victorian brothers in the south. The South Australians, for their part, had copper fever badly. Copper had helped the tiny handful of folk in that vast, so very scantily watered colony tremendously. What those fabulously rich copper-mines of Kapunda, Burra Burra, Wallaroo, and Moonta would be worth today would take the breath away.

As Peterborough was only a hundred miles or so south-west of the Barrier hills, and the Burra mines but fifty miles farther south, it was these South Aussies who led the White Quartz Rush across the border. After the disillusioned return a few of the hardier and more thoughtful ones determined to refit more carefully, bide their time until news by drover or camel-team drifted across the border that rain had come, then make a dash back to prospect those queer hills again. They did so. And the search began in earnest.

Thus Fate slowly played her cards in time as it suited her. But to the very last she would keep the joker up her sleeve.

I was fascinated by the old shepherds, as any lad would have been. Dad's job of poking about into out-of-the-way corners of New South Wales brought him into contact with them, and he had with great solemnity introduced me to a few among them. If they were as amused at the solemn-eyed, silent little boy as I was fascinated by their grizzled, weather-tanned old faces, their inquiring eyes measuring you up, their casual, effortless movements, their secretive ways, then we are square.

Surely they must have been the last of the shepherds, relics of a period just gone, as the horse almost is today! They had swung into being naturally, as the first sheep began to grow into flocks. Probably the early settlers believed you could not keep sheep without shepherds, and they would certainly be necessary in the days before fences. But the crook of these shepherds would be a muzzle-loading gun; these would not be the old-world shepherds who would tuck each little baa-lamb into bed at night, for this was a great, unknown continent of wild bush, frighteningly different to the centuries-old, pocket-handkerchief farms of older lands. This shepherd's job was to feed his flock on green grass handy to water, to keep them clear of bog and dangers, to guard the lambs against eaglehawks, crows, and dingoes, and the whole flock and himself, too, against wild blacks, bushfires, flood or thirst, against straying and strange new diseases and all the hazards, gradually becoming known, of this great new land. For all that, the shepherd knew every sheep in his flock, and was responsible for each precious one, both by day and night.

As the settlers spread out so the flocks rapidly increased; the shepherds had larger and larger flocks to tend until eventually the flocks grew into the Australian "mobs" with the evolution of the Australian stockman. And the day of the shepherd was finished.

When the early settlers came the Australian stockman was not yet born – a quaint thought, for we imagine he has always been with us. But he had to evolve, as the settlers themselves had to evolve gradually into overlanders, then pastoralists, and with labour and fortitude battle a lifetime learning to exist in this strange land. Their sons, the Australian stockmen, had to be born into the land and environment of their inheritance.

Doubtless that was the way the American cowboy also developed. It was the American continent that made the American race, the Australian continent that made the Australian.

Almost without exception, the shepherd was, or soon became, a sombre, taciturn, secretive type. Loneliness and environment made him so, even if he was not born that way, and often some fear or unhappy circumstance had driven him to seek isolation as far as possible from his fellow men. The shepherd's life offered this, especially in the drier, undeveloped areas where the scattered stations had to be of great acreage to support their stock. Rations were taken to the shepherd generally once a month, perhaps once in three months, by packhorse. Then he was left with the murmurous company of the bush again.

Little wonder that such long-continued, lonesome environment should in some cases play tricks with the imagination. Away out on the Bulloo, where the stations then were as large as many a European principality, an old shepherd came drifting up to the homestead to tell the manager he had come to draw his time. He would not be working on the run any more; he had shot himself; he was a dead man. Old Wire Whiskers was quite harmless, and actually believed himself a dead man. He mooned about the station a few months, then drifted away, no one knew where, still believing himself a dead man – which perhaps, in a way, he was.

Out in those then limitless spaces another crazed old shepherd believed himself a "working bullick". Whether he had in far distant youth ever heard the story of Nebuchadnezzar and this phantasmal memory through long years of solitude had preyed on his mind could only be guessed at, but occasionally a stockman would see him in the bush on hands and knees chewing grass. Occasionally, too, with a fork over neck and shoulders, a dead sapling he had picked up, something in the shape of a bullock yoke, there he would be on his hands and knees, grunting heavily as he "pulled the wagon along". Those were on his "workin' days". Otherwise he was morosely sane, just sitting on a log staring out at no one knew what.

When I was a lad on the Hill the day of the shepherd was finished, but in later, wandering years I was to meet his eccentric successors among lonely out-station boundary-riders. Not all were queer, of course, but quite a number were. Among the river swagmen, too, the old "Murrumbidgee Whalers", I struck oddities of the same kind. And in even later years I knew him familiarly as "the hatter" of distant North Queensland.

As a lad, when working at the Big Mine at the Hill, I would meet my friends at week-ends and holidays and we would harness up the horse and cart and go jogging out thirty miles – farther when we had time – into the hills through the night, wallaby-shooting. Or we would lie in ambush by some out-station tank for 'roos coming padding along to drink, or for that luxury of luxuries, wild duck. Happy were we to bring home game for our mothers. A shilling was money those days, 'roo-tail soup, baked wallaby, or wild duck meant that Mum had no meat to buy for a couple of days at least. And a few shillings saved meant quite a lot to any mother with a hungry family.

Occasionally on these trips we would camp at a boundary-rider's hut, or by good fortune strike a mustering camp. Each middle-aged stockman among these station-hands had well known some among the district shepherds, and assured us that, for some reason of their own, it *was* the shepherds who had really started that disastrous White Quartz Rush, using the teamsters as their "agents". Each shepherd was more or less confined to his own area of country, whereas the teamsters kept slowly travelling back and forth from the nearest points of settlement to the stations, and back again, thus passing on the news. What interested me most, though, and stuck in my memory ever after, was that the shepherds, according to those stockmen, had a strong bond, a freemasonry among them, and that, although so widely scattered and isolated, they had some queer "bush telegraph" that kept them in touch with one another, and with "the news".

That this could be so among those gnarled old hermits, each so grown into himself, so notoriously secretive, so widely scattered, so cut off from their fellow-men except for a monthly, and in some cases much rarer, visit by a stockman with rations, was to us boys a fascinating idea, kept fresh and alive in our minds by a most intriguing morsel of mining history. For we, as everyone else in the Hill, lived on mines and mining; there was nothing else. These stockmen swore that the shepherds of much earlier years, "way back east", knew there was gold in the colony long before it was officially proclaimed, knew also that some among them who had found gold in their district quietly mined it as opportunity occurred by their own extremely primitive methods, saying not a word to a soul, but letting their fellow shepherds far and wide know by this mysterious "telegraph" amongst them. So that a lonely shepherd two hundred miles away would know that another shepherd was "on gold", but never would he tell anyone else. And this was so even in the convict days, and in times when Governors threatened jail to anyone claiming to find gold in the colony lest the population become uncontrollable. Also, long years before Hargraves officially reported rich gold at Lewis Ponds and Summer Hill Creek by the Macquarie near Bathurst and Wellington in 1851, isolated shepherds here and there had quietly been mining gold in that very district.

Jogging back to the Hill through the good night under the silvery stars, we boys passed the happy miles away wondering what truth there was in this story of the hoary old shepherds. Had they really had some secret "telegraph"? Did some among them really find gold and work it on the quiet? How each of us would have loved just such an opportunity! But why had the local shepherds spread news among the teamsters of the "white quartz hills"? It was a "mineral fact", of course, that there might be gold in quartz hills, for we knew that, other mineralogical conditions of Nature being favourable, it is in such localities gold-bearing quartz reefs are found. The shepherds, perhaps for some cunning reason, had not actually said there *was* gold in those quartz hills. So that the men who came swarming in that sad rush could not logically blame the teamsters who spread the news, nor could the teamsters blame the shepherds.

It was a puzzle. We decided the shepherds must have first well tried the quartz hills, but could not find gold in the quartz. Probably they believed that gold might still be there, that it could only be extracted by methods known to real miners. Realizing that their day was drawing to a close, had they decided to spread the news and cause a rush, then quietly watch real miners at work, learning how gold was extracted from such rock? And then, of course, they knew of other distant white quartz hills which they would quietly work themselves. So we decided it. On other trips, too, we found that this story of the shepherds was widely believed among the older stockmen throughout the district. What a story it was for us to tell when Monday would find us working back among our mates on the Big Mine!

Many years later – what fascinating years, after roaming the continent! – I found myself curiously poking about old Solferino and Hill

End of magic gold history, then on to the historic old fields of Bathurst and Wellington. I couldn't resist being enticed to do a bit – it *was* a bit – of work on a claim in the Macquarie. At Wellington, I remembered the stockmen's story of the shepherds during those boyhood days on the Hill, and in a sort of amused curiosity began digging among old official records, just to see whether there really was anything at all in that old story. And eventually, with surprise and interest, found it – not only mention in half a dozen musty old journals, but a practically full account put on record by an official of that district and period. And here is the story, almost word for word as those weather-beaten stockmen told us boys years ago by Yanco Glen, west of the Darling.

Macgregor was the name, a shepherd on a Mr Montefiore's property near Wellington. A dependable laddie, very quiet, keeping much to himself, and definitely without the gift of the gab. One morning, while feeding his flock on the goodly grasses along Mitchell's Creek, he climbed a quartz ridge and idly began to examine the white stones. He broke some; presently he broke another that was held together by a soft, yellow metal.

Gold!

Almost any other man would have howled his discovery to the skies. Canny Mac kept his mouth shut for ten years, from 1840 to 1850. That is, to all but his fellow shepherds. For another old record stated that "it was common knowledge among *every* shepherd in the *Colony* that Macgregor was getting gold on Montefiore's sheep run"!

Mac, whenever he could find good excuse for grazing his sheep along that creek used to poke about amongst the quartz, selecting only those stones that were heaviest or showed most yellow metal. These he would break with a hammer, then pound into fragments until with roughened fingers he could extract the shreds of soft yellow metal. After every few hours at such laborious work he would cautiously cover up all traces.

What a picture! The secretive shepherd, his flock contentedly grazing down on the flat, he up on the quartz ridge kneeling down, tap-tap-tapping out gold. Smiling down upon him the warm sun, an inquisitive magpie peeking down upon him from a tall old tree, around him the murmurous sympathy of the bush.

What a fantastic fortune he could have made in far less than those ten years if he only had had the knowledge to work systematically! But then he was probably afraid of the authorities, who had threatened punishment to anyone starting a gold rush. Thus he hid evidence of his work.

Ah, and then Mac found a something as precious as his precious gold!

A lassie, a winsome lassie of Wellington.

Alas, what have the Helens of Troy, the Cleopatras of Egypt, the Salomes of Palestine, the Lassies of Wellington been responsible for in tumbling down the dreams of this woeful world of men!

Like most keen Scotchmen who, when once started, believe in doing the thing well, our Mac fell properly head over heels in love with the lassie, would have sacrificed his sporan for her, had he possessed one. The canny Scot must have been mightily smitten, for the presents he began to bring her left her bewildered with joy and – an all-consuming curiosity.

And when a lassie's curiosity is aroused!

She knew very well the few shillings a month that were a shepherd's wages. From whence then did this wild man from the hills get the money for these expensive presents?

Difficult indeed to drag it out of a secretive Scot who had kept his precious secret these long ten years past. But the Lassie from Wellington must have had It. At long last, after we know not what whispered promises, what starry-eyed vows of "I'll never, never tell", what honeyed beguilements, she wheedled it out of him.

Under promises of the most heart-to-heart secrecy he at last showed her – gold! Imagine her breathless astonishment – she must have been speechless for once.

One morning thereafter Mac awoke to stare at a wild scramble of two hundred men – one account says three hundred – running all over his precious quartz ridge.

How *could* a man expect *any* woman to keep such a secret!

I'm sorry the old record does not state whether Mac and the lassie married and lived happily ever after. It does casually mention, though, that Macgregor eventually left the district in search of other goldfields, but that he occasionally returned. And ends up by stating, "Macgregor is now a wealthy man."

So perhaps the canny Mac had yet another golden quartz ridge up his sleeve, which he did *not* brag about.

Mac let the cat out of the bag in 1850. In the following year came the official report of Hargraves's discovery at Summer Hill Creek, a discovery which at once put unknown Australia on the world's map.

But that is the story as written in the old record, exactly as told to us boys five hundred miles inland on that West Darling station forty years before.

11. SILVER!

However, away back west of the Darling the land-seekers, more than sceptical after the tragedy of the White Quartz Rush of minerals ever being found in this wilderness, consolidated their holdings. Unfortunately they overstocked during the good seasons, beginning to destroy great areas of the mulga also unaware of that delicate, elusive balance of nature in this deceptive country, ignorant as yet of the thinness of the vital blanket of topsoil that can so easily be loosened and sun-powdered and blown away by the winds, unaware as yet of those wheels that grind so slowly yet so surely towards a gathering vengeance for any rape of the land. Thus men toiled and battled while Destiny marched on, reaching a momentous mile-post in 1869 when, east of the Darling, two young Danes, Tommy Hartman and Charlie Campbell, riding to a job at a well-boring plant, camped at a lonely native well. It was really an aboriginal mine, the little hole now filled with that which is more precious than all minerals – water! The two young fellows were attracted by the bright green, blue, and red colouring on the sides of the well. Blessed with the curiosity which has brought so many discoveries to human kind, which in fact has led to what we call civilization, they broke off some of the soft stone before riding on their way. As they met people they would show this pretty stone to learn if it might be valuable.

Thus were the rich copper-mines of Cobar found. The aboriginal "miners", of course, for centuries past had used the bright, cupreous ochres as body paints in the corroboree. They called their "mine" Copar.

These two young fellows were not the only white men who had seen the copper. A dreamy old shepherd in that red-earth loneliness, tending his flock by Mount Hope, a small hill right beside it, had often fed his flock over it, speculating on the "queer ways of the blackfellows", wondering what these brilliantly coloured stones could be. His wages were but £1 a month "with tucker". And yet he camped many a time upon a million pounds. Perhaps some nights under those lonely stars he tossed uneasily in his blanket and dreamt of wealth, and the wonders it could buy. We all have our dreams. His could so easily have come true.

Thus these exceedingly rich copper-mines were found, not by the real copper men searching under such heart-breaking conditions west of the Darling, but by two Danish new-chums travelling along to their job, and not knowing copper ore when they saw it!

Many a fortune has similarly been tumbled into the lap of innocents by the luck of the game.

The old-timers, energetic and great workers, quickly opened up the new find. Their job can be admired today. No roads out there of course, and five hundred miles from Sydney Town; the nearest railway even when it reached Blayney seven years later would still be nearly three hundred miles away. A sun-parched country of unmapped distances, the nearest decent water the Bogan, eighty miles away. Teamsters, using bushmanship and their wagons, formed their own road, the first team slowly following a leading horseman through the bush, silence but for the call of birds, creaking of the big wheels as they broke into the first virgin dust, snap of dried branches under straining hooves, lurch and rumble of the heavy wagon breaking down into some weather-eroded gutter, encouraging, exasperated, goading, guiding shouts of the teamster, sharp shrill note of chains snapping taut, occasional crack of the whip as the team laboured slowly onward, carting the heavy ore north to Bourke on the Darling. Other teams would follow those first tracks and thus a road from a spot away out in the bush now called Cobar, to Bourke on the Darling, would be formed.

Almost all Australian roads were "made" that way.

Again the old river helped the battlers laboriously opening up her near-arid lands. For by steamer the rivers carried the ore from near the Queensland border right down through western New South Wales, then along the Murray through Victoria into South Australia, to arrive eventually at the Port Adelaide Smelting Works where the copper content was extracted. Thus bustling South Australia, despite its small population of only a few thousand drew yet more trade from the despised arid lands of western New South Wales. South Australia's copper-ore refinery works had been established through her own early copper discoveries and through those keen, knowledgeable men who could "smell" copper, the "Cousin Jacks" from Cornwall. But then their forefathers had been mining tin and copper in the savage British Isles since Julius Caesar was a boy, and long before that.

This discovery of rich mineral was a startling discovery indeed to the far western folk, who had dreamt only of cattle and horses and sheep. Some now wondered still more at this strange earth of theirs.

The opening up of Cobar took time, of course, but how the news heartened the few lone prospectors west of the Darling, those who had mused on the possibility of minerals after the White Quartz Rush! Here and there among those sun-blasted hills, at Wertago and Nuntherungie, Grassmere and Koonenberry and Ponto, they found copper, but it was not rich enough for the insurmountable transport and other difficulties.

Paddy Green from Wilcannia was one of these men, and a dogged type of bloke was he. He became convinced that away out west from Wilcannia, in an area of the scorching wastes vaguely called Thackaringa, near the South Australian border, there was mineral and rich mineral of some sort hidden in the heavy reddish and blackish rocks. He determined to strike it, and stuck doggedly at it until one day he broke a rock and stared amazed at glistening silver!

It really was galena, or lead sulphide, a bright, silvery looking lead ore when freshly broken. John Stokie and Johnny Nicholls, two bushmen friends who visited his camp excitedly, thought it silver, too. Alas, when they drew it across paper it left the trail of lead! Stokie wrote, "Paddy Green", with it.

But the more they examined the heavy rocks, sometimes brightly coloured when broken, the more they became convinced there was rich silver there somewhere.

The difficulty was to prove it. And, if proved, to have the ore treated and the rich minerals extracted.

But the only silver-ore treatment plant that Paddy could find out about was in England. A long, long way away from here, far inland in an Australian wilderness.

Paddy dug out thirty-six tons of the heavy ore, carted it through the trackless bush to Wilcannia, and in due course shipped it by Darling Dreadnought to South Australia for reshipment to England. Then he stoically took on other work to keep the tucker-bags filled while awaiting a reply.

John Stokie and Johnny Nicholls went west a few miles farther where low rocky hills among the mulga attracted them. Going their separate ways, stubbornly they began prospecting this lonesome wilderness, which in time coming would be known as Umberumberka. This was in 1876.

Eventually Paddy Green's thirty-six tons of stone were shipped to England. On the voyage his "worthless rocks" were thrown overboard. Similarly Sturt's samples had been treated years before. If the men who did such things had only to brave the hardships that the explorer and the prospector braved!

It was a long time before Paddy learnt of this. What he said, so old-timers have assured me, scorched even the sunburnt rocks.

Paddy, with his brother Dick, set to work again. Dug out one hundred tons of the ore, shipped it again to England.

Two *years* later he received an effusive reply. The ore was rich in both silver and lead.

This was in 1880.

Cobar Smelting Works 1880.

Thus was struck the famous Pioneer silver-mine that set that western country ablaze with excitement.

That silver should strew the baked earth out in that "barren" wilderness was the last thing men had dreamed of. Maybe there might be a little copper out in those sterile ranges, a cautious few admitted. An odd man thought possibly there might be a little gold hidden here and there. But silver! Rich silver!

Bush telegraph spread the word far out over the mulga, whispering ever farther out over the saltbush plains, "Silver!"

And then, a little farther out in the wastes, John Stokie struck the Umberumberka mine.

"Silver! Silver! Silver!"

"Fortunes lying out in the Barrier Range ... Slugs of silver to be picked up for the digging ... No water, but silver lying around everywhere ... Jeweller's shops on every second hill!"

So sped rumours far and wide.

And the rush started, the first of the great silver rushes.

The Rush to Thackaringa!

The Rush to Umberumberka!

The Rush to Purnamoota!

The Rush to Apollyon Valley!

The Rush to Silverton!

The greatest rush of all was to be last of all.

Unlike those that started the tragic White Quartz Rush, the dazzling rumours proved sometimes true. There was no "jeweller's shop" on every second hill, of course, but many were found for all that, silver in rich and varied forms utterly unknown in the continent before. Not only so, but forms of silver ore previously unknown to the world were presently to be found.

"Bush telegraph" had told the truth about John Stokie.

High up on a rough outcrop of broken rock he found a cap of gossan, the weather-beaten, reddish-brown rock stained from the juices of shrubs that had lived and withered there during ages past. He dug down into this yellowish, crumbling ironstone and unearthed chlorides. Thus the Umberumberka mine became a magnet drawing weary camel-men and horsemen from every point of the compass far across the saltbush plains. The era of the Silver Kings had dawned.

One of these early lucky ones was a camel-man prospector, speculative eyes on a low line of hills as his camels mooched across a bluebush plain, nonchalantly treading the glorious scarlet of Sturt's desert pea under their dirty big pads. Trudging some distance behind him were his two weather-beaten mates, nursing two sore-footed camels. Valuable indeed were camels out there.

The prospector climbed to the summit of a scrubby little hill, a dark-grey, dull-green hill, and lying insignificantly there was a little heap of stones, as they had been lying there for ages past among the roots of the few dwarf mulga, the dead-finish and snake-bush and bullocky-bush, lying loosely on the grey-black crown of gossan and ironstone rock, a nest of dirty, sunburnt, weather-beaten rocks, partly brownish, partly dirty greenish in colour. The prospector looked down at them, then bent over, stared closely. With heart in mouth he swung up his pick, striking down and in under one, then using the handle as a lever to wrench the stone over. Its underside rolled up, smooth and shiny. With a gasp he drove the pick into it – it felt something like swinging a pick into tough horn – his hands and arms were trembling as he stabbed his foot upon it, wrenched with the pick-handle, and broke the stone. It opened out into the unmistakable waxy green of silver chloride, green, soapy-looking silver chloride! He threw up his hat with a wild, exultant yell. His mates farther down the hill jerked up their heads and listened. "Yes! He's struck it –

found a nest of silver chlorides!"

Yes, slugs of chlorides, slugs of native silver amongst them, too! Slugs of nearly pure silver going thousands of ounces to the ton! And so yet another "jeweller's shop" had been found.

Joe Meech and Allan Sinclair found a little rough valley hidden in among the rocky hills, very soon to prove a "silver valley", the famous Apollyon Valley. Then one day Joe Meech, bushed and nearly dead of exhaustion, stood and saw a hill, yet a farther hill where everywhere around were hills, but up on this hill boldly stood out big rocks upon which a dull-red sunset was playing in strange colours. With the prospector's urge tingling his leaden feet he trudged wearily on, barely made the hill, and stumbled up among the pretty rocks now black and chill in the dying sunset. His few tools clanking down on the rock, he sank down there, too dead beat to move another foot. When the stars came out he had fallen into exhausted sleep. A cold, hard bed indeed.

At long last dawn came. Silver-grey the dawn comes over those sombre hills, a pearly grey that veils their rugged harshness until it is torn away by the fierce light of the sun.

Joe Meech awoke, groaned as he rolled and stretched to bring life into his numbed body, wearily sat up, and gazed around into brightening sunlight. Mulga down on the flats, a honey-eater singing his heart out from his nest in a bunch of mistletoe. Little grey, rocky hills all around, partly scrub-covered, hills rough as the hobs of hell. His tired eyes looked down at his bed of rock. He stared, stared harder, then, more in exasperation and numb misery than in hope he jumped up, snatched his pick, and sank it into the rock – into silver chlorides and pearl-grey horn silver and slugs of native silver that seemed as if long ago they had been poured upon the earth from the melting pot of some playful Titan. And beneath it all lay buried bromides and iodides.

A great fortune of dirty old silver rocks, just lying there snug as a bug in a rug. Just a tumbled mass of slugs, the surface ones warmed by the sun, chilled by the night, a great nest of silver nuggets cuddling together in the topsoil blanket of the earth.

Thus the riches of the fabulous Day Dream were blazoned far and wide – a Day Dream come true in the dawn of Christmas 1882. And Silverton was born.

Out past the dazzle of a dead kopi lake, near a line of ridges quivering in the heat, stood a grey hill glittering with schist. And there Tom Crisp found the Hen and Chickens. That rocky hen sitting on her chickens was nearly all silver, sufficient to buy all the hens and chickens in Australia with enough over to buy and stock a sheep-station.

And now men west of the Darling talked, thought, dreamt of silver, as far to the east and south men had talked, thought, dreamt of gold.

Alas! More men, in proportion, perished in the search for silver than perished in the quest for gold.

Johnny Nicholls found the Maybell – he was a Silver King at the stroke of a pick. The *lucky* stroke, for the blows he had struck in vain could not be counted.

The Maybell quickly proved to be another silver treasure-house; dust-caked men came trudging up to the silver rocks just to stand and stare, then bend and lovingly handle them, those big, greenish, soapy-feeling slugs of silver chlorides, to absorb the feel, the weight, the awe, the wealth of them, to lay them carefully down and walk away with shoulders erect in the wild, wild hope, "My turn may – *must* – come!"

Then Morris and the Nolan brothers found Morris's Blow, it was a wonder of wonders, as if the earth had blown up just there and rained down upon the ground again a tumbled mass of rocks of silver.

What can be the mysteries of Nature's mighty laboratory – that here, as if merely in play, she melts rock down, then blows it up into the air and it tumbles down in boulders of rich silver ore? Just as if to add a final touch to this fantastic largesse, as if to add spice to this feast of the gods, she rains among the silver boulders slugs of pure native silver!

In their dazed astonishment, it was a long time before Morris and Nolan realized that they, too, were now Silver Kings.

Little wonder that now to the stampeders hurrying to seek their fortune the very leaves of the mulga, the mallee, and the gidgee seemed whispering, "Silver! Silver! Silver!"

Then the Pluck Up was found. And louder the breezes whispered, "Silver! Silver! Silver!"

Thus in quick succession the rich silvers of Thackaringa, of Umberumberka, of Apollyon Valley, of Silverton were found, and the silvered riches of Purnamoota lying out there among its sand and scrub and bluebush, and its something more priceless than all the silver in the world – water! Not much of it, but so important that Purnamoota was known as "the Soakage" for a long time. And to this sun-drenched oasis in the wild hills came prospecting again the Crisp brothers, Tom and his dogged brother, with Lady Luck again guiding their footsteps as if to flaunt in the face of luckless victims how devilish contrary she can be. She breaks the hearts of men in their lifetime struggle for the rainbow they never quite grasp, yet flings her treasures in extravagant abundance before the feet of her very few favourites.

For here in this wild setting Tom Crisp and his brother found the

Lubra, a treasure chest of native silver from Nature's laboratory, pure in form as the primitive girl who gave it its name.

There is a deep secret here – guess it if you can. Australians will never know how much we owe the development of the country to the lubra.

Men went silver crazy just as the deathly hand of a terrible drought was ominously settling over all the saltbush plains. Far away up through south-west Queensland it stretched, right across the north of South Australia and on west into the unknown lands, away east far past the red country of Cobar out over the hot dry plains creeping towards the rich Riverina, and away south right to the Murray itself.

Silver mines, small in comparison to fabulous discoveries to come, but startlingly rich, were soon opened up. The Day Dream and Pioneer and Maybell, the Lubra and the Hen and Chickens and the Pluck Up and Morris's Blow, for instance – each one of these was many "jeweller's shops" rolled into one. What fabulously rich propositions they would be today!

Surface slugs found on the Lubra mine yielded 16,000 ounces of silver to the ton, while selected portions of the reef itself assayed over 8000 ounces to the ton. The Christmas mine, War Dance, and Gipsy Girl produced silver as fabulously rich, while at Silverton the Day Dream and Maybell in particular seemed to be "all silver"; from the Maybell slugs of horn silver assayed up to 20,000 ounces to the ton. Nearly as rich was the Hen and Chickens, where the silver chlorides occurred in beautiful forms with the azure blue of copper. There were silver bromides, silver glance, and silver iodides, too, often in beautiful combination and richness with other metals.

From South Australia horsemen, camels, and drays came toiling east across the border on the long vanished tracks of the White Quartz Rush. The old shepherds had never dreamt of a Silver Rush.

From townships and stations east of the Darling also, men rolled up swags, loaded the old packhorses and set their faces to the west. From the Queensland Corner Country both horsemen and camel-men came steadily plodding south. From the South Australian border for thirty miles east towards the Darling, then away north towards the Queensland border, rough mining camps sprang up as if by magic. Wee tent towns, like mushrooms down there along the sombre gullies and drab grey flats, bag and shack townships springing up amongst the rocky hills where richer strikes were unearthed. Lazy dust arising far over the burnt-out plains where fresh teams were slowly coming, plodding doggedly on through now breathless heat, on dry tracks away out there where many a dog sought in vain for a sapling's width of shade.

The Roaring Silver Days had come, bringing in their dawning what
Australia had never known before, the Silver Kings.

Silverton Silver-field and the Road to It (detail), 1884.

12. WATER OUTSHINES BOTH SILVER AND GOLD

In an amazingly short time Silverton mining camp sprang into a rough, jolly hearted township of 1500, "open" night and day, restlessly alive in feverish excitement as fresh discoveries were reported by stumbling, dog-tired men on foot, horsemen riding into town on weary, thirsty horses caked in sweaty dust, on surly camels with eyes dust-rimmed lurching up the dusty track between the town shacks to the Mining Warden's "Office" to register their claims. In view of Australia's tiny population at the time, and in this utterly isolated district, practically waterless and normally so sparsely populated, a roaring camp of 1500 men must have been an amazing sight.

Certainly the desert quietness was rocked by the "ball" held to commemorate the opening of the *Silver Age,* that vastly important, aggressive, and game little bi-weekly newspaper.

A newspaper out here in the wilderness! Ye gods! For that "feed and ball" the boys came rolling in from the hills to the bag and shack township, with enough whiskers among them to have feathered a mattress from Purnamoota to Timbuctoo. Keen rivalry for the few lucky women! The night of their lives as breathlessly they enjoyed themselves to the rattle of the rickety piano brought on camel-back from goodness knows where. The boisterous fiddling, the rollicking strains of the concertina and accordion, the lively clacking of the bones to the stamp of feet and rollicking chorus of "The Old Bullock Dray" – a haunting melody that. But the fiddlers and concertina men fairly sweated into "Waltzing Matilda", encored again and again. When the musician boys at last were allowed a breather, then up jumped the Wild Cat, seizing this chance to deliver the one and only item on his repertoire, "The Swagman's Farewell to Matilda", followed by Saltbush Bill as he thundered, to howls of applause, "Out Where the Dead Men Lie!" A stranger stockman then obliged with "How Mad Harry Drove the Phantom Mob" – which, being "new" out there in the saltbush, was a noisy success. Then, to oblige the ladies, a Silver King who fancied himself gave a dramatic rendering of "The Girl at Native Dog". They all joined in the chorus then of the inevitable "Wild Colonial Boy" and its fellow sob-wringer, "The Sick Stockrider", followed by the pleasantly pathetic:

"Wrap me up in my stockwhip and blank-it!
And bury me deep down be-low!
Where the dingoes an' crows won't molest me
In the shade where the cool-ey-bahs gro-o-ow!!"

Chloride Jim then gave them "Hay, Hell, and Booligal" supported by Stringybark Joe fittingly delivering the epic, "The Man from Ironbark". And the dance was on again.

There were the usual crusty old rock-choppers, of course, who growled, "This place is getting' too bloody civilized with women comin' about! I'm pushin' further out!" But the boys laughed good-humouredly at these sand-bugs who shied at sight of a bit of skirt, and in keen rivalry busied themselves looking for a bit themselves. Those who were unsuccessful seized a buck partner, even though he wore hobnailed boots – even the Silver Kings wore hobnails then. And didn't floor and roof thunder to boots and bodies and voices as they roared accompaniment to "the Sets" and the Lancers! The mob of aborigines, crowding at the doors had the night of their lives, gleaming eyes staring from entranced black faces as they took it all in to copy in corroboree out in the hills nights later. Ah, yes, it was a lively night when the clarion call of the *Silver Age* blared out into the arid quietness from sunset to long after sunrise. And the *Silver Age* proved to be a good little fighting paper for many years to come.

As the sunburnt land blazed into "The Silver Barrier" still others kept coming. Lazily in the heat-haze now rose dust from the hooves and wheels of the teams forming a road as they brought supplies from Menindee, rushed up river from Victoria and South Australia by the Darling Dreadnoughts. Yet again, of what incomparable value the Murray and the Darling, those long riverways acting now as roadways to and from the far inland practically to the sea, were to prove to the Far West now!

Victoria, to the south, had a shrewd ear to the ground in trade and commerce in this silver treasure. She was enjoying a sweet taste of the wealth the river brought from the transport of inland wool, now already grown into great volume as the rich Riverina developed.

From across the western border also dust was rising above the shimmering saltbush plains as the camel-teams brought supplies from South Australia's northern railhead which was creeping up from the Burra to Hallett, from Hallett to Terowie, and now creeping along from Terowie to Peterborough. Tiny places indeed, but each doing a goodly job along the borderline of South Australia's own great, dry northern plains.

There was. one more camp to reach, Cockburn. And then the line would be right on the border.

From early times, by teams, then by riverway, and finally by railway, the canny South Australians fought tooth and nail for whatever share of business they could drag from that huge, despised area away up near their own semi-arid north. South Australia earned her trade, though never dreaming of the wealth her enterprise was to bring her in the swiftly coming years. It was only New South Wales that took practically no interest at all in these shadowy events developing in her own Far West, Sydney Town being far too engrossed in her own localized interests. No wonder the silver men of the great discoveries would soon become organized to manage their own affairs – they would be forced to.

Meanwhile in that Far West stock had increased vastly. Sheep had gradually followed the cattle; in a very few years from now many of the great stations would stock sheep alone. That country was only really "safe" with one sheep to ten or twelve acres, but there was plenty of country. Corona station, then of 3,200,000 acres, was shearing 80,000 sheep. Albermarle in a year or two would be shearing 200,000. The stations now, from away up by the Queensland border right down through the Far West, shipped 45,000 bales of wool a year by the Darling Dreadnoughts to Echuca on the Murray to be railed to Melbourne wool sales. In another few years this western country, with much of the Riverina included, would be shipping by river 100,000 bales of wool to Melbourne a year. Since the coming of the quick and cheap river transport the isolated west had developed astoundingly.

Life within comparatively easy distance of the rivers was now much easier, though hard indeed compared to the luxury of the present day. And the farther out from the rivers the harder the living.

And all this time, over this thirty-six miles of now proved silver-bearing country a lonely black outcrop still rose above the saltbush plains – Willyama, that Broken Hill on Mount Gipps station. Such a rugged landmark ever and again drew the attention of wandering silver-seekers. They climbed up among the black rocks, knapping a piece for examination here and there along the outcrop, only to throw the stone aside and ride away in disgust, calling it a "hill of mullock"!

Surely Destiny really *was* playing her hand step by step in the opening up of this sombre country. First, the finding of the river. Then the coming of the cattle. Then the sheep. The discovery of rich stock food on the apparently barren plains. Then the finding of the rich copper mineral in the sun-scorched loneliness of Cobar. Then farther west still in brazen aridity the discovery of thirty and more miles of silver pockets among the

Silverton hills. Slowly one page after another of the mysterious book of Nature's treasures was being turned in land believed by the early explorers to be the Heart of Desolation. And with the earliest silver discoveries came the greatest discovery of all, and in that arid land by far the most amazing – the discovery of artesian and sub-artesian waters.

It was made at Wee Wattah and Mullyeo on the Kallara pastoral property between the Paroo and Darling rivers. In 1880, when away sou'-west Paddy Green was at last becoming a Silver King in the opening of his pioneer mine, David Brown, manager of Wee Wattah for the Officer brothers, was attracted by some queer mud springs. He wondered if by any possibility these could be an indication of hidden underground water. He acted, and at his direction the bore which first tapped artesian water at shallow depth was put down. Other stations quickly followed the example. Within a very few years – in 1884, so rich farther west in great silver discovery – the Government commenced putting down bores along the far out, very scantily watered stock-routes, thus opening a number of previously impassable routes to traffic, such as that from Wanaaring to Milparinka.

What this first pioneer discovery, which led to proof that there are lakes and rivers of underground water even in our driest areas, has meant to Australia can probably never be estimated.

Yes, a strange country, west of the Darling, slumbering with hidden surprises. Men by their toiling lives had learnt that it could give. Then bitterly they learnt that it could take.

Many died in the learning.

It was in 1881 that a lone prospector was quietly working in Depot Glen, one hundred and fifty miles north of that Broken Hill. Just he and the sun-warmed rocks, the shadowed water pool, the busy birds, an inquisitive wallaby peering down from the scrub-lined cliffs as it hearkened to the ring of the pick. Johnny Thompson dug deep into the gravels lying on the bedrock bottom of the creek, filled his prospecting dish, knelt to wash yet another dish. How many hundreds now – no, thousands – his hardened fingers had washed! Steadily, stubbornly he washed on until – he stared, with a wild thumping of the heart.

Gold! Bright yellow gold gleamed up at him from the wet bottom of the dish.

For Johnny Thompson, his world out here in this wilderness was wonderful. Laughing with excitement he pegged out his prospecting claim, snatched his bridle and hurried to catch the old horse to ride into Wilcannia with the great news. A ride of one hundred and seventy miles to the big old river winding there – how short those miles would be! – a ride to tell border civilization that gold at last had been found west of the Darling.

That discovery was in Depot Glen Creek on Mount Poole station, the glen where Poole had perished, where Sturt and his disheartened men had been marooned those long six months. If they had only known, how differently then they would have employed that weary time! Instead of slaving at a cairn of rocks to pass the scorching days away they would eagerly have worked at digging gold. Instead of nightmare dreams of perishing in that drought-stricken loneliness their dreams would have been golden.

Dreams of a Golden City. Never, of a *Silver* City!

Thirty men saddled up at Wilcannia and were soon at Thompson's Find. But the gold proved to be payable in one claim only, it was only a "patch". However, added impetus was given to the search, and a year later little Wilcannia crowded excitedly round a dusty horseman who held out to them pellets of rough gold in his horny palm. Thus Evans brought the news to Wilcannia, "Gold at Mount Browne!"

A few months later, along the same harsh range, Warratta and Tibooburra were found.

Tibooburra is a quaint prank of Nature, a pigmy range of granitic boulders rising from the drab grey plain, piled one upon another as if thrown thus by giants in play. No soil there, just those barriers of big, grey-black rocks, divided by small, sunparched flats. Running through the largest flat was, and still is, a creek. No water in it, of course. Nature was not going to make things as easy as that; there was not enough water within miles to fill the beak of a thirsty crow. Just the weird granitic rocks, the sunburnt flats, the saltbush, the brazen sky. But Nature had sprinkled those little flats with gold – find it if you can!

Little flakes of gold, as if the giants, tired of their heavy play, had climbed the granite boulders and, standing silhouetted in line along the ridge, had thrown handfuls of golden corn away out over the flats.

In what incomprehensible Mind was such a joke born? The sowing of those golden grains millions of years ago, to await the evolution of a hungry insect called Man who would defy even death as he came toiling against sometimes incredible hardship to reap the scanty golden harvest.

As there was no water for working the ground – drinking water had to be carted from eight miles away – bush ingenuity came to the rescue. Here, according to the old-timers, was invented the dry-shaker, made from bush timber, the only tools being tomahawk and penknife. This ingenious machine was used to separate the heavier grains of gold from the powdered earth, the principle being that when the machine was shaken by hand vibration and gravitation, helped by a rude but effective system of sieve and rippled trays, brought about separation. This clever bush apparatus was developed years later in Western Australia into the wonderfully efficient dryblower.

In no time, despite the isolation, a thousand men were sweating upon the "Giants' Playground" of Tibooburra. The quaint little township of today thus first sprang up as a line of huts built of bush saplings with calico stretched over them, being the shanties and stores of the more solid township to be. Away sou'-east dust would be rising where teams came toiling as they formed a road from Wilcannia, just two hundred miles away, with added activity by the Darling Dreadnoughts, racing with thunderous splashings up river all the way from Victoria with supplies. Meanwhile little Wilcannia was growing very busy and excited at this added proof that the wilderness could produce wealth apart from beef and wool.

Alas! The little gold won west of the Darling was won under conditions of heartbreak, constant lack of precious water, typhoid, the horrors of sandy blight, and the far too frequent presence of Death.

Thirst, typhoid, and sandy blight I have experienced myself, years after these men and women chanced all these and more when there was no doctor within two and three hundred miles, long before the marvels of modern medical discoveries. There was horror in sandy blight, even with a doctor in a town. I put in six weeks with it in a hot room blackened to darkness to shut out the agony of light. When folk enthuse about "ye good old days" I think back but to yesteryear, in the days before painless dentistry, when such common scourges as typhoid and pneumonia and lead-poisoning and dysentery and other now easily curable diseases meant a horrible, and nearly certain death.

And my hat goes off to those vanished women who, well before my day, so bravely trudged forth with their families out into the western wilderness.

A few miles away the Mount Browne gold-bearing area soon proved to be some thirty square miles in extent, but with only patches of gold here and there. Its harsh ridges and rocky gullies were toiled over by two thousand thirsty men. In later years, when climbing among those conglomerates, those tough quartzites of Torrowangee, those barren sandstones of Mootwingee, the burning granites of Mundi Mundi, those jagged slates, those dry gullies reflecting burning sun-heat, my boyhood mates and I would wonder how the old-timers stuck it out in those days of utter isolation, no roads, no stores, no transport but the horse or camel owned by the man himself. And, very often, no water. On week-ends and holidays from the Big Mine we'd go on shooting trips among those queer, forbidding little ranges, examining the old mining camps with all the eagerness of young fellows whose lives then were "minerals". So often thirsty ourselves, many a time we've seen the drooping-winged birds with open beaks gasping the hot hours away.

As men gathered to the Mount Browne rush lack of water became acute. So the main camp had to be formed on a waterhole at Evelyn Creek, twelve miles distant. From this camp of tents was soon to grow the little township of Milparinka, where eventually the teams came toiling with supplies from Wilcannia, two hundred miles distant. So now the harsh land was building tiny townships hardily won from its own wilderness, the earliest through horses, cattle, and sheep, with the river's help – such as Menindee and Wilcannia and Bourke – the later ones by minerals. Away east the harsh red soil was now rapidly building Cobar, and away west of the river were Silverton and Apollyon Valley and the silver camps, now Mount Browne, Milparinka and Tibooburra.

Meanwhile still more stations had been taken up, still more teams came rolling along loaded with wool on their long trip to Wilcannia. But still all men and women wresting their living from the land were doing it the hard way.

Typhoid struck Mount Browne, a particularly virulent type. Strangely, in this particular instance it was the young men who were struck down, most raving to their death within a few days. Their mates could do nothing for them, except bury them in their blankets when they died. In this first epidemic only one of the young men survived, so I have often been assured. His name was Ted Murphy, destined to be one of the greatest opal-buyers the world has known.

But young Ted Murphy, raving alone in his tent, even in his most fevered dreams knew nothing of this, his life-work to be.

I was to know Murphy well in years to come, and also was to sell him opal, black opal, in a place far from here.

We did not know it, of course. But then no person in the world then knew there was such a miracle as black opal.

13. WHEN THE SALTBUSH TURNED TO SILVER

But now at long last Destiny was ready for the unfolding of her big secret. In September 1883, on Mount Gipps station, was working a boundary-rider, Charles Rasp. Lean and sunburnt, with a yellow beard, he was a quiet young fellow, a steady worker, a poor talker but a good listener. Brooding upon these tales of silver bonanzas thirty miles west around Silverton, he sent away for a book on prospecting. He studied it by slush lamp in his hut at night. And as he pored over the book in his mind's eye was that broken hill out there in the Broken Hill paddock, that rugged mass towering above the saltbush. And the idea grew within him that that sombre black hill, which often he had meditatively climbed, was really a hill of tin! For did not his prospecting book say that though tin ore may be greyish, reddish, or nearly any colour it was nearly always somewhat like coal, or blackish-grey? And very heavy?

Charles Rasp and George McCulloch, members of the "Syndicate of Seven" that founded the Broken Hill Mining Company.

The rock of that hill was of varied colours, particularly like a scorched reddish black, but mostly it was dull black. And very heavy. Yes, it *was* a black mass of oxide of tin, he grew certain. It could not be gold or silver or lead, for practical prospectors had tried its rocks and ridden away in disgust. But now he had "book learning". As his enthusiasm grew he became obsessed with the idea that that grim, hog-backed hill was really a mountain of tin!

The serious young boundary-rider thrilled to this theory of his. But he could not work the hill alone. Quietly he rode out to Jimmy Poole and Dave James, who were toiling away out on the run at dam-sinking by contract. After earnest talks he partly convinced them. They promised to "go in with him". When they had finished their present job they would "give it a go".

"*You'll* be in for it when McCulloch hears of this!" warned James.

"He'll break your neck!" grinned Poole.

The young fellow looked abashed, feeling somewhat uneasy.

"He's a good boss," he said quietly. "I've got nothing against him. He's rough, I know. But I'm going to work that hill, do what he likes."

George McCulloch, the manager of Mount Gipps station, a tough Scot, was known far and wide as an unpleasant man to cross. A big, raw-boned man, "powerful as a horse", he would fight at the drop of a hat. Used to getting things done, determined to have his own way, he was as hard as the country. Men were wary of him, but liked him because of a saving grace of grim humour. And perhaps it was this trait in his character, combined with a determined will, that eventually defied bitter disappointment and enabled him to battle stubbornly on to wealth undreamt of, and a name remembered in pioneer history.

At this period, when so many bushmen worked restlessly because of the "mining itch", this same McCulloch had gruffly assured all and sundry on the station that if any man of his left his job to peg that "flaming Broken Hill" or any other worthless hill on the Mount Gipps run then he'd "break his flaming neck"!

And men knew him capable of carrying out at least part of the threat, and knew the reason for it. The silver rushes had caused acute labour shortage on the stations. Just as men had left jobs and towns far to the east and south during early gold rushes, so here they were downing tools to trek away out to the silver finds – a serious matter to the station folk far west, where population was so very sparse. So the young boundary-rider well knew that, so far as this touchy station manager was concerned, to peg out the Broken Hill would be like flaunting a red rag to a bull.

Despite which, Charles Rasp, Dave James, and Jimmy Poole pegged out a forty-acre mineral lease on the Broken Hill. After many heart-breaks it was to become the world-famous Block 12.

On the afternoon of the pegging Charlie Rasp rode thoughtfully back to the homestead. He would say nothing at all about the pegging, would let the manager find out for himself.

But at the rough-built little homestead he met McCulloch outside the kitchen soaping his brawny arms from a bucket after the day's toil. And then as he dismounted the boundary-rider decided to take the bull by the horns.

"I'd like to draw my pay, boss," he said quietly. "I'm leaving. I'd like a change for a while."

McCulloch straightened up, glowering, for he had picked this quiet young fellow to be a sticker. Something in the young man's face set his wits ticking.

"Ah, I see!" he growled. "And so you've gone and pegged the *hill!*"

At Rasp's guilty expression McCulloch opened his mouth to roar, then hesitated, frowning at the young fellow. McCulloch judged him as not the type to throw away a job foolishly. Glaring his resentment, he thought quickly. Unknowingly, and though very much against the grain, he must have subconsciously absorbed some faint taint of this mining fever since these mad silver rushes. What if this quiet young chap had really stumbled upon something – maybe something rich!

"Tell me all about it," he ordered gruffly. *"Everything,* now!"

Rasp told him of the pegging with Poole and James, and that he really believed the hill to be a hill of black tin ore.

McCulloch listened quietly, finally cautiously impressed. He well knew that the Broken Hill had been declared worthless, but then men prospecting for gold and silver would very likely know nothing about tin! It was just possible that this secretive young boundary-rider might really have got on to something while out on the run. Now that he came to think of it, this fellow had spent quite a lot of time riding that Broken Hill paddock these last few months. That paddock was of only fifty thousand acres. What had kept this man out there so long? Why had he so often unnecessarily, as it appeared now he came to think of it, ridden that paddock? There flashed through his mind the expression "new-chum's luck". Yes, in his own quiet way this young fellow might have stumbled on something! If so, then George McCulloch was going to be in on it, too!

"You and Poole and James have no money." He frowned thoughtfully. "Only enough for a couple of months' tucker. It takes time and money to sink a shaft away out in this country. I've a few pounds put by. We'll form a little syndicate – among any of the station hands who care to throw in. Say we'll need a capital of £500. A few pounds each for a share, and a pound a week towards working the ground. Then we'll be able to finance you and Poole and James while you sink the shaft, and when you've proved it a duffer and come to your senses then you can all come back to work on the station again."

To which the considerably relieved boundary-rider willingly agreed.

So that night, in that rough-hewn homestead, over a bare plank table, sitting in their shirt-sleeves, by the light of a hurricane lamp the men drew up and signed the "Syndicate of Seven".

Charles Rasp, boundary-rider.

George McCulloch, manager.

George Urquhart, sheep overseer.

George A. M. Lind, station storekeeper.

Philip Charley, station hand.

David James, contractor.

James Poole, his mate.

That scrap of paper with its scrawling signatures was a momentous document in Australian history, I believe in the world's! For not only did it start a chain of events, of developments and industries in which hundreds of millions of pounds would be concerned, not only was it also to build towns and ports, but it was to build a mighty framework of heavy industries just when this coming nation would need that strength the most, and be the base and framework of a young nation's industrial power.

Today, seventy-two years later, the ghostly echo of that first pick striking into the broken hill has grown into a thundering chorus of mighty steel-works and vast allied industries that encircle half our continent.

The next morning McCulloch, growling that he was just as big a — fool as young Rasp, who was working quietly beside him, pegged out all the rest of the Broken Hill, the canny station manager not risking late-comers pegging the best claim, if claim there should prove to be.

After which McCulloch straightened his big form and gazed up at the hill, wiping a sweating brow with hairy forearm. The sun shimmered on the black, steel-hard rocks. Somehow or other, now that he had done something about it, he felt a surprising interest in this sterile-looking rock mass. Surely the hill was not beginning to grow on him! He frowned.

"Well, there you are!" he growled. "If there's any tin in that hill we've pegged the lot! I'll bet you'll find the only tin in that hill is in our heads. But now you and your smart mates Poole and James can start breaking your backs sinking that shaft. And I hope you'll weep bucketfuls of sweat. Which you surely will, on that rock in this heat. The three of you will soon wish you were back at your station jobs again. Anyway there's your wild cat, so get stuck into it!"

And thus began the sinking of Rasp's Shaft. Slow, laborious toil, lacking the efficient explosives of today. And the buckets of sweat they "wept" should have satisfied even McCulloch.

Meanwhile, at Silverton and Apollyon Valley thirty miles west, word had spread round of the pegging of the Broken Hill – to hilarious laughter from those wide-awake silver camps. The idea of a new-chum boundary-rider, a station manager, and a few station hands pegging out that "hill of mullock", as their own good silver men had long since proved it to be! This romance of a handful of men on an outback sheep-station was greeted with derision, and the aspirations of this Syndicate of Seven caused many a hearty laugh in which some among the far-out station-men joined. But not to Georgie McCulloch's face. He became savage as a wild bull when diplomatically these jokes came to his ears, swore he'd show them, challenged any who fancied themselves to come along and slog it out with him!

Silverton merely laughed the louder, while busily picking up on the surface among the hills heavy slugs of almost pure silver, native silver chlorobromide, horn silver, and red silver. And then a few enterprising blokes got together and marked out a "township site", to a great roar of laughter from the camps. The idea that there could ever be a *town* in this wilderness of saltbush and mulga!

But "the blokes" persisted. "Blocks" were surveyed over the saltbush, then on one humorous day were actually offered for sale! A few men bought an acre or two for a pound or two; there are always a few men in any crowd willing to take a risk for a few pounds, even if only in a half-hearted, joking kind of way. But the joke these jokers little knew was that each acre they gave a pound or two for within five years or less would be worth £20,000.

So a block or two were bought. And then I'm blessed if Delamore didn't get the absurd idea to sell his outback shanty and build a "hotel" on this saltbush and mulga now called Silverton.

The boys just simply could not understand it! They had thought Delamore was a pretty shrewd bloke, but now they knew he was nuts – as were a few other blokes who presently were cautiously giving up to £25 for a "block" of land! Twenty-five pounds for an acre of saltbush! Yes, that was big money in those days.

They could not know, of course, that soon over this sea of saltbush money was to lose all proportion; £25,000 was to have less meaning than £25 in the struggling days.

To the opening of "Delamore's Hotel" men came riding from far and wide, in some cases even from some hundreds of miles away. So to the saltbush came its first "real hotel", the opening of which was so momentous that it was still talked of in Silverton when I was a lad.

But while the teams were slowly carting the timber and iron and calico for this "fool" venture of Delamore's, out in the hills the picks were slugging down into the lodes, the drills were shrilly singing, hammers clang-clang-clanging as the drills bit down into the lodes to open out parcels of ore of fabulous richness. No wonder that now men all over that far nor'-west suffered feverishly from the "silver itch", bitten by the "silver bug", every whit as bad as the gold-fever of earlier years in the coastal lands. Now, away out here in the saltbush, Silverton and Apollyon Valley and the thirty miles of silver camps went silver crazy. Life was hard indeed, but as hectic and as brimful of dreams of fortune as it was in the stirring days of the earlier New South Wales and Victorian goldfields.

It was only the fact that silver has not the glamour of gold, the lack of news, and the extreme isolation that prevented this great silver-field from becoming known as widely as the goldfields in *their* day. How little anyone dreamed, even fifty years later, that the silver would far outlast the gold!

And still among the grey plains of mulga and saltbush, broken at long intervals by low, rocky ridges under a scorching sun, the growing camps at Apollyon Valley, Umberumberka, and Thackaringa boomed yet more feverishly, with richer finds still of slugs of native silver tarnished greyish-black from the sun, of argentite, of slugs of horn silver like huge lumps of greyish-green, sun-dried wax, of iodides and bromides of silver, of fahlerz and silver glance, of stephanite and ruby silver, and slugs of dirty-looking embolite weighing anything from ten to fifty pounds and often containing half their weight in silver. Just nests of dull weather-beaten stones lying upon and in the sunburnt gossan outcrops amongst the dwarf mulga, sombre saltbush, peppermint and needlewood and dead-finish – surely the last place in this wilderness where a man would expect to find the brilliance of a "jeweller's shop". But there they lay, these fabulous pockets of silver ores, thrown there by the magic of the Great Engineer, silver in plenty where water was more precious than silver, where men perished for the lack of it. And away back on the broken hill the angry George McCulloch drove his men both on the station and the "mine", in dour mood now, determined to prove mineral wealth where before he had believed there was but a chance – and a mighty poor chance at that!

But the toiling months dragged by, and the shaft proved a duffer. To make worse this disappointment, the land was gradually becoming stricken by the terrible drought that was to leave all the Corner Country festering with the carcasses of some millions of sheep, cattle, and horses, while the course of the Darling for hundreds of miles shrank to a chain of putrid waterholes, thus cutting off the far-flung stations, the tiny townships and mining camps from all river transport and contact with civilization. Horse- and bullock-teams perished or were marooned on the banks of widely scattered waterholes. The burning red earth, the terrible grey earth was now a true desert barren of grass or shrub, with camel-teams like gaunt spectres coming wavering up out of the mirage. These, now the only transport to stations and camps, mainly loaded up at the South Australian railhead that had now crept north to Peterborough, one hundred and sixty miles west across the border from Silverton. The nearest New South Wales line was hundreds of miles away.

Among the low, flat-topped ridges, the dark bluffs rising above the burnt-out plains, the countless broken scarps, dead watercourses and precipitous slopes, in rocky gorges just here and there lay gleaming wealth unbelievable – a natural well of clear, cool water. Such a hole, churned out through aeons of time in these old, old rocks, held water throughout all but the longest drought if only protected by rocky walls from the sun. Alas, they were far and few between, bitterly contested for by white men, aborigines, perishing stock, dying wild animals, and drooping birds. Elsewhere, under the burning sands where big dry creeks ran out on the plains from among the rock-bound hills, were occasional soakages of water. Eagerly indeed men dug for these in competition with skeleton survivors of wild horses, wallabies, and euros.

In other places men sought water at the drying waterholes stinking from the carcasses of bogged beasts, straining the filth and maggots from the slimy mess through mosquito net or tattered shirt into billycan or quart-pot. And on noiseless pads the Black Camel came spreading the scourge of death far over this strange, harsh land. By lonely camps typhoid-stricken men crawled deliriously from their blankets, following the Black Camel out into the pitiless day, out into the black night.

14. THE BREAKING OF THE DROUGHT

At Mount Gipps station work went doggedly on, mostly toiling to save a remnant of the stock, only desultorily at "the mine". The heart had gone out of both jobs.

Rasp's Shaft had proved there was no tin, of course, only plenty of black manganese, worthless there: A few assays did show ten ounces a ton of silver, worse than none at all, it seemed, for that value was quite unpayable. Silverton, Day Dream, Apollyon Valley, Umberumberka, Thackaringa, and other ores were showing from hundreds to thousands of ounces a ton.

Under the frightful conditions of the drought the disappointment nearly broke young Rasp's heart. The others shrugged their disappointment away. But McCulloch, as if defying Fate itself, in a sort of dogged stubbornness drove the others on.

Such is Fate, or the Game of Chance, or Destiny, look upon it as you will. They were convinced now that they were chasing a will-o'-the-wisp, and even when they began their wildest dreams had fallen far short of the truth – that they possessed the greatest silver-lead-zinc mine the world has ever known. How were they to know that along all that mighty Line of Lode, in all that great hill of silver, they had chosen the one tiny barren spot to sink a shaft? Even so, had they sunk still deeper they would have struck silver. But their pockets, their bodies, worst of all their hopes, were exhausted.

Finally, Urquhart and Lind threw in their hand.

"We just can't keep going," they explained dispiritedly and justifiably. "Just can't afford the money, especially in these times. We'll sell our share to anyone who will buy – if anyone is fool enough!"

Trafficking then began in shares and part shares, mostly to rare passers-by tempted to take a faint chance at the risk of a few pounds. Lind sold his share to Rasp and McCulloch, who bought only in a half-hearted attempt to keep the show going, to try to hold some sort of syndicate together. Soon afterward Urquhart sold his share. So for a few pounds they sold shares eventually worth millions.

One man bought three fourteenth shares for £330. He sold one for £100, another for £200, but kept the third. Twelve months later this share was worth £30,000. In six years its market value with dividends and bonus was worth £1,250,000. Where in the history of the world have such fortunes in mining been made – and lost! Urquhart sold two fourteenth shares for £10. Cox, the blacksmith, bought a fourteenth share for £30, and sold it later for £60, well pleased.

One day a young fellow came riding along, droving a little mob of bullocks. A long, lanky lad, with a drawling voice and a smile and eyes that missed nothing. He pulled up at the camp of Jimmy Poole and Davy James. He had met them before and liked them. Enthusiastically they told him all about the mine; they were going to make a great fortune out of it. But he noticed they had eyes only for his wee mob of cattle.

"Your mine sounds like a dream," he said with a smile.

"It's not. And we'll let you into it!" And Poole's eyes were on the cattle.

"It's the real McKay, Sid! But we want ready money quickly to help work it properly, and we haven't enough bullocks to complete this well-sinking contract. We'll sell you a fourteenth share in the mine for ten working bullocks – or sixty pounds!"

"Right. You can have the bullocks."

And the young fellow rode on his way, smiling at the idea of selling ten precious bullocks for a part share in a mine! He would never have done anything so foolish, only that Poole and James had put a deal his way when passing through Mount Gipps station some time before. And all his long life he was to be noted for handsomely paying back any good turn done him.

That lanky lad was Sid Kidman, destined to be known throughout Australia as "the Cattle King". Starting out with a one-eyed horse and five shillings in his pocket, he was to build up a hundred stations. And, though he knew it not, he was to bring cattle in their tens of thousands to this apparent wilderness, to a hungry market that would help to build him up into the greatest Cattle King ever.

Within a few months Weatherley and Bowes-Kelly bought that lad's part share in Silverton for £150. The lad was quite satisfied; he had repaid a good turn and made a profit on what was to prove his one and only mining venture.

Bowes-Kelly was soon to become a familiar name in the mining world.

That part share, if held throughout the years, would have been worth some millions of pounds. I have seen an estimate worked out that it would have been worth £5,000,000. I reckon that was the greatest stock deal in the world's history. Ten working bullocks for £5,000,000!

Long years afterward I asked the grizzled old Cattle King whether he ever looked back on that deal.

"I never regretted it," he drawled with that whimsical smile of his. "I made a profit on it. And I believe in the other man making his profit, too. I never was cut out for a miner, and I knew it. The profit I made on that deal helped me buy horses for a mail contract I was angling for. And I made money on that contract also. No, stock was my line. I would have been a lamb among the silver wolves."

But what in soon coming years must have been the feelings of the men who sold two of the original seventh shares, for less than £100 each!

In a matter of a few years each of these shares was worth £2,500,000

But in that lonesome area of the Far West, especially at the time of that terrible drought, of course neither buyers nor sellers had the faintest idea that this would be. Had a dreamer ventured to suggest that perhaps the Broken Hill might after all turn out to be worth a thousand or two they would not even have laughed, so dispirited were they by the duffer shaft, by the state of the country under the frightful conditions of that drought. The money paid for the shares at that time was valuable indeed to the seller. As to the buyer – well, he just happened to have the few pounds to spare and the urge to "give it a go", somewhat shamefacedly, knowing he was taking a foolhardy risk.

A fourteenth share was played for over a game of euchre, surely the greatest card stake in history. McCulloch, with the canny idea of at least getting his grub-stake back, tried to sell a fourteenth share for £200 to a pleasant-mannered new-churn, a young Englishman who had ridden across on a visit from Momba station. He did not want the fourteenth share, but toyed with the idea that it would be great to write home that he owned a share in a mine. But he shied like a brumby at the mention of £200. McCulloch, scenting a fish nibbling, persisted. Finally the young fellow very diffidently offered £120, at which McCulloch urged all the more for £200, little knowing that his rosy picture of the wealth that *could* be in that mine would be multiplied 100,000 times over in fact.

At last the new-churn declared, "Well, Mr McCulloch, I won't pay £200. But I'll tell you what I'll do! I'll challenge you to a game of euchre, the winner to fix the price of the share."

"Done!" agreed McCulloch, who fancied himself with the cards.

He lost. Within six years, that fourteenth share, on market values with dividends and bonuses represented £1,250,000 – won in a lonely station homestead west of the Darling. Compared to such a stake, breaking the bank at Monte Carlo is but tobacco money.

As a lad working in the Big Mine I sometimes found myself wallaby-shooting at week-ends among the rocky little hills on Mount Gipps station. I have gone into the little old homestead, actually hardly more than a hut, and easily pictured that game, the sunburnt bushmen sitting round on boxes, cross-legged, elbow on knee with chin cupped in hand, quietly puffing their pipes as they watched the game. The two men sitting opposite at the rough plank table, the brawny McCulloch in shirt-sleeves with alert eye on his cards while watching his opponent's every move, the fresh-skinned young Englishman thinking hard, cautiously playing, warily guarding his precious £200. Above bearded faces there would be tobacco smoke floating up to the dull glow of the hurricane lamp with the moths flying round it, silence in that hut except at each deal the whispering shuffle of the cards, the puff of an onlooker's pipe. Out through the open hut door the hot night, the moveless air noisomely tinged with odour of decaying carcasses, shadow of the mulga-clad hills, the ageless stars like diamonds above, over the ridges the howl of a dingo calling his mates to feast upon some drought-stricken beast.

Within the hot, silent hut, unknown to the players, a vast fortune waiting upon the fall of a card. I wonder if that fourteenth share had been held in its entirety, how many millions it would be worth today!

The dry months dragged on, and news came that south of Silverton Maiden and Pretty had discovered the Pinnacles. Silver! Silver seemed everywhere, on a day when the sun was a furnace, the rocks so hot a man could barely touch an ironstone surface with his hand, a day when even the saltbush was dying, even the mulga grey and drooping, not the voice of one single bird – a silence as of death itself, slowly settling over all the land. Above a quivering plain, half chopped from the earth by flickering rays of heat, the Pinnacles appeared as pyramid shadows floating in a leaden sky.

Despite deadening drought blighting the life of the country on the one hand and the crash of all their mining hopes on the other, McCulloch still clung grimly to the Broken Hill. By cajolery, wrath, jeers, and his own stubborn will he kept a syndicate together. Though disheartened members might sell their share, pack the swag and trudge away, he clung to the hill.

In 1884 William Jamieson, surveyor of the New South Wales Mines Department, received orders from Sydney to survey the Silverton mining areas.

He drove from Bourke, ninety miles south of the Queensland border, straight across the Far West to within fifteen miles of the South Australian border, through a country now dead, a desert inferno. The widely-scattered folk still remaining – station folk, teamsters, and miners – were marooned beside well or waterhole, existing only they knew how, grimly holding on until the drought should break – if it ever would. Only the hardiest of the camel-teams now ventured to travel. As these had to carry feed for the camels and water also, you can imagine the cost of one weevily bag of flour. Jamieson had to travel through this desolation under a blazing sun with loaded buggy and – *horses.*

Dad used to wax enthusiastic about Jamieson's trip, and when I was a lad at the Hill old hands there still marvelled how Jamieson had made it.

It is a pity that many little bush epics such as this, which all over the continent shone for a moment like vanishing stars, should disappear in their picturesque variety from our pioneer history. Future generations, intent on a monotonous trip to the moon, surely would have been interested.

George McCulloch, brooding in his rude homestead to the howling of the dingoes tearing the remnants of his perishing flocks, little knew that his lost hopes now lived in the life of a man slowly travelling away out in the hot night, night that still was merciful to the panting horses laboriously trudging in a cloud of suffocating dust so fine that the dragging hooves stirred up the misty powder as by a fan, though there was not a breath of air. The patient driver, nursing every ounce of his horses' strength, encouraging them as if they were his own toiling children, his eyes red-rimmed from sleeplessness, dust, and heat, his nostrils, mouth, blistered lips, and ears clogged with dust, plodded slowly on with for company the steely stars, the hot night, the labouring breaths of his horses, the sickening odour of decay over the land, the dismal howl of dingo.

I have known that country in its strange beauty, have battled through it when it was hell on earth.

Jamieson's outfit crawled into Silverton in a violent electrical storm. The red sky broke into blinding flashes that bit the dying earth with an instant smell of brimstone as the heavens burst in frightful thunder. The bottom dropped out of the sky as solid water smashed down.

The Great Drought of 1884 was breaking.

Jamieson's entry with the life-giving storm symbolized the dawn of the long-forgotten dreams of the remnants of the Syndicate of Seven. They did not know it yet, but they were happy. Each was conscious of a strangeness, of something unusual, which puzzled them until they realized that it was the smiling faces. None had seen a smiling face for – how long! Theirs now the joy of breathing in cool, sweet air instead of heat and stifling dust, and the foul tang of rotting carcasses. They tingled to the moist kiss of rain, the new breath rising from the dead earth tasting already of life; they were crazy with delight that the drought was breaking; life would be born again. As for the mine, they barely gave it a thought.

Meanwhile, Jamieson, in his weeks of painstaking survey along the Silverton fields, eventually came riding to the Broken Hill, his interest immediately attracted by this towering buttress. In the next few days, carefully examining it, then thoughtfully turning over in his hand a fragment of black, heavy, hot rock, he seemed to smell there was something there. Earnestly then he examined Rasp's duffer shaft. Then, to the amazed incredulity of McCulloch, he asserted that there were probably great values of ore concealed deep within this hill.

Those of the Syndicate watching him working smiled wryly and shook doubting heads. True, this was a man of wide and practical mining experience. But, after what they had gone through, after those bitter disappointments ...

To convince them that he really believed what he said Jamieson bought three fourteenth shares. Two he later sold.

By degrees, bucked up by Jamieson's earnest regard, urged on by the rekindled enthusiasm of McCulloch, the Syndicate of Seven expanded to a Syndicate of Fourteen and decided to "give the hill another go".

Jamieson eventually brought along two geologists, C. S. Wilkinson and Norman Taylor. Their report was enthusiastic. Work recommenced with a new born hope on the Broken Hill.

It was in January 1885 that Charlie Rasp, laughing in crazy excitement, came galloping to the homestead waving a fistful of silver chloride. He had picked the specimen out of the hill with his knife. The sample assayed eight hundred ounces of silver to the ton.

Then Low found a specimen amazingly rich in silver. Jamieson decided this stone must have fallen from, or been washed down, the hill. Accompanied by a blackboy carrying a sledge-hammer he climbed up to the rocky crest, the crest where Sturt had stood. A rock smashed by the hammer shattered into a mass of silver chlorides – over one thousand ounces to the ton.

Broken Hill was born.

Sturt's look-out rock that was so very, very old when it had overlooked his Inland Sea was to make a Silver City, to forge a silver link destined with steel to build a chain of new towns and mighty industries in the now swiftly coming development of the last continent.

But out over the grey saltbush plains all they knew then was, "McCulloch and Jamieson and the Mount Gipps mob have struck it rich!" The "hill of mullock" had made good.

How greater their amazement had they even vaguely guessed the treasure deep below within that sombre four miles, the Line of Lode!

Jamieson and McCulloch and their little band of bush workers moved swiftly now. Like excited schoolboys they gathered at Mount Gipps homestead and agreed to draft out a prospectus to form the Broken Hill Proprietary Company Limited. And Jamieson was in the saddle for Silverton. In a group they stood and watched him speeding across the saltbush plain, swiftly he would cover that thirty odd miles. That same night the prospectus was being printed on the little hand press of the *Silver Age,* Silverton's mighty atom of a newspaper. Just before dawn Jamieson was packing bundles of the prospectus in the boot of the overland coach and was rumbling across the plains towards the South Australian border, thence to Peterborough railhead for Adelaide. No cars or planes in those days, but the boys could move when they wished to.

While the young company was being swiftly and successfully floated away south in Melbourne and Adelaide the men back at Mount Gipps were digging through the ironstone cap of the broken hill to break through into amazing silver treasure, green chlorides and kaolins assaying thousands of ounces a ton, slugs of native silver, oxides, and presently bromides and iodides of silver, argentite and sulphur-yellow iodyrite. From sunrise to sunset they toiled in a feverish excitement, their sweat now dripping down on to silver ores of fabulous richness.

Hurrying horsemen appeared; in haste the Line of Lode was pegged out for miles and the greatest silver rush in Australia's history began. Silverton had seemed to spring up overnight, but the town of Broken Hill appeared as if by magic, a tent town firstly, then swiftly developing until along the foot of the scrubby ridge the Argent Street of today formed even as business buildings, hotels, and houses sprang up each side of it. Shacks they were, of course, but it was the start, the first sign of permanency after tents. Fortune-hunters swarmed all along the crest of the ridge; others worked feverishly at buildings below, while a new mushroom town of tents spread far and wide out from the rapidly growing "main street". Lazy little clouds of dust arose from the hooves and wheels of ever-increasing bullock- and horse-teams, packhorse-teams, and camel-teams coming from now busy Menindee as the Darling Dreadnoughts made rush trips, in keen rivalry racing one another, the crews even fighting one another at times for the prize and honour of the swiftest trips all the way from South Australia and Victoria with stores and trade to this new inland bonanza. Away west over the border the teams were coming from the Burra where the loaded trains from South Australia were vying for their overland share in this trade. The wilderness west of the Darling was springing to life with a vengeance.

At the Broken Hill Proprietary, soon for many years to be familiarly known as "the Big Mine", Aladdin's Cave would not even have been cigarette money to the riches they now were digging out. Then along the Line of Lode other mines now from day to day were striking silver ores, amazingly rich. Down below the rising town, in the grip of the wildest silver fever ever, seethed in hectic activity day and night. The Roaring Silver Days had come! In time fast coming the saying, "The Silver City never sleeps", was true indeed.

They named their streets after the ores from which the town was growing – the main street, Argent Street, which means Silver Street, Chloride Street, Blende Street, Iodide Street, Telluride Street, Sulphide Street, Oxide Street, Bromide Street, Crystal Street, Mercury Street, Mica Street, Zinc Street, Cobalt Street, Beryl Street – all names of wealth of rock dug from deep in the earth under that so recently despised "hill of mullock"!

And now officialdom in distant Sydney gradually woke up to the fact that something big was developing in the despised Far West. So a proclamation came through reserving the very land upon which the town was already being built.

The miners held a monster indignation meeting and decided that, as the Government had let the country west of the Darling stew in its own juice these man years past without the slightest help or even interest, they would carry on on their own as they had been compelled to do. They would keep on building the town where it grew. And they did.

And that was the start of that go-ahead independence which in time, with canny and increasing organization, has made Broken Hill the most remarkable town in Australia, and its way of life unique.

Tom Mann Addressing the People at Broken Hill, May 8th

15. THE HOME OF THE FIRE STONE

Meanwhile, on Momba run, a bearded old shepherd was seeking water in the wilderness one hundred and forty miles north-east of the broken hill – water, more precious by far than any mineral.

Around this old veteran was no sign of habitation, just distance, saltbush and bluebush plains, a far-off patch of mulga, an uprising of small hills here and there, a dark serpent of trees marking the course of some dry creek. Summer, but a beautiful day, he was walking dreamily along the bottom of an ocean of purest air. Far above a sky of faint blue, around him a breathing stillness, though a brown lark was singing joyously as it fluttered high up in the sky.

I have dreamed through many days like that west of the Darling – and have battled through other days very different.

But our grizzled old shepherd was seeking water. Scant hope of finding it, he knew. But you never can tell. You might come across a waterhole in a sun-sheltered gully somewhere or other, perhaps a shallow gilgai hole, maybe a soak. Just enough to water a few head of sheep, that was all he wanted. If he found it he would keep it "back in his head". After a thunderstorm there sprang up good pickings along these flats here and there. When hard times came on other parts of the run such knowledge would come in handy to him and his flock if only he could find water – or a hole that he was sure would hold water for a week or two after a thunderstorm came.

Leisurely, with a movement that would conserve energy, he began to climb a gently rising slope. He would come to the top of these little hills, then, eyes shaded by hand from the sun, gaze far out, turning ever so slowly round, seeking some sign of depression, a clump of moisture-loving vegetation, or the flight of a bird in the grey country below that to practised eyes might betray the existence of a waterhole.

Queer little hills these, he mused, seeming to be made up of a greyish-white chalk, sheltering under its cap of "Grey Billy". An actual "helmet of the hills", this Grey Billy, a dense, extremely hard cap of rock by means of which Nature had jealously preserved the remnants of so many of these little hills throughout how many millions of years of storm and stress? Under the caps, just here and there, the hills reminded the old shepherd of little white cliffs. This was where time and weather had eventually worn away the thin layer of overburden on the steeper slopes under the caps, the rains of ages finally leaving exposed the softer rock, like little white cliffs.

He came to one, of which sections had fallen and, broken up by fierce suns, lay frittered in powdered fragments before him. He stood, gazing curiously down, then stooped and picked up a small dark-grey stone. Oblong in shape, almost square, flat, perfectly smooth, a quarter of an inch thick, as clean-cut as if it had been moulded – as indeed it had, by the miraculous, timeless, titanic forces of Nature. Curiously he turned it over in his horny palm.

"Seems like it mighta bin glass one time," he mused aloud, as often these old shepherds did.

He picked up another similar piece and hit the two sharply together. With a crackling sound they splintered.

"It *is* glass!" he cried delightedly. "I thought so! An' it's all clear like glass inside. But nobody ain't ever bin near this place to leave glass here!" Seriously he examined the fractured pieces. "Bin here a hell of a long time," he mused. "Long before the white man came. See how dirty grey the outside has bin burnt be the sun. An' all sand-scratched, too ... fair polished by wind-blown sand."

After a while he concluded, "It's glass right enough, but not man-made glass ... the natives never made no glass. I believe it's bin burnt out by a volcano ... I've heered somewheres that volcanoes spew out molten glass."

How near, yet how far, the old shepherd was in his surmise! We believe that great heat, with subsequent cooling and contraction and pressure, was partly responsible for this particular "glass" the old shepherd had stumbled upon. But here at least there is overwhelming evidence that something else, and the reverse of volcanic action, had been at work, too.

The sea – a long-vanished sea.

For here a sea had been, long before Sturt's sea.

The proof is that petrified, otherwise opalized, shells and fish almost in plenty, even long-extinct sea monsters, were to be found here where the sun was now beating down upon the old shepherd trying hard to use his brains, here where the coarse, tufted grasses were flourishing upon the warm earth, here all around him were the sands of that sea long since compressed into layers of sandstone rock.

What fantastic mysteries lie all around us!

This old shepherd was seeking a tiny waterhole where once, far around and above him, had rolled a great sea.

And that sea had dried up even before the sea of fresh water from the northern and nor'-eastern rivers had come pouring down into the dead sea bed.

How right Sturt had been, how right the old shepherd! Yet so far, far away in time.

The old shepherd picked up a stick, began scratching round in the fallen, whitish dirt. Presently he unearthed a line of little stones where the dirt was more solid.

"They seem to be all laid down flat in a seam," he mused. Which they actually were – by the hand of Nature.

Sitting down, he broke a number. To his amazement he saw a flash of fire, then an orange glow, then gleaming many-coloured flames as he broke stone after stone.

"Can't make head nor tail of it," he muttered. "Never heered of stones before what was all the colours of the rainbow."

Squatting there under the sun's warmth, slowly he turned the flashing fragments round and round in his stubby fingers, frowning his bewilderment.

"Can't make it out at all," he mused. "Seems as if the volcano has left orl the colours of hell an' heaven in these glassy stones. But you can't keep fire prisoned up in a stone ..: no, not even a volcano can't!"

At last he stood up, quite reluctantly, prepared to move on. His job was to find water for "them there sheep". Suddenly a thought struck him. Cunningly he stared round into the great loneliness. Then carefully he covered the broken fragments with earth, smoothing over everything to look as nearly as possible as it had before he had begun rooting about.

"Dunno what these stones is," he muttered, "but if I keeps me ears open I might hear somethin' about 'em some day. Might be somethin' valyable ... perhaps."

Then he walked steadily on, seeking a waterhole where once had rolled a sea.

The shepherd did not know what he had found. But then there must be many discoveries that we all miss likewise.

In later years, in telling of his experience the shepherd used to philosophize: "I sat me tail down on a hill of fire, an' it didn't warm me one bit. I was lookin' for a pannikin of water to water a few sheep for a few shillings a week. An' all the time I was sitting on what could have bought me Momba station, an' Mount Poole, an' Yancannia, an' Weinteriga, an' Wonnaminta. Damn it all, enough money to buy all the country west o' the Darling. All waiting there under the seat of me pants ... where me brains orter been."

But the old shepherd was not the only lone man to climb that hill and curiously break pieces of that "glassy-looking stone" and not recognize it. Even as a boy I used to wonder what would have been the feelings of the handful of settlers, storekeepers, stockmen, drovers and teamsters, the bargemen and crews of the Darling Dreadnoughts if they had known that in the wilderness sixty miles north of Wilcannia lay a blazing wealth of "fire-stones", treasure piled upon treasure of precious opals such as the world had never seen.

Interesting indeed how that harsh Far West had disguised her good stock food in the apparent barrenness of her shrubbery, had held back her rich mineral treasures, her varied gem secrets within the heart of seeming desolation.

A few years later, in December 1889, a party of kangaroo-shooters – Alf Richardson, Will Clouston, Charlie Turner, and George Hooley – were shooting in the vicinity of those same sparsely grassed, tiny hills a hundred and forty miles north-east of the now booming Broken Hill. Richardson and Clouston, eyes searching the ground, were slowly tracking a wounded 'roo over one of the little whitish hills when blood spots upon several small, dull-grey, flat stones set like a mosaic upon the whitish earth attracted their attention. Curiously they examined the pebbles and found, like the old shepherd, that when broken some gleamed with dancing lights.

"I wonder," mused Clouston, "could these be opals? Couldn't be, I s'pose. You remember that story we heard in Wilcannia about some Queensland blokes finding fiery opals 'way up Cunnamulla way?"

That night over the campfire, in a half shamefaced, joking way, they decided to collect a few of the little stones and on their next trip back to Wilcannia risk asking the Mining Registrar if they might be of value.

"The boys will poke borak at us if they're not," said Turner, grinning.

Thus were opals discovered in New South Wales, at White Cliffs, destined to be the greatest light-opal field ever yet found in the world.

Truly that harsh, sometimes deceivingly lovely country carried strange, fantastically rich secrets in her sunburnt bosom.

Opals were practically unknown in Australia then, of course. So very few men had even seen the desert sandstones, "home of the opal", let alone opal in the rough. Only about, perhaps, a hundred men in all Queensland, which meant all Australia so far as the opal was concerned.

With opals, as with copper and silver, it has seemed to me that Destiny unfolded her secret riches in her own good time. She clung to her "hills of fire" until slowly, and with what hardship, despair, and heart-break to humans, the way was prepared.

Away north of the Silver City, away north of those little "white cliffs", across the Queensland border running right up through south-west Queensland is a strip of desert sandstone hundreds of miles long, up through Cunnamulla, Eulo, Yowah, Quilpie, and on towards Windorah through the coolabah, box and gidgee to the queer Kyabra hills where the rocky gullies, the fantastic escarpments of long-dead ranges, the ironstone boulders are thrown out over the scrubby flats as if belched from some mighty furnace.

Here and there in this forbidding, continuing strip of strangely fascinating country – alas, also so short of water! – an occasional lonely wanderer, mostly nameless now, first found opal in Australia. It was purely by chance, for in that lonesome country where a wanderer's ceaseless thought was to learn the whereabouts of water and not get bushed, in those drab, harsh surroundings, whoever would dream that he was in the home of the most colourful and vividly beautiful gem the world has ever known?

The first wanderer who found the first "Yowah nut" picked it up, curious as to its shape, much like a brick-red, wrinkled walnut. Maybe, turning this ugly little stone over in his knotted, sunburnt hand, he wondered if it could be a petrified nut from a long-dead forest. He had probably seen petrified logs down in the Lake Eyre country. He cracked the "nut" with a tomahawk and there blazed at him a miracle of flashing orange and green.

What must have been his feelings, kneeling there among the coarse grass in that lonely wilderness, staring at the most beautiful thing Nature has ever made!

Thus were the Yowah nuts discovered, and almost similarly the strange form of boulder opal, another treasure of Nature so cunningly hidden in a dirty shell of apparently worthless rock – and of pipe opal, and matrix, and other strange, fascinating forms of Queensland treasure stone.

Away back in 1872, at Listowel Downs station near Adavale and at Springsure, opal was thus first found. From 1875 onwards, just here and there in that unpeopled bushland, an occasional wanderer, blessed with the curiosity that urges a man to examine anything unusual, stumbled upon the gem. Some merely rode away, not understanding what they had found. A few at long last rode back to civilization to inquire if their find was of value, and were told there was no market.

Then in 1878 – while Paddy Green far south was still toiling like a Trojan to keep his tucker-bag filled while awaiting result of that shipment of ore from the Thackaringa hills – they found the Aladdin mine, where the opals were so plentiful and beautiful they simply blazed their own path across bush gossip. The prospector, in the lonely silences by the campfire there, had silently wished he could find Aladdin's lamp whose

137

compassionate genie at his wish would lead him to a mine of blazing gems. But his wildest dreams never brought him the beauty he stumbled upon in fact.

The Scotchman mine was then found also at Coonavalla on Euronghella station, and the Yowah away down by Eulo. The quantity even as much as the quality of these magnificent gems caused folk to say, "Surely there *must* be something in them! These beautiful things must be of value *somewhere* in the world!"

Herbert Bond of Toowoomba, then a struggling little town, took a parcel of the gems to London in a sturdy attempt to find a market. A little company was formed. Back in western Queensland a few more wonderful mines were quickly found when word spread round that Bond had returned to buy opals. But it all died out. Bond's efforts had met with failure. The London jewellery merchants simply refused to buy. They shrugged their shoulders, declaring these were not, *could not* be opals.

Overseas, the experts were used to the pale, milky, watery Hungarian variety of opal. For centuries the largest, best-known opal-mines in the world were in Cyscherwentza in Hungary. These had been worked since the end of the fourteenth century.

But these "new" brilliant opals, blazing with all the colours of the rainbow, these flashing Australian gems were utterly unknown to the world's experts who suspiciously refused them. Some did not even know there was such a country in the world as Australia, and smiled knowingly at the suggestion that precious opals had been discovered in unknown wilds.

Thus this early promise of an Australian opal industry was quickly killed.

It was revived eleven years later, in 1889, seventeen years after opals were first found in Queensland, when Wollaston took his first parcel of Queensland opal gems to London and began a heart-breaking struggle for recognition – while that party of 'roo-shooters was still shooting down south on Momba run in New South Wales, north-east of Broken Hill.

Tully Wollaston was a young South Australian, a little bloke, but with brains and grit, whose passion in the study of gems was, after great hardship and heart-break, to put the Australian opal on the world's market. Since then the world has asked for no other.

David Tweedie, an Adelaide solicitor, impressed by the lad, agreed to go into partnership with him, formed a little syndicate, and arranged finances. Nearly crazy with joy, Wollaston threw up his survey job, said farewell to his wife and baby, then with his mate Herb Buttfield travelled north to Hergott Springs, plodding by out past the silver camps, riding ever on into the frightening mirages of South Australia's far north, to cross the Corner Country into south-west Queensland, heading for some phantom locality called the Kyabra Hills. A wild goose chase, said his friends, from which he might never return.

Their prophecy almost came true, and yet again on succeeding trips. Almost, for Death was beckoning away back in the mirage for Herb Buttfield, his mate – it was he who would perish of thirst.

It would really seem, though, as if this young fellow was taking a great and utterly foolish risk in more ways than one. Throwing up a steady job when jobs were so very scarce, leaving his wife and baby, only a few weeks old – and he was passionately attached to his family all his life – going out into some far, unknown country, seeking an unknown gem, which even if he could buy it from a very problematical miner was of no marketable value.

It was true that Wollaston was going on a mere rumour, a report that a miner called Joe Bridle had made a rich opal find somewhere in south-west Queensland, in a district vaguely called the Kyabra Hills – and that three years ago. Wollaston could not even learn whether the report was true or not, let alone whether the man was still in that unknown locality a thousand miles away in another State. If ever the old saying, "Nothing venture, nothing win!" was true it was so in this remarkable case. A gambler would have shrugged, declaring the odds against success to be a million to one.

It seems rather quaint also, to me at least, that it was to be a South Australian who, mainly through White Cliffs, was to make Australian opals famous throughout the world. But then Destiny had already decreed that little South Australia was to benefit exceedingly well from the treasure-houses west of the Darling, in the future to an almost unbelievable extent.

Wollaston and Buttfield, reaching Hergott Springs, set out by camel and horse on a seven-hundred-mile ride, crossed the Queensland border and eventually, after what we would today call incredible hardships, found the Kyabra Hills. Far more surprising, they at last found tough "Old Joe" Bridle, camped at Stony Creek. Above all, to young Wollaston's almost crazy delight, Old Joe had really found an opal-mine. And what opals! But he did not show them at first. With the secretiveness of the opal-gouger he showed only the poor stuff. For several days he quietly weighed this young fellow up. Not until he felt sure the stranger was genuine did he show the true gems. And the deeply disappointed Wollaston nearly went crazy with delight.

Torn by dreams and impatience, after three thousand gruelling miles by camel, horse, buckboard, coach, river-boat, and train, Wollaston eventually returned to Adelaide with a brilliant parcel of gems and a heart alternating with feverish hope and determination. Would the little syndicate be able to scrape up the few pounds necessary for him to go to London and sell the gems?

As it turned out, they did. But before that he received news from the Windorah police that his mate Herb Buttfield had perished of thirst while tracking runaway camels in waterless bush.

In London bitter disappointment awaited. Wollaston found, as Bond had found, that the big gem-merchants of Hatton Gardens first looked at the brilliant gems with curiosity, then glanced at the seller askance. They shook reproving heads.

"No," they declared quietly, "there is no market in London for such opals."

They did not believe them to be opals, knowing only the pale, milky variety. Some were openly suspicious, wondering how such ignorant "primitives" as "wild Australian bushmen" could have made these brilliantly coloured fakes.

It seems unbelievable today that the most beautiful gem the world has ever known should be rejected and in some cases looked upon as a fraud by the acknowledged experts of the world's gem markets. But such is fact.

After three months' heart-break Wollaston found Hasluck Brothers of Hatton Gardens, who were ready to give the "new" opals a chance. They examined them with every test known to the trade, experimented with a few, then decided to cut a small parcel and try the American market.

It was a small opening, but it was something – a trickle, destined to grow into a flood. For that firm, once they started, stuck to Australian opals as Tweedie, far away in Adelaide, was standing by the struggling Wollaston.

16. THE SILVER CITY GROWS

The crowding together of so many people at Broken Hill, under such primitive health arrangements as then existed in that hot, almost waterless country, again brought the "Terror of the West", typhoid. A brand-new cemetery received its harvest with a frightening greed – alas, there was to be more than one cemetery filled before medical science finally overcame typhoid. Pneumonia also took its toll. But silver riches now pouring from the Hill stifled men's fears of death. During the epidemics they buried their fellows, then those who felt they needed it hurried to the riotous hotels and drank to their late mate's passing "over the Silver Range". At night the dark bluff above the roaring town was now splashed with glowing fire from the smelters, suns of scarlet flame flickering in vivid green and drowned in fiery orange rolling and splashing down the growing slag dump. High up there the dark trucks came rumbling on their curving way like some reptilian monster creeping along the skyline, each iron pot emitting a glow as from a score of monstrous eyes. As the trucks came to a clanking standstill darkness swept in, smothering the glow while the toilers seized the lip of a pot with their long iron levers. Cautiously, expertly, they stretched up and forward, tipping it. And darkness vanished as the guts of a furnace spilled out, loosening a rolling ball of liquid fire that flamed down over the dump, spreading into a wave splashing over the red-hot cliff in sprays of starry foam. As each pot tipped so the figures of the two men sprang out of the surrounding night, scarlet as toiling demons.

In distant Cobar also the slag dumps glowed, but far more brilliantly in dazzling colours painted into them by the unmeasured variations of coloured copper ores. Gazing up thus at the tipping of slag from a smelter's fires, the watcher feels his imagination shiver with a faint intuition of what Primal Night must have been when the earth was one vast melting-pot.

Some ores of the earth when in specimen form are very beautiful, often, too, shaped in entrancing forms. We are familiar with the beauties of flowers and birds and butterflies, of a cherry orchard in bloom, of golden wattle along a hillside, of the delicate fernery in a shady gully, of the flashing beauty of a satin bird in flight. Some know, too, of the gorgeous brilliance of many tropic fishes, of the fantasies in colour and shape of underwater life along the Great Barrier Reef and other treasuries of the seas. There are beauties all around us, for those who have the eyes and the time to see. But few of us indeed know of the lovely things deep within the impenetrable darkness in the bosom of the earth.

Of these many, the opal is the unrivalled Queen of Beauty. But, apart from gems, specimen ores of metals common to us in everyday life occur at times in colourings of transcendent beauty, of breath-taking shape. Sublime pockets of ores of silver were commonly unearthed thus in the early years of the Silver City, little treasure-chests of unearthly beauty and form whose loveliness far outshone in value their intrinsic worth as silver. Silver ferns as delicately shaped as the most delicate of maidenhair fern and infinitely more lovely in their varying colours, forms like corals also, miniature jewelled birds and "bower-bird tails" and lizards of cubes and crystals, jewelled silvers of infinite variety and shape, with wonderful specimens of lead ores. As I write this I think with a sigh of where most of those few beautiful collections must have vanished to now. I remember one publican who had collected a little museum of these entrancing specimens that surely would have been priceless today. His collection was known far and wide in the district. Only a few enthusiasts collected these beautiful things, for with development they grew comparatively "common" within that fabulous Line of Lode.

Even when I was a boy such specimens were still common enough, but the lovely treasure pockets were found less and less as the mines worked deep down through the oxidized into the sulphide zones. I suppose those beautiful things have long since been melted down for their silver, or sold here and there to some buyer who fancied some particular piece. Perhaps a mining museum here and there may have a little collection. I hope so.

The beauties of colouring and form found in the copper ores of Cobar, and of course of the great copper-mines of South Australia, are beyond description. There are colours and shades of colour among copper specimen ores that have never been put into man-made paints. Doubtless the collections of those often fantastically beautiful copper ores have vanished also. They were so very common in the early days, and with the early days they vanished. Just what might be far down in the very centre of the earth? I wonder. It was the liberated colourings of coppers in the molten slag that made the rolling balls of liquid fire so vividly beautiful at night.

However, west of the Darling by the Silver City came the clamour as of an army at work from all along that long black crest of the developing Line of Lode, while down below among the thousand lights of the town shadows were ever moving. Riotous life went ceaselessly on day and night, a feverish life thrilling now to still wilder speculation as other mines were opened up on the field, hectic speculation, too, on the distant stock exchanges of Melbourne and Adelaide. Thousands of men who would not even know native silver, let alone silver ore, if they saw it, many who would never even see the Silver City, many living five hundred miles, a thousand miles away, were feverishly buying "silver shares", blindly ignorant whether they were dabbling in wildcats or a genuine silver-mine.

This speculation commenced soon after the finding of the first rich Silverton mines, and later rose to a frenzy with the first boom of the Silver City. Thus a small army of otherwise level-headed men who would never even see the saltbush chased the will-o'-the-wisp of quickly gained wealth without leaving their city homes. That very small minority who "got in on the ground floor" along the real Line of Lode reaped rich reward indeed, but the majority of hopes faded into the silver mirage.

This phase in the life of the Silver City lasted but a few years, wild and woolly years indeed. Fortunes were changing hands daily, yet not a soul even on the field itself dreamt of the vast wealth actually there underground along that Line of Lode. To the majority it was a God-forsaken ridge of barren hills which by some impish freak of nature mothered a silver-mine here and there.

The scrubby timbers of those hills and gullies and flats was now falling fast to feed the ever-hungry, ever-increasing furnaces.

By now unhappily aware of the periodic changes in this country, the inhabitants raised a cry for railway connection with Sydney. For with recurring droughts the Darling would surely go dry again, and this would ground the Darling Dreadnoughts; supplies would be cut off from the town, from settlements, from camps and stations until at long last the rains should come and the river run again. Now that it was obvious a big mining future lay out here west of the Darling it would pay the New South Wales Government handsomely to build a railway.

The Government refused. Not so South Australia. The line was pushed on from Peterborough to Cockburn, a village right on the border, the first train puffing up there in June 1887. Even then the New South Wales Government refused to build a connection of only thirty-six miles and thus link the South Australian railway with the New South Wales mining town.

Indignant men of Silverton decided to do the job themselves. They formed the Silverton Tramway Company and built the line – away back in 1888. Thus was Sturt's lonely outpost connected overland with the distant coast and a little Australian capital. Never could he have dreamt, as half blinded and in near despair he wrote in his journal of the desolation there, that time would bring a locomotive following in his footsteps.

Greatly was South Australia to benefit from its enterprise as the Barrier rapidly developed into the Silver City.

Within the first three years, despite handicaps of isolation, with the only transport bullock-wagon, dray, camel-team, buggy and horse east to the Dreadnought transport of the Darling or west to the railhead on the South Australian border, battling against dreadful lack of water and primitive conditions in general, the Big Mine alone produced over seven million ounces of silver and twenty-eight thousand tons of lead, returning over £1,500,000 at the low metal prices of that day. Dividends were just over half a million.

The boundary-rider and his "hill of tin", George McCulloch and his dour determination, had made good indeed.

Despite this, the rapidly growing town in the saltbush wilderness was to remain isolated in men's minds for long years to come. That Silver City which arose as if by magic in aridity began to boom in 1887. The railway from Sydney did not connect with the Hill until 8th November 1927 – just forty-four years after Charlie Rasp's discovery. No wonder the Hillites had long since organized to manage their own affairs. Had it not been for the continuity of mineral in the Line of Lode, the sturdy independence of the Hillites, the far-seeing Australianism of the mine management, the engineering achievements, and the wonderful mineral-separating discoveries of the Big Mine metallurgists, Broken Hill would have been abandoned many years ago.

And painfully we should have been buying our steel – and at what a price! – from overseas.

That is, if we could still have held Australia without our own steel!

However, back in those roaring silver days slowly the developing town below the Broken Hill began taking some form of organization and order as yet more wealth came pouring from the lode. The Australian Broken Hill Consols, not content with being a good mine, started turning out bonanzas in silver, for mixed with the lode were patches of almost pure silver ore. In one such patch, one slug alone weighed sixteen hundredweight, more than half a ton of eighty-three per cent silver valued at £3500. The value of that slug would, of course, be far more today. Another slug was of six hundredweight, with a slug of chlorides of 600 pounds, and there were numerous lesser slugs. Thus, in the main Lode itself occasional patches of a few tons' weight of almost pure silver "sweetened" the already rich lode. Perhaps in the earlier years when the workings were going down through the oxidized zone the Australian

Broken Hill Consols may have been famed even more than the other mines for the diversity and beauty of its silver bonanzas – the rich hues of red silver, of sulphur yellow iodyrite silver, of yellow bromyrite, the fresh green of "new" chlorides, the vivid of antimonial silver slugs, the freshness of silver glance, the loveliness of crystallized dyscrasite in calcite, the great beauty of various silver ores intermixed with antimony.

The Great Lode, now partly cleared of scrub, was now scarred with gaping chasms appearing along its rocky face where in time the great open cut of the Big Mine would eat away all the crown of the hill. From away up there smoke poured from the tall chimney-stacks of the smelters, whose hungry furnaces by night blazed far out over the saltbush plain. Such tiny smelters compared to the gigantic machinery, the mighty mills presently to be! Coming from and toiling up the rough track cut along the ridge creaked bullock-drays loaded with ore and wood – quaint, laborious transport compared to the long trains heavily loaded with coal and coke that eventually would constantly be rumbling right up to giant mills.

Thus this good earth, this harsh barren earth, this "land of desolation" of the explorers rapidly now began helping its sons of enterprise and toil to another kind of richness than the steady growth of stock – the quick wealth of minerals. This harsh, good earth also helped not only in fabulous silver but in labour, industry, and commerce. For the Big Mine in particular, followed by the mines extending along the Line of Lode, wanted labour in increasing numbers, eventually an army of miners, tradesmen, technicians for the mills soon to be, chemists and metallurgists for solving the problems of treatment of this, the greatest silver-lead-zinc ore body in the world. And all these folk and numerous others concerned needed food and clothes and houses, which meant ever-growing commerce to supply them, while year by year the rapidly developing mines required more and more materials in ever greater variety and quantities. So demand and supply have kept increasing to this day, from 1884 to 1956.

Very soon the Silver City was crying aloud for a water supply – a voice in the wilderness indeed.

With increasing population and dry seasons muddy water for drinking and cooking had to be trained from the South Australian Government Tank seventy miles away. Not only was this expensive, but each housewife had to cherish every precious drop, for there was little indeed to be had. The mothers in the Silver City, throughout the summer dust-storms, the typhoid and pneumonia epidemics – and especially those poor unfortunates whose bread-winners were choking their lives away with lead poisoning – the mothers for a good many years found life hard indeed.

The position was becoming desperate. The mines had to pump undrinkable water from wells eight miles distant just to keep the mines working. The distant Government refused to do a thing, thus again arousing in the growing population the stubborn independence which long since crystallized into the unique community that is Broken Hill. They formed their own Broken Hill Water Supply Company and built a storage reservoir across Stephens Creek, a large dry creek eight miles distant. They began the job just in time, each gang toiling doggedly under a blazing sun, determined to beat both unsympathetic authority and the recurrent drought if it were humanly possible. There was no slackening on *that* job; their wives and children, mothers and brothers and sisters and fellow townsmen were stifling in the deathly quiet town sweltering below the Line of Lode eight miles away.

Have you ever breathed under an iron roof suffocatingly hot from a blazing sun, knowing that your muddy drinking water for the day is measured in but spoonfuls, staring away from an agonized wife trying to keep a moaning child cool? I have seen such things.

As week after rainless week went by, it seemed that the town must be abandoned or the community wiped out. Grimly they held on, straining the muddy liquid through mosquito net then boiling the often stinking, precious stuff. It was hell for the doctors and nurses slaving among the gasping patients in the little hospital.

Nature, Fate, or Destiny must have been looking on, and been satisfied at long last that her children had learnt the lesson that they must help themselves. Just as the reservoir was completed a torrential storm burst over the very catchment area.

Thus, at the dawn of her career, the Silver City was saved through the energy of her own sons. But often since she has held her breath for rain – just for water to drink.

As a lad, when the great rabbit plagues came at the height of a drought, I have seen the parched earth round Stephens Creek a moving mass of rabbits as far as the eye could see. The brown water fast drying up in the catchment was worth far more than its weight in silver to the humans back in the sweltering town. But time and again it seemed the rabbits would finish it off before the drought broke, while their countless carcasses everywhere in putrid pools helped bring typhoid yet again.

CENTRAL MINE - MAIN SHAFT - 1907

17. ROMANCE OF THE FIRE STONE

Wollaston was forced to return to Adelaide with nothing to show for his trip but the small opening made by Hasluck Brothers, but more determined than ever to put Australian opals on the market. And Tweedie, the solicitor, eventually to become his working partner, still stuck by him, though the little syndicate was quite disheartened.

Wollaston made several more trips to those far-away Queensland hills where the few tough gougers, existing as best they could, toiled and hoarded their parcels, doggedly hoping for his successful return. And those men did live hard, in those days when living hard in the dingo lands meant living hard indeed. It is a fact that one human wombat lived almost entirely on carney lizards.

Have you ever tried to eat a carney? "Carney Jim" ate them until he looked like one. But he lasted it out until the day came when he really could sell his opals.

Peculiarly enough, such is the perverse streak in some human natures, when that day did come, after Carney's physical being had satisfied its ravenous demand for real foods, Carney did not want to sell his opals – not his best stones. He hoarded the gems among them, as has been done since by gougers among whom the Fire Stone exerts its magical influence, slowly growing into the heart of the owner – that strange living power possessed by this most beautiful of inert things. I have felt it myself, have gloated over some particular gem stone and just hated the dire necessity that at last compelled me to sell it. Carney, when the opal days did "come good", hoarded his gems, selling only the poorer ones for his simple necessities of life.

Where did he hide his precious gems, down there below in the dark catacombs of his diggings?

Long years later the withered old Carney died, but they never found his hoard. Man after man dug in those gloomy tunnels, seeking Carney's hoard. But the man who possessed the heart to exist on lizards until at last he found the Fire Stones developed the primitive cunning to hide his treasures deep.

However, Carney did not go back to sleep in his Mother Earth in which he had found the Fire Stones until long after Wollaston had made good.

Overseas in London, Hasluck Brothers were now managing to sell a small parcel of stones from time to time and encouraged Wollaston to keep going.

It was after another trip overseas that he returned beaten to Adelaide. He had hoped to bring back sufficient capital to set out and buy more opals from those scattered men working and waiting in those far-away Queensland hills, but he had made barely enough to pay his meagre expenses. The syndicate seemed beaten, too – they "had had it". Wollaston's only consolation was in his wife and child, and in the support – "Never mind young man, just have a spell for a while, then we'll think the whole matter over again" – of Tweedie.

Very despondent, Wollaston packed his swag again and set out on the long, long trip for Euronghella and the Kyabra Hills. There he found again the rough camp of the "Old Man of the Hills", Old Joe Bridle, who gave him a welcome and his quiet sympathy.

One morning Old Joe, saddling up his two old horses, lit his pipe, then with a nod and, "So long! Be back soon", mounted his horse and rode out into the scraggly timber towards Kyabra for stores.

That night Wollaston sat by the campfire in a mood of black despondency. How utterly ridiculous to think that he could put Australian opals, even if any could be found in quantity, on the world's markets! He, an unknown man crouched over a gidgee fire in a God-forsaken, uninhabited loneliness ... He glanced around. Silhouetted on the skyline were the small, dome-shaped hills with flattened tops; he knew by day he would see the harsh red outliers pitted with weird caves that had been pounded out by some long-vanished sea, caves tainted now by the wild-animal smell, shelter places of the euro. The dense black patches between the red sandstone ridges, he knew, were broken gaps strewn with monstrous ironstone boulders; broader black shadows were stunted mulga, dead-finish, gidgee and wild-apple. And a frightening loneliness over all here down on this flat that seemed sighing in the night to the everlasting stars up in the unreachable sky.

As if the great outside world far across the seas would ever know of *this* wilderness! Opals! London! Markets! He must have been crazy ever to have dreamt of such a thing! London! Why, London was twelve thousand – no, more than thirteen thousand – miles away from this grim locality, a locality that had not even a name! Memory flashed him the bright lights of London, the wealth of New York, Paris, Vienna, Berlin. What did *they* know, what would they ever know of Australian opals? Why, not a handful of souls among all those teeming millions even knew there was a place in the world called Australia, let alone that there were opals there – let alone that a poor devil called Wollaston was staring into the coals of a dying campfire.

Presently he crouched rigid, staring – and suddenly jumped up! He threw kindling on the coals until they crackled and blazed into cheerful flame, for morbid thoughts had led him to his mate, Herb Buttfield, to a shrivelled skeleton lying away out in the mulga somewhere, perished of thirst.

Wollaston has told me of that night when he was alone with despair.

He must pull himself together, he decided. At least he had something of value even beyond opals here, the little soak which supplied Old Joe's camp and which the shy creatures of the bush shared with him. He stared at the banks of the soak, watching the timid things as they came hesitantly to drink and finding comfort in their presence. Here from the shadows was creeping a bilbie, ears pricked, sharp nose sniffing for lurking enemies. As it came out into the open by the soak its fur was speckled silver by starlight. It put its little forepaws to the water's edge and daintily drank, anxious to hurry back into the safety of the shadows again. He loved these quaint little creatures. As a fleeting shadow it vanished and he was aware of the liquid green eyes of a dingo staring from across the soak. One ruddy sundown several days later he pricked his ears to the eager hoof-beats of Old Joe's thirsty horses. Then he was looking into the old bushman's weather-beaten face, all screwed up in what he imagined was a grin of cheery sympathy.

"Good noos!" Old Joe croaked as he dismounted. "I've heered as Old Bill Johnson has struck it rich twenty mile back from Euronghella. Ori-right stuff, accordin' to mulga wire. He rides into the station about once a fortnight for meat. What if we ride through bush an' try an' cut his tracks?"

Thus, next dawn, again full of hope as a butcher's pup is of meat, Wollaston was riding through the rain and timber with the old bushman, seeking some faint track that might lead them to the opal-gouger's hut – riding not only through heavy timber and a hissing rain, but through a misery rain of beetles. And don't smile, for up there, just occasionally such windy rain, due to some seasonal climatic condition in combination with the birth of a plague of beetles, literally brings with it a rain of beetles. And the constant smacking of the hard, clammy things on face and neck, driven by the hissing rain, is a misery only known by those who have experienced it.

In later wandering years, after I had left the Hill, occasionally I ran across Wollaston. He never tired of telling of that never-to-be-forgotten day when eventually with Joe Bridle he came to Old Bill Johnson's "Little Wonder". He brought before my eyes the vast arc of sunlit sky, pure after the passing of the storm, the deathly quietness, the little grey hills so harsh and primitive, the two old battlers squatting there amongst the needle-bush and gibbers, their gnarled hands and deep-lined, sunburnt faces, their steady eyes speculatively watching his face as he stared down with parted lips at such magnificent opals as in his wildest dreams he had never imagined could exist within the earth.

This treasure, such as lovers of opals like Pliny and Caesar never saw, such as the proud Roman Senator Nonius could not flaunt in his so envied "Treasury of Opals", so infinitely more beautiful than that which Antony risked a kingdom to give to Cleopatra, was parcelled in a worn-out leg of Old Bill Johnson's blue dungaree trousers. This glory of gems, wrapped in the fragments of brown, earth-stained singlet, and thrust down a worn-out denim trouser-leg.

In my day, too, I was often to see beautiful opals wrapped away like that, waiting the visit of some long overdue buyer.

I have often wondered – and Ted Murphy, with his vastly greater experience as an opal-buyer has helped me try to calculate – what, if the Little Wonder opal-mine could be refound today and its fiery treasure resold at today's prices, the final total would be.

The old gouger asked Wollaston what to him and his fellow bushman seemed an utterly fabulous price for that parcel of opals.

"One thousand quid!"

Wollaston tried to keep his hand from trembling as without a word he wrote out the cheque. He would have to ask the gouger to hold that cheque for a while.

A very few years ago Wollaston told me he would willingly give £20,000 for such a parcel today. "And," he added with a smile, "a keen bargainer might drive me up to thirty thousand."

He was to buy many a parcel from the Little Wonder.

His mind afire from the fiery gems that he felt certain no jeweller in the world could resist, he travelled almost night and day back to Adelaide in a fever to catch the first boat back to London and Hasluck Brothers.

If he had dreamt of the aeroplane travelling of today! But then he had to be content with Cobb and Co's coaches, which were express in the back country.

Wollaston arrived back in Adelaide, surprised to find a letter and small parcel awaiting him. It was from Charlie Turner, a surveyor acquaintance of boyhood years, now working at some little township called Wilcannia on the Darling River, far west in New South Wales. Turner wrote that he was sending him a little parcel of what looked like opals, found by a party of kangaroo-shooters – one of whom, as we have seen, was also a Charlie Turner – about sixty miles north of Wilcannia.

The specimens might be of interest to Wollaston. But if so he had best contact the shooters quickly for they were fed up, and just about starved out of the place. They couldn't sell these stones that looked like opals, whereas they could make good money 'roo-shooting. They had promised to stay in the district only so long as it should take him to get here.

With mixed feelings Wollaston opened the parcel, and was immediately interested. These were opals certainly and, though they were of no great value, this was only because of inexperience of the miners. For these had been weathered out by the hills, to lie bleached by the sun. Deeper in the earth there must lie beautiful gems. But the strangest thing about them was that they were quite different in shape to any opals he had ever seen before. And what a wonderfully easy and inexpensive shape for the jeweller to cut into gems! This latter would be a great point to appeal to that hidebound oversea gem market.

Raking up the few hundred pounds he could lay hands on, Wollaston two days later was travelling north again. A luxurious trip compared to the west Queensland trips, for now by train he could travel all the way to these recently discovered great silver camps just across the New South Wales border, travel right to the last found but apparently greatest of all, some broken hill which men were now calling the "Silver City". And from Silverton to the Silver City he found it the Roaring Silver Days indeed. But he was an opal man and the wealth and tumult and hectic life of the Silver City, the feverish atmosphere of big things doing, made him all the more anxious to hurry on in his own ambition of putting Australian opals on the map. He booked in for the first Cobb and Co. coach he could and was off to Wilcannia, twenty-seven hours in good company on the rolling coach. From Wilcannia to Mount Browne goldfield he covered the rough track by buckboard. And there one of the 'roo-shooters met him with a led horse and they rode the rest of the way to the 'roo-shooters' camp near some low whitish hills soon now to become known as White Cliffs.

They showed him their opal. They would not name a price, insisting that *he* should do so.

This opal was utterly unfamiliar to him. Besides, he had very little money. At last he offered £140.

The four of them nearly knocked him backwards reaching out their hands. As laughingly he counted out the money, they told him he could have had the lot for a tenner! It was worthless to them, they could not sell it, they were going to throw the stuff away and carry on with shooting.

Cheerily Wollaston advised them to carry on with opal-gouging which offered them not only good money, but the chance of a fortune. He also gave them practical advice on how the few old Queensland gougers worked the gems, enthusiastically assured them that he would soon have a ready market for opals overseas, and that he would return as soon as possible from London and pay them a fair price for all opals they had dug.

And thus, at long last, came the dawn of the "Fire Hills" west of the Darling.

In London Hasluck Brothers were immediately enthusiastic over the beautiful gems from the Little Wonder, immensely intrigued by these promising stones from White Cliffs that were so easy to cut into any shape for any jewellery design. Wollaston assured them he could now guarantee a continuity of supplies.

Cutters were engaged; Wollaston has told me how there the work now went on in a fever-pitch of excitement as stone after stone turned into a flashing gem under the cutters' fingers.

The first parcel of gems placed on the American market were quickly bought. Followed inquiries for more, with more sales. Cautiously then the English market commenced inquiring.

Within twelve months Wollaston knew that at last he had won a market for Australian opals.

Within a few short years it was to be a world market with the only opal wanted the Australian opal, with buyers from the capitals of the world pouring out to the Australian fields eager to compete for the gems.

Does it not seem to you that it was a Pattern in Time that stage by stage brought to a wilderness a few venturous white men whose flocks surprisingly increased, whose discoveries brought population and wealth in the development of a Silver City, then, of all things, brought hurrying expert gem dealers from the capitals of the world, from Paris and Berlin and Vienna, from London and New York, to a desert hill in a wilderness west of the Darling?

Now, while Wollaston was happily examining those "opal specimens" handed him by those four anxious 'roo-shooters there was working on the banks of the Darling at Wilcannia a tall young fellow helping unload a Darling Dreadnought. Young Ted Murphy – you've met him before, he was the lad who recovered from typhoid at the Mount Browne gold hills while so many strong men died in the sun-scorched camps around him. Fully recovered now, half listening to the sighing of the leaves of the big old gums as some breeze from God knows where whispered by, absorbing the lisp of the current as the waters flowed on to strange waters far away, vaguely restless as he watched the churn of paddle-wheels as a Dreadnought waddled downstream on its noisy voyage towards the coastal world.

So when excited 'roo-shooters rode into town to peg out an opal claim in untried country sixty miles west, young Ted Murphy instantly decided he would ride with them and try his luck with this strange gem. And thus was decided the destiny of the greatest opal-buyer of all time.

On his return trip from overseas Wollaston met and bought a parcel from Murphy, and during succeeding years Murphy came to work for and buy for Tweedie and Wollaston. Eventually, when Tweedie resigned on the fulfilment of his lifelong ambition to join the ministry, Murphy bought exclusively for Wollaston. During Wollaston's continued absences developing the oversea market Murphy was travelling and buying on the widely scattered Queensland fields, on White Cliffs in New South Wales, on Lightning Ridge when later it was discovered, eventually on Coober Pedy in South Australia. These three men – Wollaston, Tweedie, and Murphy, but particularly Wollaston – driven by their own enthusiasms and ceaseless toil, during many years of travelling in which they took risks that more than once brought them within an ace of death by misadventure, finally succeeded in bringing to Australia the world's market for opals. This benefited thousands of families, put many a man successfully upon the land, helped in part to develop the country, and gave Australia a unique recognition overseas. For though Australia then was "unknown" the Australian opal came to be sought by all who loved gems. And then the black opal came, the only such gem ever found in the world, and to this day it still has been found only at Lightning Ridge, New South Wales.

So those three men west of the Darling did a job for Australia, as others quietly have done in other paths of life. Sometimes I muse on the men who toiled thus, did some such job along the track of Australian development, then quietly passed oil quite unsung. Every here and there men, in city as well as country, are steadily doing the same today.

But this is not a book on the fascinating story of Australian opals, it is but a wanderer's vagrant memories of the Silver City and the wilderness then west of the Darling, of the wonders it slowly unfolded, seen as if through a mirage. And, still as through a mirage in blazing summer across the gibber plains, just a little of what those wonders have meant to Australia as the ghostly years slip swiftly by.

154

18. AS TIME ROLLS ON

Meanwhile, nearly three hundred miles west as the crow would fly through that limitless sunshine, lone men in South Australia had heard of the wonders of the Silver City. These were the station-hands of Coruma and Middleback, dwelling in even more waterless plains of red earth and drab grey of saltbush, dwarf myall, and mulga.

This was particularly lonesome country, west of little Port Augusta away up Spencer Gulf. In their huts at night and when camped out on those vast runs the station-hands spoke with bated breath of the news drifting through of the Hill of Silver three hundred miles to the north-east just across the border in New South Wales. They marvelled that this bonanza had been found by a station-hand, sunk upon and proved by a tiny syndicate of station men, men just like themselves. And their thoughts, then their words, then actions turned to the Knobs.

Might these not be hills of silver, too? Just like the Broken Hill! The same sort of country almost, according to the few lone travellers. The same barren hills!

Their eyes were questioning as they glanced at one another, dreamily then they sat puffing their pipes. They thought of it, too, in the silences of the night as they rolled themselves in their blankets before the campfire.

The more they discussed it and thought of it, the more certain they became. So they formed a little syndicate, just as McCulloch had, and began to sink a shaft on one huge outcrop.

Strangely enough – or was it written in the Book of Fate? – a great sea explorer first mused upon the rock of this district as Sturt, our greatest land explorer, had wondered at the possibilities of the broken hill. Matthew Flinders, sailing these lonesome waters in his tiny *Investigator* found space in his precious journal to record his impressions of the "reddish, argillaceous, smooth, close-grained, heavy rock".

That was in 1802. What amazement would Flinders feel if only he could sail up Spencer Gulf today!

So those station-hands were now swinging the pick under the broiling sun upon the tough red rock, the sharp, clear song of the drill trilling out over the lonely plain as the hammer clanged rhythmically upon it.

Above the red plain this thin line of isolated hills rise like gigantic knobs in the vastness, massive outcrops of brick-red rock towering like sun-baked castles over the sea of saltbush.

As the syndicate toiled they sweated, for, believe me, it is hot there.

They forwarded samples of the ore to England. At long last came back the reply, "Iron!"

The syndicate gave up in disgust, just as others had ridden away from the broken hill. The Knobs slept again in the sunbaked silence, their crags the warm basking place of the lizard, the outlook of the eaglehawk.

Rasp, the young boundary-rider, had pegged the Broken Hill hoping to find tin. Instead, it was silver, which had made the now famous Silver City.

The syndicate of bushmen at the Knobs had sought silver, but found iron instead. How utterly amazed they would have been could they have known what that "worthless" iron was going to mean not only to this locality but to Australia in the years coming!

With what derision they would have greeted a prophet had he declared their iron would prove of greater value far than silver!

Meanwhile the Silver City continued pouring out wealth as year by year the mines developed, to the good content of all concerned. However, the mine managements were glum, for they were not getting a fair price for their metals. Moreover, for years, as with early Australian copper-mines, some precious metals in both concentrates and ingots was simply being pirated. As only one mere instance, the gold content in Cobar bullion was never accounted for by oversea refineries.

The pirates were the oversea refineries and the "Captains of Industry" who manipulated the oversea metal market.

In those days – some would have us so now – we were looked upon as hewers of wood and drawers of water. At our own risk and cost and by our own labour we found, worked, and developed our raw products. Oversea interests then "took over", at *our* expense, the refining and selling of these products. What the Australian producers at long last got out of it was a crust to enable them to carry on with the good work.

So far as minerals were concerned, the Big Mine determined to do something about it. To build new, much larger smelters on as modern lines as possible, to plan a refinery of their own on Australian soil, to train a staff of Australians as metallurgists, chemists, technicians, engineers, and mining staff. A long-sighted view indeed in those days, but by now they had faith in the Big Mine, above all in the future development of Australia, and were determined to put something back into the country in return for what they took out of it.

That was sixty-seven years ago.

Those men and their successors were workers and men of vision. But in their most ambitious dreams they could not have foreseen what a mighty aid that far-seeing, determined, long-continued policy was to mean in hastening the development of Australia; in educating skilled workers in practically every branch of industry, in helping develop a spirit of national independence, and in building urgently needed strength for the future peaceful development and defence of the continent.

The new smelters and refinery were erected at Port Pirie, 282 miles away, on the shores of Spencer Gulf in South Australia. The first giant stride of the Broken Hill to the distant shores of another State. As that baby giant rapidly grew up it was to stride with increasing momentum south-west, south-east, east, west, and north-west, was to skip across Bass Strait to Tasmania. And from each footstep would spring up a new enterprise, a new industry, a new town, a new port in far-flung, rapid development increasing as the years sped by. All from a sombre, sunburnt hill out in the great loneliness, its riches but above all its potentialities developed and harnessed by the brains and labour of Man.

Port Pirie, away down on the shores of Spencer Gulf, was then a tiny place indeed. I have heard it alluded to, by folk used to the amenities of town life of those days, as "that dismal mangrove swamp". But it was the shipping place for a handful of battling South Australian wheat-farmers in their back country. To this port the wagons carted the wheat when seasons and market price allowed them any to sell. Up the big gulf the white-winged schooners came sailing to load the wheat at the little piers and unload supplies for the struggling farmers. Those stores were mostly "hard tack"; there were no luxuries those days for the battling settlers and their toil-stained wives.

But the building and operation of the new smelters and refinery soon began to change the face of "the mangrove swamp". Thousands of tons of ores and concentrates coming continuously rolling in from the distant Silver City created an immediate demand for labour where jobs had been so very scarce. Building activities on waterfront and land also meant money, and money meant more and better stores and more people. A big new jetty was built, then steamers came, and the town began to expand. The increasing activity began spreading out in various ways into the back country. As away back in the New South Wales interior the Silver City developed fast more and more trains came rolling down from west of the Darling and "the mangrove swamp" eventually disappeared as it grew into busy Port Pirie.

When the Big Mine started work at Port Pirie larger and larger quantities of ironstone were needed for a flux in smelting the silver-lead as the smelters developed and grew. What more natural than that the management should cast eyes upon those ironstone Knobs across the gulf, the Knobs the station-hands of Coruma and Middleback had abandoned in disgust when they found these were but ironstone bastions and not another Broken Hill? These knobs lie west across the gulf from Port Pirie, thirty-three miles inland from the then lonely, mangrove-studded shore. The ironstone as a fluxing material proved an immediate success at the smelters and a lease was taken up. Thus the Iron Knob and the Iron Monarch, hitherto for so long despised except as landmarks in this other wilderness, were called upon to fulfil their part in Australia's destiny.

But men did not know this as yet, could not yet know that from these iron-girt sentinels would come the chief material in building a mighty steelworks just in time to help Australia in the greatest of all wars, and mightily so in the Second World War, when her very existence would be at stake.

As time went on, the Iron Baron, the Iron Knight, Iron Duke, Iron Duchess, Iron Prince and others of those massive pyramids were to be taken up and developed by the Big Mine.

Thus the influence of the Broken Hill of Sturt, of Charlie Rasp and McCulloch, was to reach again into yet another area of South Australia, an area even more waterless and as lonely as the country west of the Darling had once been, and here build; and yet again at a mangrove swamp, an entirely new modern port, and thirty miles inland a new town in that waterless waste. And those same influences were to bring water, which means life, in a huge pipeline from the Murray, a distance of over two hundred miles.

And to build yet again, this time in its own State, far to the east. For the Port Pirie Works demanded coke on a vast scale. So Bellambi benefited by the construction of a great coke works in 1900.

Truly, the influences expanding from development of that once despised "hill of mullock" were now beginning to exert a growing momentum upon Australia's Wheel of Time.

It was soon after the new works opened that I first saw Port Pirie. In the early years of the new smelters lucky families from the Silver City enjoyed their Christmas holidays at Port Pirie or Adelaide, thanks to the enterprise of the South Australian railways and Silverton Tramway. Otherwise transport would have been by horse. All Broken Hill who could manage it longed for that holiday from the hot, dusty summer in the cool sea breeze, though but few indeed could afford more than one wonderful fortnight. Those were the days when a shilling was a shilling; many families could not afford the holiday; most clung to every spare shilling fearful of the breadwinner's being out of work, or of disastrous strikes. For the mine managements and unions had not yet got together, as they eventually did, to solve in amity the recurring troubles which were so ruinous to family economy and district progress. Dad somehow managed nearly every year to scrape the few pounds together and sent us entranced kids and harassed Mum by train to that long-dreamt-of fairyland by the shores of the sea.

What a never-to-be-forgotten sight for youngsters from the land of the shimmering mirage! Here, plenty of cool, sweet water to drink, and a cool sea breeze. The placid waters of the gulf, with a real steamer with foam at her bows ploughing towards us – sometimes she'd whistle, deep and hoarse, and that delighted us. We were fascinated by the bustle at the wharf, the loaded wagons creaking on their way to smelters and refinery and piers, the wagons rolling in over the rutted roads of the back country loaded with wheat for the port, new buildings going up, the carts, the buckboards, the sun-browned horsemen riding into town. And then to watch the schooners, and the fishing vessels sailing down the gulf, gulls circling above them!

We sent them voyaging far across the sea, of course, to find King Solomon's mines and come sailing back to Port Pirie laden deep with gold. Sent them out to far Cathay, and to the land of Sinbad the Sailor, to return laden with diamonds, with the Old Man of the Sea clinging to the masthead. To us youngsters from the saltbush Port Pirie's waterfront and the gulf scene was of entrancing activity, a childhood's Port of Dreams. Unhappy hearts were ours when the sun sadly set on the last day of the holiday.

Time marches on, while transformations take place within a few short years. Some years after the 1914-18 war I again saw Port Pirie. The district had expanded almost beyond recognition. And the port was a real port now; the smelters and refinery and treatment works of the Broken Hill Companies had grown to huge proportions; the old steam machinery that to us had seemed so grand had given way to a network of electrification; giant electric loading and unloading cranes were working on the wharves; the poor old horse-teams and carts had almost gone, their power multiplied many times over by locomotive traction. The back country had developed also; decent roads were creeping out while numerous modern homes showed a prosperity in farming probably undreamt of by the early battlers.

Yet again, but a few years back, my wanderings took me to Port Pirie. Gazing at the busy port, the big works, the power plants, the giant smelter works, the highly modern engineering plant, the busy town, I tried in vain to bring back the village by the mangrove swamp where Mum and we kids and our lucky holiday friends had built our castles in Spain. Where were the schooners? Where were the teams? The carts, the buggies, the sulkies, with their wheels stained with mud or dust? Now were fleets of motor trucks and cars, good roads spreading away out to a prosperous farming hinterland. How very, very different to the early years of the distant Silver City! That city of boyhood days vanished in memory's mirage as I turned again to the bulks of the great works. Throughout the years, what vast tonnages of concentrates and ores had come rolling down here from the Line of Lode that I had known even while mulga still grew in places upon it! What vast wealth of refined silver, of lead bullion, of zinc had been shipped from here to the world's markets – to England, the Continent, to the East, to other oversea markets!

During my boyhood days in the Silver City the very few people in countries overseas who had even heard of Australia vaguely imagined it as an island somewhere or other peopled by savages. As to the Silver City, why, even Sydney hardly knew it existed! But now the mining world, the metallurgical world, and the steel world of the greater world knew all about the Silver City. And even Sydney knew a little.

What would Sturt have thought on that now seemingly far away day if the mirage that beckoned him towards his Inland Sea could have shown him the Silver City instead – a phantasy of reality? What utter amazement would have been his at what that sombre broken hill out in the mulga wilderness west of his Darling was to mean!

19. WHEN THE MINE CREEPS!

Occasionally, while working at the Big Mine Assay Office, a lucky lad would be detailed to accompany sampler or assayer down the mine to lend a hand in collecting special samples. Thus to the gigantic poppet heads, the engineer sitting high up in his little cabin above the enormous drum round which was coiled the gleaming steel rope. Into the iron cage, then a drop of a thousand, two thousand feet it seemed, in a second, as a fellow's belly whizzed over and shot straight up out of the roots of his hair. Then stepping out on to the dark plat with the heavily timbered mouths of tunnels converging on the plat, the thousand-, two-thousand-, three-thousand-foot level as the case may be. Rumble of oncoming wheels, shadowy forms of heavily loaded ore trucks clanking towards the plat. An electric light here and there. Then the long walk down the heavily timbered drive, those closely set, massive baulks of Oregon giving you confidence as you dimly realize the mighty pressures bearing down upon you within those millions of tons of rock between you and the open heaven now so far above. Down in the bowels of the earth now in fact. You shiver a moment, trying to blot out the thought of the "Creeps", faintly hoping no Creep will take place while you are here like a mouse creeping, in a different sense, along in the bottom of the earth.

Occasionally a disastrous Creep, a great crack torn by the stresses of the rock, would open up at the surface and, slowly widening, creep far down, relentlessly rending its way through the living rock to crush like matchwood timbers supporting any tunnel in its merciless path.

Just here and there water drips through the roof as we plod on and on. There are miles and miles of such drives here, on levels above and below, a gigantic honeycomb of tunnels and stopes and galleries far below the Silver City. From far away, like distant thunder heavily muffled, comes gruffly, *"Boon-oom! Ooom! Oooom!"* Somewhere, in some gallery, they are shooting down a face – tons, hundreds of tons perhaps, of ore.

Comes an increasing hum, as you walk on growing into an infernal, vibrating chattering of sound. And then you step out into the open.

So, after the enclosed drive, for a moment it seems. For you are in a huge open space torn out of the hazy rock stretching out into darkness. Here and there along the walls, high up, cling threads of electric light. As your eyes sweep away up towards the roof and around you gradually visualize an Aladdin's Cave of silver. But this is a vast chamber, no little cave this. And hazy around a light, on walls and roof are gleaming pin-points, billions upon billions of twinkling silver pin-points. It is really lead sulphides that are gleaming in this way. High up, on benches cut out of the rock near the roof, bare-chested, white-capped men like clinging spiders are handling a diamond drill that vibrates in deafening clatter as it bites deep into the rocky ore. Another shadowy group is toiling over there, another away up there, yet another in dim distance. Towards the shift end those drill holes will be charged with gelignite. When the men are safely away back at the plat by the shaft the shots will be fired and thunder and smoke and flame will erupt in shuddering convulsion all over the cavern as in the fume-filled darkness tons and tons and tons of ore come rending, crashing down from roof and walls, wrapped in whirlpools of invisible dust.

Underground, those miles of drives, tunnels, caverns were shored up with a forest of Oregon, the drives timbered in solid square-set. Imagine a forest of big trees out in the open bush. Your eyes would have to sweep a long way indeed to cover the extent of that densely packed forest. And yet a forest of Oregon tree-trunks was used as very necessary timbering underground in the Big Mine alone. That Oregon, the most suitable timber for the job, came in shipload after shipload, all the year round, steaming from Canada to help support the miles and miles of tunnels under the Silver City. Thus a sturdy Canadian forest stands up deep underground in an Australian city west of the Darling – which helps you realize the size of that underground ore body, and the vast amount of work done deep down there by day and while the city sleeps.

In the risky portion of any dangerous drive, or in time of Creeps, it is difficult to imagine anything more frightening away down below than the whispering, wheezing, shivering, grinding, straining, crackling, splitting, then shrieking of heavy timbers as they strain against the slowly increasing, implacable pressures of mother rock that finally explode the great timber baulks into masses of splinters. These, alas, have sometimes caught fire. Trained teams of men throughout all the mines were constantly alert at any danger point, men trained to scent the slow combustion of a gathering fire, or the growing heat of rock or straining timbers threatening to burst into flame, men trained to scent out foul air, or the accumulating of poisonous or inflammable gases. There is far more in mining than merely digging out ore.

The hot climate of that country, the dryness underground, added to natural heat at depth as the workings deepened in all the mines along the Line of Lode, eventually grew into a problem for all mine officials, and all men working underground particularly. And an ever-gnawing, secret fear for wives at home.

"Fire! Fire underground!"

Such can be a terrible alarm, deep down below in a big mine. For the retreat of men working in some distant stope or tunnel can be cut off by thunderous blasts of flame, or by a grinding, rending, shrieking fall of rock, or by poisonous gas stealthily creeping along the tunnels, or with sudden blasts of hot, foul air, often in a terrible darkness.

If a fire were not quickly smothered, walled off, or otherwise overwhelmed then disaster would follow. For eleven nervy years the Big Mine had to ward against and fight such fires until at last by ingenuity and toil men learnt how to beat, or at least control, them.

While I was a lad working at the Big Mine the Big Fire broke out, the worst of the series. Heroic work was done by the fire-fighting teams in the inferno below. Unhappily, there were tragedies; it is amazing there were not more. For along the underground caverns blasts of flame flashed through the rolling smoke. From side tunnels came roar of fire as new areas of timbers burst into flame, then the thunder of falling rock as the blazing timbers collapsed, the concussion shooting blasts of poisonous smoke and fumes away along and into the main drives. Here and there men were trapped. To add horror to horror poisonous gases in sulphurous fumes which tore into the lungs were presently generated by the action of the heat on arsenical pyrites and sulphur in the ores. It was hell down below during the Big Fire.

It took months of sweat and ingenuity to overcome this particular disaster even partially. The fire danger was eventually controlled by "cutting it in pieces", then smothering it in its own fumes behind solid brick walls, by isolating great sections of timbering, and by an ingenious arrangement of "water curtains". These were built strategically across drives and tunnels and very effectively helped check the spread of flames. This cleverly contrived safeguard really was an actual water curtain. Imagine walking down a dark hall. You come to a closed door. Well, you are walking along the still darker mine tunnel. But the door you come to is all agleam under the light, and there is a reassuring coolness and dampness here. For that closed door is a barrier of drops of falling water. You step straight through, again into a reassuring coolness. That water curtain is a door all right, a very clever door to drown, or check, or very efficiently discourage heat, quickly dampening the ardour of smouldering timbers eager to burst into flames. There were many of these water curtains in dangerous ground when finally the Big Fire was brought under control. It took years to accomplish it, though, and to control the danger of underground fires.

One job given to us lads on occasion was to help assayers get samples of the foul airs, gases, and waters down below as section by section the great drives were walled off and the fires gradually suffocated or imprisoned. The giant fans used to roar in the shafts as good air was pumped down and foul air sucked up.

During the early years of the Big Mine a long-sighted policy, destined to pay rich dividends, was followed in the bringing from overseas of experts to train Australians in phases of mining and industry with which this young country was unfamiliar. From the very start, phase by phase as the Big Mine gradually developed into the gigantic chain of industries it is today, teams of experts trained Australians who then quickly trained others in problems of mining, engineering, metallurgy, chemistry, and various intricate technical problems. And there were many, indeed, in that great romance of "from Silver to Steel".

It was natural that nearly all these experts were Americans. The great silver-mines of the world were in America; the Big Mine heads in the early years took advantage of the experience gained by Americans in working their Great Comstock Lode of Nevada, where conditions were somewhat similar to those existing along the Line of Lode. It was American miners, engineers, chemists, and metallurgists who were most familiar with the problems connected with the mining, extraction, and refining of complex ores and metals. Similarly in later years, during the transition from silver to steel, picked teams of American experts were of outstanding help in training our men.

The Australians were so keen that the objective, to develop a highly skilled staff that was ninety-eight per cent Australian, was quickly achieved in each succeeding new branch of industry. After this, our men began to branch out on their own.

In a very tiny way I was privileged to see, or partly see, one such phase which has long since passed into world-wide renown. This was the work of Australians in the metallurgical field, in the discovery and adaptation of entirely new processes in the extraction of refractory minerals from ores. I was working in the Assay Office of the Big Mine, where a number of us young fellows were employed as off-siders to the assayers, while learning assaying ourselves. In the same building were working the chemists and metallurgists on their intricate experiments, which after some years of heart-breaking failure occasionally brightened by brilliant results were eventually destined to achieve a series of amazing successes, the practical fruits of which have long since become world-famous.

I still, after all these years, remember the thrill when one of us lads ever and anon would be detailed to crush the special samples for these particular men. Bradford, Carmichael, Horwood, Henderson, Potter, were the metallurgical stars that linger in memory, though only so far as my little day was concerned. They worked under G. D. Delpratt, one of Australia's greatest mine managers, I believe one of the world's greatest. Born in Holland, his was an international reputation both in mining and metallurgy when he first came to Australia as Assistant Manager, then General Manager, of "our" Big Mine. He proved himself to be a big man, and a wonderful Australian. Also, despite the great difference between his position and ours as "boys" in the Assay Office, he always had time to give us a friendly smile and nod of encouragement when passing through the building into the laboratories to watch our metallurgical stars test some difficult process.

It was under Delpratt then, that this team of Australian metallurgists eventually solved, year by year, problem by problem, complex ore treatment processes which up to then had defied the best mining brains.

That strange, sombre strip of country west of the Darling had produced successful pioneers and beef and wool from apparent desolation, then the greatest silver-lead-zinc mines in the world, then incomparably the loveliest and most plentiful opals in the world. And now the brains of her sons were unearthing secrets that were to produce work and wealth not only for Australia but for every corner of the mining world.

Truly, a strange country out under the saltbush mirage!

We lads of the Assay Office, of course, stole far more reflected glory than our humble positions entitled us to. But then, we were immensely proud of the men slowly but surely solving those deep secrets in the laboratories, unravelling secrets so jealously guarded in Nature's laboratory since time began. For, just as there are secrets in the flower and butterfly, in the bird and the deer and man, so there are secrets in the Mineral Kingdom. As the medical man and the botanist and biologist had to study hard and long to unravel secrets of the Animal and Vegetable and Insect Kingdoms, so the geologists, the chemists, and the metallurgists had to study hard and long to unravel the secrets of the Mineral Kingdom before reluctant Nature could be forced to part, little by grudging little, with her mineral wealth. At night time, in our own little laboratories at the School of Mines, we would try to emulate the work of the experimental chemists – to the hidden amusement, I realized later, of the principal, Mr Ford, Mr Wood and his assistants, who so patiently were trying to impress upon our jackass minds the mysteries of practical chemistry, metallurgy, assaying and physics. Meanwhile we, with heat and pressures and acids and alkalis, in unholy glee were mixing chemicals and gases in the weirdest of quantities and proportions just to see what would happen, filling the laboratory with amazing smells, and occasionally a hair-raising explosion. No one was ever killed, fortunately, but there were numerous burns, scorched eyebrows, and gasping coughs and choking lungs when some violent liberation of chlorine gas sent us and the staff, urgently holding our breath, racing out into the open for God's own pure air. Little we knew that some of us would gasp out our lives, vomit up our own lungs through this very gas on the battlefields of France.

Thus, in between hard study, we coming chemists experimented with furnace and acids in most atrocious mixtures, once coming within an ace of setting the whole School of Mines alight. By the way, some among my boyhood "alchemists" have since made goodly names for themselves in the world of industrial chemistry and metallurgy.

Those few men then, between them, by different processes eventually developing into the wonderful Flotation Processes, solved all the problems of extracting minerals from complex ores, particularly sulphides.

But for these hard-won discoveries all of Broken Hill, all that mighty Line of Lode, would have had to be closed down and abandoned years and years ago, because, after the mines had been worked to a certain depth, there was no known process which could economically extract the minerals from the poorer and increasingly complex ores. Those leading discoveries were made approximately fifty years ago and, with the exception of the Big Mine, the mines have been working ever since, with many years' work yet ahead of them.

The Flotation Processes solved not only the problems of mineral extraction, but of the profitable treatment of low-grade ores, which previously it had been uneconomical to mine.

They also solved the problem of the Dumps.

The Dumps were hills of "worthless" tailings, refuse from the mills. These sands from the treated ores were dumped around the mines until they grew into a ring of big, grey hills. Wherever you looked towards the Line of Lode, even from a few miles away, these hills caught the eye. Ever growing, ever spreading out until finally they were rolling down into the very back yards of the town, indeed, right into the back yards of shops below the Line of Lode in Argent Street. The Big Mine alone was pestered by a million tons of these "worthless" tailings, while there were millions of tons along the Line of Lode.

Years and years later, revisiting the Hill, I was puzzled by the familiar old place. There was the Hill all right, there was the Line of Lode. But – something was missing.

Suddenly – the Dumps! Where were the Dumps, those big grey hills of tailings?

Vanished completely. All those hills of "refuse", to the last shovelful, had been put through the treatment plant, and a wealth of mineral extracted – proving how marvellously efficient are those Flotation Processes.

The mining world, of course, soon availed itself of the Australian discoveries. Unknown millions of tons of otherwise unworkable silver-lead-zinc and other ores have since been worked throughout the world because of those processes.

So you can guess why I get a bit hot under the collar when every now and again some thoughtless folk remark that Australians cannot do really big things because we are "too-young", or for some other equally stupid reason. And remember, at the time of which I am now writing Cobb and Co's coach was still King of the Roads, energetically jogging along the dusty tracks west of the Darling.

As in most industrial communities, constant strikes, some very ugly, marred life in the Silver City for years. The isolation of all, the feeling of being so far away from all other interests, of being forgotten and abandoned by the outside world, made these fights between companies and men all the more bitter. Maybe, though, it was this very isolation, this being "left on the outer" by the rest of Australia, that eventually brought about an almost unheard-of but very happy result.

Miners and companies pulled together in practically complete agreement for the good of the unions, the companies, and the civic affairs of the town. Instead of tearing themselves to pieces to the bitter end they got together and decided that, with give and take, there was sufficient and plenty along the Line of Lode to give a good living to all hands concerned, also to make living conditions ever so much better for the whole town and everyone concerned. This happy union of all for the common good did not materialize until some eight years or so after my time, but in later visits to the Hill I saw the remarkable and highly satisfactory results.

The main point of the arrangement as I – now merely an onlooker – saw it was this. The industrial agreements were made between the unions and the companies. The agreements are made afresh every three years. Each union supplies a representative to voice its views. These representatives become then the Barrier Industrial Council. The companies are represented by the Mining Managers' Association.

The unions present a Log of Claims. The Mining Managers' Association study it. Both sides fully understand the position. Negotiations proceed amiably and sincerely, generally over a period of several months, until final agreement is reached. This is the law for the following three years, and companies and unions loyally stick to the letter of the agreement.

Since this arrangement was made strikes are unknown, while industry and all concerned have benefited very considerably. So have the town, home life, and the entire community. There is practically no crime at all. I have walked through the city by day and night and have seldom seen even a drunken man. And, thank God, the typhoid, pneumonia, and lead terror have gone.

Miracles have been brought about in the Silver City since the days when we lads shouted with glee at sight of scarlet quandongs upon a sombre hill slope.

20. BLACK TUESDAY

Yes, the fever terrors have gone. Not so the occasional summer dust-storms, though the misery of these has been vastly reduced by the work of the Zinc Corporation and the mining companies that backed the genius of Albert Morris. Refusing to be beaten, he was a voice crying in the wilderness for twenty-five years, ever crying that the desert could be made to blossom as the rose.

The result was that Broken Hill by 1942 had grown a Green Belt, three parts encircling the town, half a mile in width, of luxuriantly growing Australian trees among many acres of waving grasses that formed a complete barrier to the encroaching sands, which in places had threatened to overwhelm part of the town. Parks also sprang up, and thus came beauty as well as impenetrable barrier to wind-driven dust and sands that for many and many a summer had caused untold misery in the loss of health and comfort to the citizens, and especially to the housewife.

The difference in comfort and utility and beauty this Green Belt has brought the city can only be realized by those who have lived there before and after its making.

But though the dust and sands and ordinary dust-storms have been beaten by Nature's own barrier of trees and grasses, there comes, very occasionally, a real Terror from the skies – just as other countries suffer their occasional much worse tornadoes.

The climate of the Far West from autumn to October nearly always is exhilarating and makes a man feel full of beans. But the summers, before the fevers were beaten and while the voice was still crying in the wilderness, were pretty dreadful.

In earlier years the town would be periodically overwhelmed by a real Terror, coming rolling on in a darkening storm that seemed to reach from earth to sky, a limitless wall of rapidly advancing dust. Brick-red, it sometimes was, and should the sun be slanting through it it was like rolling billows of flame. At such times the housewives in the poor little ant city ran to fasten doors and windows, to shelter baby in the cot, hurriedly to stuff bags or "anything" into every crack and cranny under door or windowsill. Alas, how futile to try to keep out altogether such a dust-fiend as this! But I am enclosing here a description of one of these "Black Fridays", "Black Mondays", and so on, as these old-man dust-storms were called, according to the day on which they came. This description is from the *Barrier Miner*, 31st January 1945. The writer is

Constable Sowerby, Branch Secretary, Broken Hill. It is a far better description than I could write myself, and I should like you to read the best there is. This storm occurred nearly forty years after I left the Hill, but the account will give you a vivid idea of the Dust Devil we used to periodically know on black days. So here is Constable Sowerby's description of the Black Tuesday of 30th January 1945.

A dust storm which raged with unprecedented ferocity over Broken Hill yesterday afternoon caused a total black-out at 4 o'clock, which swallowed up the city in a "midnight" blackness for over an hour. The famous "Black Friday" storm of the early days and all previous black-outs were outclassed by yesterday's terrifying storm. All old residents, including some who came as early as the 1890s, agree that this was the worst blackout ever experienced.

It brought all traffic to a standstill for an hour, reduced street lights to pin-points, covered pedestrians in a few seconds with a grimy coat of dust, and unloaded hundreds of tons of fine dust throughout business shops, over their stocks, and through all residences.

A feature of the black-out was its deadly swiftness. There was no warning tide of rolling black clouds. One moment there was the familiar dense red of the dust storm which had been blowing with gradually-increasing intensity since about 3 o'clock, and then the next instant all light was blotted out as suddenly as when a blind is snapped down over a lighted window pane.

The pitchy blackness of a very dark night was a pale thing compared with this blackout, in which it was literally impossible to see more than a foot ahead. Although city business shops and houses had turned on electric lights half-an-hour before because of the red dust, the black pall swirled over these blobs of light and drowned them completely.

The powerful intersection lights in Argent Street were the only street lights visible, and these had been reduced to small star-points. From the Sulphide Street corner, for instance, only two of these were visible.

It was an incredible blackness and one that bewildered and stupefied people. Many workmen, who were coming back from the mines at that time, were lost. A few who attempted to drive in cars were lost within a few minutes and had to pull up. There were also more amusing instances of people who had been sleeping in the afternoon and awoke to find the world blacked-out.

While the storm was at its height, much of the dust was black soil dust, and people who were out in it were coated with a grey powder. Nevertheless, the black-out appears to have been caused mainly by a red dust storm of such density in the centre that the sunlight was completely shut off.

After the black-out had been maintained for about an hour, there was a very slight lifting for a minute or two, and in that time there was an indescribably eerie red glow struggling through the gloom, like the first flush of light through a thundery dawn. After two or three minutes the red glow vanished, and the black-out was total again. It maintained this density until ten minutes past five, and then the red light began to filter through again. There were further waves of darkness, but by 5.25 p.m. conditions had improved enough for people to venture out and try to reach their homes again.

Until the development of the green belt in the 1940s, wind-blown sand threatened to engulf Broken Hill and summer dust-storms were frequent. Even the green belt could not tame "a real Terror", which, as the picture shows, could blot out the sun in mid-afternoon.

At that stage, the dust storm was still severe, but there was a reasonable visibility. Temperatures dropped, and there was an icy touch to the wind. The storm continued until towards 11 o'clock last night, when it tailed off, and by midnight the skies were clear again.

The phenomenon was eerie and fantastic throughout. One of the strangest and most fantastic touches given to it was the groping of a funeral cortege through the main street in the darkness. The funeral was that of the little daughter of Mr and Mrs J. Olsen, of 502 Argent Street.

The cortege was just opposite Pellew & Moore's when the black-out occurred. Lights were snapped on, and these were just sufficient to give an eerie shadow shape to the hearse as it went on at a snail's pace.

The funeral pulled up outside the Palace Hostel, as further progress seemed impossible. Some of the staff came out with lights and assisted the mourners to the lounge, where they were given iced drinks.

Ten minutes later, the undertaker, Mr Norman Woodman, decided to move on again. The cortege groped its way on again through the intense darkness, but again had to halt at the Globe Timber Mills for a time.

The burial was in the Roman Catholic Cemetery, where the Rev. Father M. J. Higgins, assisted by the Rev. Father Clancy, officiated.

"It was two and a half hours before the funeral and the service were finished," said Mr Woodman. "It was very distressing to the mourners, and a great ordeal for all of us. We all greatly appreciated the kindness of the people at the Hostel."

Another touch of fantasy was given when the Fire Brigade received a call at 4.10 – when the black-out was complete – to a grass fire in the vicinity of the Congregational Church in Chloride Street. It could only proceed at a slow pace and had to depend on an emergency spotlight rather than headlights.

"We were informed by a man that there had been a grass fire, and that he had put it out," said the District Fire Officer, Mr Howell. "Dust storm or not, we had to turn out and make sure the fire was out. Because of the great danger of colliding with traffic or pedestrians in the total darkness, we put the brigade into first gear for the trip, which fortunately was only short. The visibility was so low that the headlights only showed a few feet, and we had to use the big spotlight.

"This shows a very powerful beam, but the dust was so thick that the light only extended about thirty feet. At the corners, we had a man out in front making sure that there was no traffic danger, and throughout the journey we tooted the horn."

From the onset of the black-out at 4 o'clock, the dust seeped into all buildings with an amazing rapidity. By half-past four office and house lights were showing dimly through a fog-like haze of dust which piled up on every exposed surface.

Worse still was the immediate effect on eyes and lungs. Within a few minutes people were choking and gasping from the effect of the dust. Throats were sore, and many others found that their eyes were quickly affected, becoming inflamed and smarting.

By 5 o'clock all interior effects and business places and residences were covered with a quarter to a half inch of dust which was the despair of those who knew they would have to clean it up. In shops, stocks were quickly covered with red dust. The effect was particularly striking in drapery stores.

It is no exaggeration to presume tons of dust were deposited inside the buildings alone. Meantime, outside the streets were being carpeted with dust, at least an inch thick, and inches thick whenever an obstruction caused a wind-break. Sand drifts were deep against window sills and ledges.

When visibility improved, it was found that streets, footpaths and lawns had been covered completely with sand, marked with rhythmical wind pattern marks, and for all the world like a strip of windswept beach. Many people were lost during the black-out. Mr R. O'Keefe, who was riding back from the Zinc Corporation, said, "I was riding a bicycle, and got to the bottom of the South Hill when the black-out came on. I nearly collided with another chap, and, in trying to avoid him, swerved. I was confident I was still on the main south road, but it was not till I neared the children's playground at Railway Town that I realized I had wandered off the route and become thoroughly lost."

His experience was typical of many workers who were caught by the storm. Motorists had a similar experience. Some of them became lost and took a wrong turning after travelling only a few yards. The bulk of city traffic was suspended for an hour. 'Buses pulled into the kerbs and stayed there until about a quarter past five.

Dozens of parents had an anxious time inquiring about their children who were out in the storm, and the telephone exchange was kept busy as they made inquiries. There was a great crowd of children at the baths at the time. To avoid all chance of panic, the caretaker immediately locked the doors and asked the adults present to look after the children. They were allowed to go home later on when the visibility was better.

There was no picture show last night because of the ravages of the dust storm within the theatres, caused by the thick coating of dust over seating, and also because of the fact that few people were prepared to venture out under these conditions.

At the height of yesterday's storm, Sergeant Durbin, R.A.A.F. railway transport officer stationed in Broken Hill, was advised from the aerodrome that two Air Force 'planes were in danger of being damaged. One 'plane had been blown a distance of 90 to 100 yards.

With a companion, Sergeant Durbin left in an Air Force utility truck for the 'drome, but had to wait en route for the black dust to subside.

They proceeded at a slow pace, the road just being discernible. On arrival, they found that the two pilots had been able to move the 'planes to safety, but not without much difficulty. Every time they started the engines, the tail of the 'planes lifted.

Mr H. Hyman, manager of a Sulphide Street grocery store, said, "I left in the car to see if my wife and family were safe, but got lost somewhere in Blende Street. I tried tagging along with the Fire Brigade by following their lights, but even then lost them, and had to pull up the car and stay there until the black-out lifted."

During the height of the storm there were no such things as brunettes or blondes. Women who were caught hatless in the dust had their locks coated thickly with grey dust. Glamour had a tough time as young and "grey-haired" girls smiled from dust-smeared cheeks.

Even food was not exempt from the attention of the dust, which penetrated cupboards with a deadly thoroughness. Many housewives, when they set for tea, found butter, sugar and milk covered with a ... red-dust film.

Miners, who are issued with respirators at the mines when work conditions are very dusty, had it all over the ordinary citizens. Two men were seen struggling home through the storm with respirators strapped over their faces.

Two railwaymen took an hour to walk from the "loco points" to Crystal Street Station, which should normally take no more than ten or twelve minutes. They could not see each other for dust, and could only find their way by clinging to each other's arms and walking between the lines.

A guest at the Soldiers' Hostel lay down in his room at 2.30 to take his usual afternoon nap. On waking, it was pitch dark, and he went to pull up the blind. Finding it was up and feeling sure that he must have slept through tea, he began to upbraid himself for being too convivial during the morning. Muttering "Good God, drunk again," he went out to find his tea at a pie cart. It was then 4.10 p.m.

Mr R. Coates, licensee of the Grand Hotel, was resting in the afternoon and went to sleep. He awoke at 4.15, and was astonished to find that the room was pitch dark. He rang the office, but could get no answer. He was firmly convinced that he had slept right through the afternoon and the night.

Guess the chagrin of certain ladies and young women who had appointed this fated afternoon for hair-sets and perms. Local beauty parlours had a full quota of clients on their hands when the storm broke. Some of the unlucky lasses, after paying well for the hairdo, had it ruined within a few minutes after they left the shop, as the hair was coated with grey or red dust.

Cafes, restaurants, and hotel bars were obvious points of refuge for pedestrians. These places were not only crowded with dust, but with people. Cafe staffs had an embarrassing time trying to serve food before the dust spoiled its appearance, but customers showed plenty of goodwill.

Many horse-drawn vehicles, mostly produce carts and carriers' vans, were isolated in the black-out. Drivers found the horses became restive and frightened, and in nearly all these cases they had to dismount and hold the horses' heads during that black hour.

Bar-room enthusiasts had no difficulty in appreciating their refreshment under the circumstances. Barmaids were kept busy washing down counters to try to free them from dust. Lounge-room patrons were more unfortunate, as the stifling curtain of dust turned even the most luxurious corners into a shambles in a short time.

The dust storm appears to have been general over a very wide area in the outback and caused black-outs from as far afield as Lake Eyre, in South Australia, over to places on the Queensland border.

Wireless operator of the Flying Doctor base, Mr F. Basden, said that he had received outback reports to this effect.

"Nearly all the outback stations reported black-outs of outstanding severity," said Mr Basden. "The worst effect seemed to be on a belt running north-east to east from Broken Hill through the White Cliffs area and up to the Queensland border.

"It seemed to hit the White Cliffs district about 7.30. It reached Owen Downs Station, which is towards the Queensland border, at 11p.m.

"Lake Stewart Station, in the north-western corner of the State, also reported that they had a severe black-out.

"A severe dust storm and black-out were experienced at Lake Eyre and many other places in Central South Australia.

"One man at Royal Oak Station said that at sundown the dust storm became ablaze with colour, with reds, yellows, blues, and other colours shining in the dust. It was like a painted dust storm."

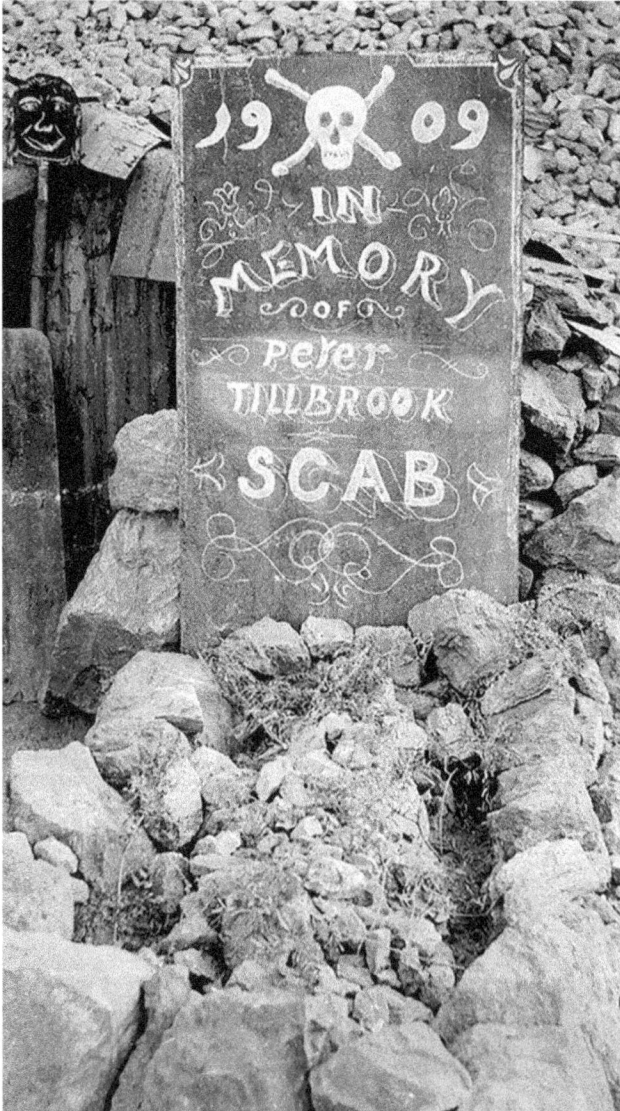

21. WE FIND MINERALS IN OTHER WORLDS

One trip of ours opened up an amazing new world to us boys, such a fantastic mineral discovery that we just could not believe it. You see, the world for us was Mum and Dad and the kids, the Big Mine and our work with the earthy minerals we so familiarly handled each day, and the week-ends and longed-for holidays when we could load up the cart and jog out into the hills. That was our little world, enclosed by the sky above, the familiar earth around us, the sun and moon, the day and the night.

On this particular holiday trip we were seeking a lost silver-mine believed to be somewhere in the Coko Range. So there we were, happy as Larry, jogging along in the old spring-cart, each quiet mile taking us farther and farther away from the Hill. A rough track, of course, nothing like what we call a road today, with innumerable rocky gullies to cross, and many a stony rise. Laughing like jackasses, perched along the board seat, we "balanced" the cart when on an incline one side of the "road" would be a foot higher or lower than the other. But what did we care, so long as we drove the cart so that the precious horse did not break his neck? It used to cost us, between us, 7s. 6d. for hire of that horse and cart for a week-end, a pound on holiday trips. Low, barren-looking spurs of the Barrier Range rose all around us, drab brown and covered with mulga. Distantly, though, our "mineralized" eyes noted that on the occasional limestone belts grew the mallee with its many suckers, with an occasional dense green whitewood vivid along the dry creek banks, the shrub-tree which shoots so quickly and vividly green after rain. Good cattle food, this. And now we saw plenty of bullock-bush, and remarked that the early bullockies just loved this bush. "Wherever the bullock-bush grows," they swore, "there I can take my team!"

For west of the Darling the fodder is far more bush and shrub than grass. Saltbush for the sheep, bullock-bush for the bullock, any old bush at all for the camel. Jumping out from the cart, excepting the driver, we manned the spokes of the wheels to give the horse a hand to climb up and over Fowler's Gap. Cunning old stager, that prad would have let us push along the whole box of tricks ourselves had it not been for the energetic driver at the reins. On board again, we were jogging past Fowler's Gap Hotel, despite the old prad's outraged attempt to stop "for a drink".

The hotel, a low-built, iron, rambling bush shanty in its sombre surroundings, drew our boyhood eyes and interest, of course, for, apart from countless tales told of it, was it not a fact that it boasted its own private cemetery down by the creek? Boy-like we wondered if the ghosts of the men who had got the horrors and staggered away into the hills ever returned in the lonesome nights to wander back to the shanty by the creek.

This rough track, still used, was a lonely stock-route of hundreds of miles coming from south-west Queensland down through the Warri Gate at the border fence to junction at Cobham Lake with the Milparinka track, wandering on through the Barrier Ranges to cross the South Australian border near Thackaringa and carry on all the long, long way to Adelaide. Here we would meet drovers, teamsters, travellers, sometimes wandering shearers. And here, midway between Queensland and Adelaide, they enlivened these lonely hills for a day and a night, then passed on.

We jogged past the old-time Fowler's Gap homestead and magpies were warbling, the mulga parrots and blue-bonnets were making merry in the trees shading the deep waterholes, a slate-grey thrush in one loud, strong, beautiful note was telling the whole world that everything was lovely.

Alas, I passed this way years and years later, after the motor-car had come, after the years and years of overstocking, the rabbits, the destruction of the timbers, the erosion. True, the road was a lot better, but still very rough by modern standards. We did not have to get out and push, as often we had to put our shoulders to the wheel of the old cart. But we were held up a day by a violent dust-storm that obliterated the track and all the world. The old homestead at Fowler's Creek was abandoned, the old hotel delicensed and forlorn. The once beautiful waterholes of the creek were silted up.

Where the thirsty stock had made pads down from the hills for water thunder-storms had deepened the pads into rills, following storms had deepened them into ravines, other rills had joined the developing ravines until, with nothing now to hold the scanty topsoil, a thousand ravines were presently pouring their precious silt down into the creek waterholes.

But as cheerily we jogged along in the old cart we knew nothing of the forces silently, ceaselessly, ever more swiftly working, the vengeful forces that man by his own hand had set working against himself in this now supposedly tamed land.

The day we camped at the foot of the Coko Range we sat yarning round the campfire, eagerly discussing whether we should have the luck to discover this lost silver lode. Talk ceased abruptly as a storm came roaring up with frantic rapidity. We sprang up as a ball of lightning flamed overhead with a hissing that split the skies – then all was drowned in a roaring explosion right behind us. In that vivid flash my mates' frightened faces, the bark, the veins in the leaves of the trees, were vivid as in a dazzling searchlight. Utter silence as we stood trembling, then the agitated "ding-dong, ding-dong, ding-dong" of the horsebell as the old horse lit out for fresh horizons, breaking the record in hobbles.

It was a meteorite, of course. It had not fallen just behind us, but miles and miles away. We forgot all about the lost silver-mine, and searched for the meteorite during the few precious days left to us. We never found it.

Back at the Hill, full of the great adventure, we youths who thought we knew such a lot learnt a lot in a very short time. The metallurgists explained that it could not have been "big as a house", probably it weighed only a few pounds, maybe a hundredweight. That a meteorite is a tiny fragment broken away from a comet. That meteorites encircle outer space, travelling at unbelievable speeds. That many of them are drawn towards the earth, pulled to us by gravitation. That immediately they are drawn into the "envelope" of air surrounding the earth their speed is slowed down very considerably, and soon the friction causes such heat that it is set on fire by the oxygen in the air and volatilized before it can reach the earth. "Otherwise," they said, "life would not be worth living!" They reminded us, too, that we already knew what happens to a hot piece of iron if we put it into a jar of oxygen – we'd seen similar experiments in the laboratory at our own School of Mines. They explained also that a meteorite is almost all iron, or a mixture of iron and nickel, but that meteorites also contain practically all the minerals known in the earth. Chemical analysis had proved it so.

This mention of chemical analysis somewhat abashed my mates, for this was bringing our special visitant from another world down to our own level. Our own lives were bound up in minerals, and chemical analysis.

"What minerals?" asked my particular mate, bluntly.

"Oh, practically all. Metallic iron, nickel, cobalt, felspar, manganese, magnesium, tin, copper, siderite, angite, chromium, titanium, lead. For good measure there's sulphur, silicon, oxygen, carbon, chlorine, carbon dioxide, sulphuretted hydrogen – practically the whole box of tricks. Minerals, non-minerals, gases."

And with a chuckle, the chemists, though very interested themselves in our account of the meteorite, left us to get over it.

To youthful minds, it took some getting over. The idea that "common minerals" such as those already so familiar to us could come to us from outer space looked far too much like leg-pulling.

It was all perfectly true, of course. Time has passed by since then and I know just a little more about meteorites, but it still seems very wonderful. And, strangely enough, more homely. That in outer space whirl countless worlds, many of which are built of the same materials as our own familiar earth, makes us feel not so lonely as it were.

It was many years later that I learnt that even very tiny diamonds have been found in meteorites. I wonder if "up there" there are space-men prospectors eagerly seeking their lives away in searching for gold and silver, and opals and diamonds and rubies.

Since that unforgotten night by the Coko hills when we and the old horse "near busted" ourselves with fright Man has moved so fast he is now seeking to find out. Already he is reaching up to even past where the meteorites meet the outer fringe of air to hurtle down towards us in vanishing flame. What will happen when Man's space-ships pass beyond the protecting air, out where the meteorites are flying through space – solid lumps of iron travelling at a thousand miles a second?

Just as well there is plenty of space "out there".

Truly, Man has advanced fantastically since boyhood days of the bullock-wagon, of Cobb and Co., the Darling Dreadnought and the camel-team.

That particular meteorite was found, though. At Wonnaminta station it appeared from the homestead as a big black streak coming across the sky, passing overhead with a shrieking, whizzing sound to land in a terrific explosion, apparently at Grey's Creek but actually a mile and a half away. Con White, the manager, and the stockmen quickly mounted and cantered across, certain they could find it. They couldn't.

But they did, three weeks later, when out on the run mustering.

It had fallen near Mount Browne, sixty miles away from the homestead. It is the terrific speed that deceives the eye; it is "here and gone" almost before the eye realizes it. Where we thought it had fallen beside us it had travelled a hundred miles or so farther. In later wandering years I knew of one that fell with a mighty explosion in a lonely Kimberley gorge. Cattlemen thought it had landed but five miles away, whereas it turned out to be nearer two hundred.

The musterers found the Wonnaminta meteorite buried a few feet in the rocky shale, and Con White sent it to the Sydney Museum.

22 THE LAST SECRET WEST OF THE DARLING

Wonnaminta was one of the great far western stations those days. Some had developed to carrying a hundred thousand sheep, and more. Alas, with now rapidly advancing deterioration of the country such figures would too often be reduced to twenty and thirty thousand. It all came about, of course, by fall of markets, by overstocking, by men not "knowing the country". But this deceptive country was very difficult to learn.

After the coming of the pioneers huge areas of country were taken up everywhere. The cattle thrived, began to increase, then rapidly became great herds. Rough homesteads were already built, out-stations began to appear. The discovery of the copper riches of Cobar added impetus to settlement in the west. A few years later the discovery of the Silverton silver-fields away farther west towards the South Australian border attracted a fresh stream of people, which brought the opening of "bullock-dray roads" from the Darling west to the South Australian border just as sheep began appearing. The rapid increase of cheap river traffic in transport for the silver camps as well as the little pastoral settlements had a mighty influence in the remarkable increase in sheep, the river transport solving the wool problem. With the discovery of the Broken Hill mines with their extraordinary and lasting riches the Far West was made. Discovery of the White Cliffs opal-fields was a brilliant but fleeting comet in that intensely interesting saga of the Far West.

By now the quiet, lonely river of the overlanders was very different. Heavily loaded Dreadnoughts from Wentworth on the Victorian border were thrashing upstream right across New South Wales to Bourke, to Walgett, even to the Queensland border. Great barges loaded with their house-high tiers of wool were being towed downstream right into the Murray and to Echuca, for Melbourne. Branching out from the river, from Menindee, Wilcannia, Bourke, and beyond, wound the bullock roads with the dust of hundreds of teams – bullock, horse, and camel – rising into bright sunlight as they lumbered their way out into the silver ranges, and out into the vastness towards hundreds of stations all along the western and north-western borders of New South Wales and to South Australia and the Queensland border. Telegraph lines were being laid, a bridge or two being built here and there.

During the season shearers on horseback, with the packhorse a-jingle with hobble chains and quart-pot were jogging along the river road, or singly or in groups of threes and fours carrying the swag along road or track from station to station, or congregating at favoured river waterholes awaiting the shearing to start. The rouseabouts would be with them, too.

Many of the shearers "followed the sheds" from State to State, which as a rule left them with a three months' spell until the season started again. Some during the off season "took it quietly" in Brisbane or Sydney as the case might be, though others – and, of course, the married men – had to take on other work to keep the billy boiling. The shearers were the aristocrats among bush workers, and made big money for those days, but they earned it. The exploits of the "gun" shearers were discussed by the campfires far and wide. It was fierce, back-breaking toil. I happen to know, for I've carried the swag to the sheds as a rouseabout and once eagerly seized the chance of a learner's pen. Three days of it and I was hobbling about like a roach-backed steer for a week afterwards, my hands and arms and legs having collected all the burrs and prickles in the bush, my nostrils protesting at the smell of cantankerous, kicking old wethers. So I learnt that I was not cut out for a shearer, just as I learnt I was not born a sailor bold. They can have their girls in every port and their shearing tallies for mine.

The ambition of nearly every shearer was to save enough to "take up a bit of land" and become a cocky. Alas, many fell by the wayside; the shanties on the lonely tracks and that spell in town after a hard season fleeced them to the bare pelt and saw them back on the roads again with the coming of the next season.

A minority, though, gained their heart's desire and helped develop the lands nearer the coast, where no doubt their sons are doing well today

– far better than the old man ever dreamt of. Yet a few again, imbued with the fear we all had those days of some day growing old and no longer being capable of hard toil, strove to save enough through the seasons to buy an annuity. I don't know if that idea is still in fashion these days, I hardly think so. The idea, with confirmed bachelors, was to "sell" their life savings for so much a week. Five pounds a week was, in general, the great goal. We used to look upon a man who could command five pounds a week for life, as away up near the millionaire class. These days it would hardly pay his tax, but then it meant, or appeared to mean, a heavenly security for the evening of his days.

In much later years, when passing through Sydney I would wander through Hyde Park and could always find a few pipe-smoking greybeards sitting contentedly there, just yarning and watching the world go by. These were some I'd known in youthful days, shearers who really at least had managed to buy their longed-for annuity.

Luckily for them, they've all gone west now, for if any were still alive their "independence money" would barely keep them. And thus again, as to numerous other things, even to wealth – five pounds a week independent income really *was* wealth those days – has come a great change in the course of half a man's lifetime.

Along the Darling, and many another river, drovers were on the roads with their plants, the riding horses and spare horses, their cook and cook's cart, their buggy or buckboard or packhorses. And, of course, the wonderful sheep-dogs. The big mail-coaches trotting, swaying and bumping along the rough roads, with crack of whip and encouraging shout, with steady hand on the ribbons urging the powerful horses make time with the mail. Since Freeman Cobb and his four American partners in 1853 had imported the first "leather spring" (thoroughbrace) coaches to Melbourne in a game attempt to open up transport to the Victorian goldfields, Rutherford by 1870 in New South Wales, Victoria, and Queensland was harnessing six thousand horses a day, travelling 28,000 miles per week, an epic and an exceedingly efficient one in pioneer Australian transport. The annual pay-roll was over £100,000, which meant a very big enterprise indeed in those days when wages were round about £1 a week. Only in 1914 was the last coach taken off the Wilcannia run, in 1924 the last in Queensland.

It was the American invention of the thoroughbrace that made these coaches the ideal method at that time of swift travelling along the Australian bullock-track roads. The braces were the springs, thick strips of very heavy harness leather, the ends clamped and bolted, thus "thoroughbrace", meaning thoroughly braced to carry any load through variation, imparting to the coach a "cushion" and "spring" enough to give passengers some comfort, and yet be practically unbreakable on the unbridged, often rocky, often deeply rutted roads.

So, far around the Silver City, all west of the Darling, the country was developing fast, the life of the mining districts, and the life of the man on the land. Both distinct, yet intermingled, and each had their market and other worries. The worry of the up-and-down metal market, the worry of the beef and horse and wool market. But for quite a long while now the future looked rosy for the men on the land, with a continuous market, and the best yet known, for wool and beef. Men pushed out, seeking yet more land; there was clamour for money for improvements, for the building of decent homesteads, for the scooping out of giant tanks for water conservation, the sinking of wells, the erection of tens of thousands of miles of fencing. The banks and other institutions lent large sums of money to many who asked. Labour now was never short of a job. Tank-sinkers, bore men, well-sinking men, fencers, scrub-cutters, station-hands, teamsters, drovers – there now was plenty of work everywhere. "Money to burn", and plenty of signs of easy wealth.

But in the eyes of the old hands there was a questioning. The wind had long since blown away the ashes of their campfires, nothing but a broken tea-pot that had been some pioneer woman's treasure, a rusted hobble link, the remains of a mud chimney, now showed where an original pioneer hut once stood. These men had learnt a lot. The heat, the dust, the silence had got into their blood, the sun on the saltbush, the hazy distances had brought wrinkles to their eyes, a grimness of life away out here had slowly born within them a deep questioning as to the true heart of this strange land.

For the man on the land it would eventually prove disastrous not to be able to "learn the country". So it happened in the case of the manager of one huge border station. "The rabbits will *never* come here!" he declared. "Even if they did there is grass and to spare, they could never make an impression."

That station then was running forty-two thousand head of cattle. When the rabbits came dry times came with them. When both rabbits and dry times had passed away there were just eight hundred head of cattle left alive on that station.

"It is a cruel country," said Goddard thoughtfully. From the veranda of pretty Weinteriga homestead he was gazing out over the plain that, now well grassed, looked a picture under a warm blue sky. From the big gums beside us came a whispering sigh as the river flowed silently by.

"Yes," mused Goddard, "this country holds fortune, but only for those who learn to master its every mood. And God knows it has many. You were speaking of men like Kidman, it is such as he that have the gift, or early learnt their lesson the hard way, often bitterly. And even they can be taught again in the cruelness which is in this country, this country that grows on one, I cannot understand why. For the country looks wonderful – *is* wonderful. The stock rolling fat, the increase greater and greater each year, the market good. At last you can build that fine new homestead, you can erect those hundreds, on the big places those thousands, of miles of fencing you so badly need. You get heavily into debt, but you will soon square it all up in another such season or two. Then the market falls, the rain doesn't come, the feed dries up. But the river does not dry up, it becomes a chain of waterholes barricaded by mud. When the feed is all gone the remnant of the starving stock stagger down the river banks – they would have one last drink from the still, brown depths away below. But they never reach there, they sink in the bog and die. And the crows are waiting there in their thousands, croaking their Dead March. And when everything but the crows is dead you are ruined. Then the rain comes and a fortnight later the country is a riotous green pasture – and nothing to eat it."

Goddard had learnt a lot about this strange country, and was to learn more – that a fence can vanish in a night.

In the sandy area south of Menindee he had, with considerable expense and labour and time, built a line of fence across the run. Thankfully he completed the job and went dog-tired to his blankets. In the morning he stared out towards the new fence and could not even see where it had been.

During the night a violent dust-storm had raged, had blown masses of dried roly-poly and buckbush against the fence, thus making an effective dam, a wall against the driving sand. And on through the night the storm had piled its sand against the fence until by morning it had completely obliterated it, as a snowstorm would overwhelm and pile up over a man.

But this pile would not melt.

A strange country, yes, but – after it rains!

Everyone is cheerful after rain. The station owner feels better. The station manager feels better, his wife, the jackeroos, the hands feel better. Even the cook! Everywhere are smiles, merry whistling, cheery talk. The horses feel better, the cattle and sheep. The station dogs' tails wag eagerly, they want to jump up on you, to bark at the least excuse. The fowls cackle, the birds put vim into their flight and chirp. The moist breath of the reviving earth arises under the warm sun, the smoke in a ribbon of blue rises from the kitchen chimney. The trees and grasses stretch fresh green leaves to the sun. The mailman sings to his horses. The swagman's swag is lighter as he plods cheerily along. The air smells sweet with life, warm is the sun, blue the sky west of the Darling.

The real bushman is an earthy man, loving the life he deeply feels is within the earth. He is ever watching things springing up, withering, dying – yet springing to life again after rain. During hard times anxiously he sees his horses and cattle growing poorer, sees his breeding ewes will not have the fresh young food that will put the life into them and make them fertile. After rain he sees the life springing fresh on every side, feels it in himself. No wonder he longs for rain.

"It does me good, too!" once confided Greasy Bob the artist, the wool-scourer who never washed.

The station cook, a grumpy sort, declared later it would take Noah's Flood to make Greasy Bob smell sweet.

Yes, rain brings life. Desaile, who had learnt a lot about the country and was making good, built his lovely new outhouse of cement, using sandhill sand. Carefully sieved the sand, too. Rain came, and a week later that pretty brand-new outhouse was like a colander where wee paddy-melon vines were bursting forth.

"No man will ever learn this country!" remarked the Storm Bird one morning. It was on Culpaulin station and the Storm Bird was indulging in desultory conversation with Sweet William, so called because of his bad temper.

"Why won't no man ever learn this blarsted country?" demanded Sweet William.

"Because it's just as full of hazards as a sheep is of burrs."

"Yah!" growled Sweet William, and spat.

"If you had any brains you'd see it, too!" declared the aggrieved Storm Bird.

"Yah, brains!" sneered Sweet William. "If *yours* was dynamite they wouldn't blow off your hat!"

The resultant all-in fight was a great joke from Wilcannia to the Cliffs for many a day.

Thus, after the battling of the pioneers had come the water transport, the copper and silver and opals and settlement, with vast increase of herds. Then came high prices for stock and wool, bringing increasing prosperity. Which brought – happily in only a minority of cases, but definitely, distinctively, a mistake – the attempt to establish a rough and ready but sharply defined autocracy of its own, perhaps best summed up as "Government House", as some of the great homesteads were presently called. This was particularly marked on lands bought and controlled by oversea interests, and was a phase distastefully and very dubiously looked upon by the old hands.

For long since they had learnt that in this country a man must work. This country would heat him well enough if he nursed it, if he put back into it quite a lot of what he took out of it. "Look after your land," they would soberly declare, "and it will look after you."

They feared the rape of the land, the same old story which means disaster to both man and earth.

Already far and wide were ominous signs that the balance of Nature was being upset, and Earth was beginning to rebel. And the balance is set far more delicately west of the Darling than in eastern New South Wales and Victoria.

Perhaps a slight incident will best illustrate the changes threatening. You have met a long, lanky, drawly-voiced bush lad before – Sid Kidman. He was gradually getting on his feet now, but when passing a pretentious new station homestead he would never enter there, preferring to pull off and camp alone by the creek, later to visit the men's quarters for a yarn. For now, in this once so hospitable bush, "Government House" was no place for a young dealer in horses, a wanderer, a toy drover seeking a job of droving a few paltry head of stock. To men who now owned or managed a hundred thousand head of sheep or twenty or thirty thousand head of cattle the right place for a roughly clad bushman was the men's hut or the creek, not amidst the evening dress at "Government House". It was typical of the changes that were to come to this country that this far-seeing wanderer who rode to the creek by evening and had departed before the dawn was to become the owner of many of these great stations.

He was riding along the Wilcannia road one morning with a chance acquaintance when a squatter's turn-out passed them, leaving a cloud of dust. Kidman blew the dust from his nostrils, took off his hat, ruefully surveyed it. "I bought a new hat," he drawled, "cost me seven and sixpence. And now these jolly tinkers cover it with dust! The country won't stand it, Jack. It may run to a seven-and-sixpenny hat, but it won't run to a special train."

The squatter was travelling express a long distance to railhead, where a special train had been engaged to take him to Adelaide.

In the main, the wise man was the man who could sit down for a feed at a drovers' camp and get up saying gratefully, "Well, I'm jolly glad for that feed, there's many would be glad of it." Such were the men who had "learnt the country", even though the feed was but a hunk of salt beef and damper, a billyful of black tea.

Ah, but how I wish that I could enjoy a city meal as I have enjoyed many and many a feed under similar circumstances!

And so the good earth west of the Darling was changing. How many of us realize that the earth, the earth upon which we walk and build our houses and sleep, has a life of its own? That we can knock it about and do atrocious things to it, just as we do to our own wonderful bodies, and it will build itself up and recover and serve us again, just as our bodies do? But if you go too far it will brutally retaliate, and that part of it may even die. We have doctors and hospitals and cemeteries to try to repair the harm we so often do our own selves – and what of the earth?

Yes, the earth has life of its own. And the man on the land who has learnt this fact of his own paddock, is the successful farmer.

Long, sometimes heart-breaking years were to pass before men learnt to work this harsh land without disaster, to take of the wealth it offers without breaking their own hearts. Even now they have to be ever watchful, ever careful. The causes of this are too many and complicated for us to discuss here.

Meanwhile, with the passing of the years it dawned on these men that besides wealth of wool and cattle, of minerals and gems, this deceptive land held yet another secret – how many *does* she hold, I wonder? – the Secret of the Lakes.

These actually run from the Queensland border, those shallow depressions, you remember, that are a flower-garden after floods. But these lakes in particular came to be called the Menindee Lakes. They are much larger and deeper than those to the north; Lake Menindee if memory be correct, has a shoreline of thirty-seven miles when full, and is twelve feet deep at its deepest.

This chain of Menindee Lakes stretches from just above Menindee, parallel with the Darling, south almost to Wentworth on the Murray at the Victorian border. Only during heavy floods when the Darling is overspilling its banks miles wide these lakes fill as a backwash.

Lakes Bijiji, Tandure, Pamamaroo, Menindee, Emu, Cawndilla, Nettlegoe, Kangaroo, Tandou, Coombah, Mindona, Yartla, Popilta, Traveller's, Yellow, Popio, Milkengay, Nearie, Windamingle, Milkengar, Victoria – these are the largest, and there are many other smaller ones, and swamps.

As the Darling recedes the waters from numbers of these lakes slowly drain back into it, helping keep the main stream replenished. In the deeper lakes the water lies for a long time, to the content of stock and innumerable wildfowl. Under the warm sun as each lake dries it turns into a verdant paddock of clover and herbage. Those are the times when stock grow rolling fat, increase and multiply, and you can really hear the heart of the man on the land singing with the birds. Even the grumpiest of old sour-dough station cooks secretly sings in his sacred kitchen at such times. I have a soft spot in my memory for the station cook, for often in my homeless wandering days he has given me food and shelter on a bitter night.

Thus, the lakes blossom into a blaze of glory as the water leaves them. Alas, during prolonged droughts their hot, bare beds often become putrid with the carcasses of perished beasts.

Man, as the battling years from the days of the overlanders passed by and he gradually "learnt" the country, began to dream of a weir, a dam here and there across the Darling that even with a fresh or a light flood in the river would raise the height of water just there a few feet so that the excess water would flow along the old natural channels and thus fill lake after lake. Thus they could be filled again and again, could grow herbage again and again, not only during that rare year when an old-man flood spilled the river water for many miles far out into the bush over its banks. Thus this otherwise wasted floodwater could be held in bondage, not alone to grow new pasturage, to save and increase flocks and herds, but to hold precious water also far out from the river waterholes.

And why not? For this was Nature's own scheme many, many years ago, in the days when Sturt's Inland Sea far to the north-west was gleaming there in fact. For in those days of the Great Animals the chain of the Menindee Lakes was thus often kept filled by the river, for it is plain to the bushman to see that the now filled in channels were much deeper.

So it is a practical thing that can be done, though over that widespread distance it took years and the experiences and observations of many men to see it. But they did see it and dreamt of it and talked of it, and at long last it is to be done. The sooner the better, for we badly need land that can be made rich. And now we have the great machines to do it, and it is a comparatively easy job.

Could it possibly be Destiny again? That Nature in this strange country kept her last – *is* it her last? – great secret until the time came when we had those machines?

Nature has helped us in yet another way. Not only has she provided the chain of lakes to be filled by the excess water from the Darling, but she has also made numerous channels running out from the river towards the lakes, similar to the Channel Country of the Cooper, Georgina, and Diamantina in the Corner Country of south-west Queensland. But some of these Menindee channels are giants, really river-beds. These are the anabranches, swirling torrents during heavy floods, otherwise deep, dry channels, their bottoms littered with the fallen leaves and dead branches dropped from the gnarled old gums that so gracefully shade their deep, thirsty beds. One of these great anabranches breaks out westward from the river below Menindee, then runs south through a chain of lakes to reach the Murray near Wentworth. Thus a very considerable area west of the Darling from Menindee south, right to the Victorian border, lies there already "dug" by Nature, awaiting that slow-coach Man to do a little damming work and open up a few channels so that when flood-waters come they can fill the lakes and channels and bring rejuvenated life to a very large portion of that strange country.

And I really believe that Nature here is offering us, not only the food to increase our flocks and herds, but actually a new Mildura. For this land has long since proved that, given only moderately permanent water, it will grow fruit and vegetables equal to the best.

What would Sturt say, could his spirit see from Menindee to Wentworth one great orchard!

Silverton Tram turning into Argent Street, Broken Hill, 1908.

23 SEEN AS IN A MIRAGE

Alas, tragedy ended my active days at the Hill. On one of our holiday trips into the back country with boyhood mates I drank water impregnated with the typhoid germ. Then came nearly three months in hospital – what a different hospital to the fine, excellently equipped hospitals there today! But the frightfully overworked staff were essentially the same; the proof is that that was just fifty years ago and I still have not forgotten the tireless devotion of the doctors, nurses, and wardsmen, often "asleep on their feet" through strain and overwork. When eventually consciousness slowly returned there dawned weeks of nightmare. Men were dying night and day in the hot, overcrowded wards, some of which were but iron sheds, the lucky ones silently, others in wild delirium, still others, particularly the pneumonia cases, gasping out their lives most awfully. Lying there, trying not to listen, a lad slowly recovering while strong men were dying, I made up my mind that the only human being I should ever lift my hat to would be the man or woman who had toiled to discover some cure for disease or the alleviation of pain. My sentiments are the same today.

When at last I was taken from hospital it was to learn that mother was dead; she had caught the typhoid while nursing me. So I left Broken Hill.

It was years and years, and I had wandered all over the continent, before I saw the Hill again.

But ever and anon throughout the wandering years, in State after State, the Hill, and particularly the old Big Mine, has "come back"; its influence even reached me in a Turkish gun-pit in Palestine. In the far north of Western Australia, when from a great sea cliff I watched a catamaran paddled by a wild blackfellow of those days carelessly making his way across a sparkling blue sea to the wonderful Iron Islands of Yampi Sound.[1] In more recent days while I was crossing South Australia by car with on the red earth beside us for two hundred miles and more the giant pipe-line taking water from the Murray so that Whyalla in the waterless lands towards those Iron Knobs could live and become a modern town. During all these wandering years and throughout two world wars the influence of the Silver City, seen as through a Mirage of Life, has clung around me to the present day.

My first job after I left the Hill, still convalescing from fever, was seaman aboard a little paddle-wheel steamer trading between Sydney and

---

[1] Since then, this wild location has become scene of great activity by the "Big Mine" people.

Newcastle, and up the Hunter River to Morpeth. Such a change! A seaman before the mast, rolling through pitch-black night, lashed by spray, buffeted by howling winds – how different from the firm brown land stretching far away into mirage under the mighty dome of sunlight west of the Darling!

I made but very few trips, for the utterly changed conditions to a lad still weak from typhoid brought on that then so dreaded relapse. But I still remember the countless bugs and fleas so ferociously active in that tiny bunk, the rushing, hissing away of the water as the glistening paddle-wheels dipped and churned and thrashed their way through the ever-rolling waves, that breath-taking swaying that verily seemed to touch one "side" of the ocean, to pause, then slowly roll back in a great, tremulous arc to dip at the "other side". On stormy nights it seemed to me surely she could never come up again. When it was my watch up in the crow's nest, away up there, alert for the light of another ship, I would see the mighty heaven, ablaze with its coloured lanterns, roll slowly over us and dip right down to port, slowly right itself to roll right up over the ship and dip right away down into the sea at starboard. How that sky used to roll! With the wind gremlins whistling in my ears, I'd be ready to shout to the Officer of the Watch, "Light to starboard, sir!" when I was sure it was not a star, ready to tug at the big bell whose deep tone seemed to ring so defiantly out into the night, far over the tumbling wastes of waters as this tiny, so important human insect would hurl his shout into the teeth of the wind, "Eight bells! And – all's – well-ll-ll!"

The tucker I thought plentiful and delicious – Heaven knows what a seaman of today would do about it; but a lad in those days who had undergone that long starvation convalescence from typhoid simply wolfed it. There was novelty, too, in the company of good-natured men whose interest – except of common humanity and the struggle to earn a crust – environment, and life-work were so utterly different to those of the men west of the Darling. They were tough men who ran the little ships those days under such tough conditions, just as the land pioneers had to be tough to survive the conditions of those battling days. The seamen and men of the land are just as tough today when needs be, but I am glad that time has brought unbelievably better conditions of living to both. Fairly often I am aboard some ship of today, and occasionally I am allowed to peep at the crew's quarters. Immediately then memory flies back to the dark, smellful, unbelievably cramped dungeons of the little ship alive with their battalions of livestock, and I try to picture the amazement on my old sea-mates' faces if they could but see such a fo'c's'le as this of our modern day.

When travelling through the country that I knew as bush I am glad, too, to see the grandsons of the land battlers I knew come spinning into town in their big new cars, money in their pockets, well clothed and smiling. It is a better, and far happier world, for such vastly improved conditions make life so much more worth living. If only humanity would learn to chain the Dogs of War we could now make this world for all people a goodly place indeed.

On that Newcastle run I grew familiar with one spot as an evil-smelling, most desolate hole. This was a large area of mud flats and mangrove swamp by Port Waratah, under water at high tide as the little steamer churned past. It was impossible to visualize that gloomy waste ever being of use to man.

Today one of the greatest and the most successful steelworks in the world rears its busy buildings, its mighty hive of industry, over that very swamp. On occasion in recent years I have been through those works, for some of my boyhood friends from the Assay Office on the Big Mine have played their part in that gigantic enterprise and still work there.

I have a good memory for anything that has interested me, but more than once I have roamed through and around those acres of buildings and wonderfully organized activity and tried in vain to "bring back" that desolate swamp. It is as if it had never been; the little steamer churning past the mud flats seems but a phantom memory of some dream gone by.

Like the Silver City, seen as through a mirage.

What human mind, in those early days at the Hill, could foresee the influences that, gradually developed through the Big Mine, would build on this distant mud flat probably the greatest works of steel and allied industries in the world – all starting from a "hill of mullock" far out in the lonesome wilderness west of the Darling.

As a life on the ocean wave was not for me, it was back to the bush again, humping bluey on the long straight track from Walgett to the Ridge. And the world was wonderful. Just the blue sky ever so far up, the whispering leaves of the box and the budda and the wilga, the happy-go-lucky birds, the ears of an inquisitive wallaby peeping above the tufted grass, the brown track stretching ahead into distance where both walls of trees slanted towards each other and closed up and obliterated the road. But as step by step I plodded on, so the end of the track squeezed the trees aside, and though there were always the trees there was always the brown track steadily opening out, step by step, into the distance ahead. And now the big, lumbering Walgett mail-coach came pushing through the trees on to the track where dust rose up as horses and coach quickly grew. It was quite exciting, in that warm loneliness that was not lonely, tramping towards a coach that now had grown a voice in hoof-beats and song of wheels. And that coach was moving, for this was modern speed of the day, the horses smartly trotting to deliver mails and passengers on time. As the Mail rattled past there was a cheery flourish of the whip from the driver, a shouted "Good day! Good luck!" from the passengers as I waved the old hat in reply. And I was plodding through the slowly settling dust, alone with the brown track and sweet bushland again, to meet but one horseman in fifty miles.

Then at last the box-tree-clad ridges of Lightning Ridge rose before me.

Some years before, on this big sheep-station, the ironstone pebbles on a ridge had been struck in a blinding flash of lightning, terrifying the horse of a passing stockman sheltering from the storm. Symbolical, indeed, for deep down under the sandstone of those ridges, under that terrific pressure, in darkness nestled a blazing wealth of the loveliest fire stones the world has ever known.

The black opal.

Fervently I had wished, when camped along the Namoi and carrying the swag to the Ridge, that I would find some. My company the swirl of some big fish, the hoarse, solemn croak of a mopoke, I would fall asleep by the campfire coals under some huge old-man gum, dreaming of flashing opals, opals, opals everywhere, so many opals that I did not have bags enough to put them in; my trembling hands would become exhausted scooping up those opals that were plentiful as the pebbles down by the water's edge.

What a queer land of fantasy is that mysterious world of dreams!

Charlie Nettleton had found the Ridge twelve months before, the only black-opal field as yet discovered in the world, a treasure-house of the most magnificent gems the world has ever known. When I dropped the swag at Watty Thompson's bark store the white tents of a thousand gougers stretched between the ridges among the box-trees from Knobby's along the Flat on to the Three Mile. Wollaston had taken his first parcel of black opals to London, gems unknown to the jewellery world, and was experiencing the usual old struggle of placing unknown gems upon the market. Though long since the trade had eagerly bought Australian light opals for the big profits they were making, most firms shied off these black gems for a time, for the trade since unknown years before the Birth of Christ had only known of light and white opals. Again, unbelievable as it seems now, as had happened with Queensland and White Cliffs gems, some "experts" really believed these black opals were fakes. Oh, how often by the campfires longingly we used to wish we could make such unparalleled gems! However, almost immediately, the American market took to the new gems and all was well.

Ted Murphy was Wollaston's resident buyer on the field, and one bright day cheerily indeed I trudged along the timbered track to Murphy's bark hut with a little parcel of opals snugly wrapped away in a tobacco tin, not only eager to sell the opals when a shilling really meant a shilling, but to meet Ted again and hear news of the Hill and the Cliffs.

Long Ted Murphy wore his slow smile and big black beard. Ted was well seasoned now, older than the lad who, tossing in delirium, had awaited death from typhoid in his hot tent on Mount Browne far west of here, west of the Darling. Seated before the board table in his neat hut, he gravely examined the opals, he who now had examined and classed and valued and bought hundreds of thousands of pounds' worth. Mine was a very tiny parcel indeed, but it meant such a lot to me. Gravely we bargained. Finally he bought. I was secretly delighted as he handed me the cheque.

Long years afterwards, in Sydney one day, he brought me one of those tidy books of his and showed me the entry of the first opals he bought from me those years ago, for £26 10s. if memory is correct. And that was a big sum of money to a wandering lad in those days; I could live on the Ridge for exactly twelve months on that money.

Murphy was quite agreeable to a yarn about his beloved Cliffs and the characters he knew so well there. Then casually he mentioned a bit of news about the Hill.

"On my last visit to the Cliffs business took me to the Hill," he said. "You might be interested to know that the Big Mine tried an experiment at Port Pirie. Smelted some of that iron ore from the Iron Knobs across the gulf into pig iron. Just five tons of it as a trial. It turned out to be first-class pig iron, and had a ready sale. It would be funny if the Old Mine turned from silver to iron, or even steel!"

Prophetic words that Ted and I were to recall in coming years.

That iron was responsible for the building of a modern town and port called Whyalla in that waterless wilderness. Here, too, would spring up big jetties, the machinery of a wonderfully efficient loading system; modern ships would steam here to be loaded with the rich, red iron ore that, shipped to Newcastle in New South Wales, was to make a great industrial city. Water would be brought to this South Australian waste in giant pipes from a river more than two hundred miles away, precious water without which this model town of Whyalla, with its up-to-date efficiency, its green trees and lawns and gardens, now an oasis in a desert, could never have been built. A railway would be built thirty-three miles inland to Iron Knob, where another though smaller town would develop. All "out of iron" – iron, that in the swiftly coming future was to prove a mighty aid in the saving of Australia.

Ah, no! Ted Murphy and I, sitting yarning in his opal-buyer's hut, never dreamt of such far-reaching events. But then, which of us can see under the ground? Who can peer into the future?

Who could then have dreamt of a Port Kembla?

Few of us then dreamt that iron is of greater value far than silver or gold. Fewer still that, from the treasure of a sunburnt hill west of the Darling, harnessed by the brains and labour of Man, was to spring a chain of mighty industries and a bastion of defence for a continent. No man could then have thought so. But who can tell? Maybe some lone mind glimpsed it as a vision on a shimmering horizon – a vague thought-wave hazy in a mirage rising from the heart of the Silver City.

LASSETER'S DIARY

Transcribed with Mud-Maps

Harold Bell Lasseter had always claimed he had found an immense reef of gold hundreds of miles west of Alice Springs. In 1930, with Australia in the grip of Depression, a privately funded expedition led by Fred Blakeley, accompanied Lasseter in an attempt to relocate the reef.

Blakeley left Lasseter at Ililba, and Lasseter continued his trek towards the Olgas with a dingo shooter and their camels. Lasseter continued to be introspective and brood, prompting Lasseter to go off alone.

In March 1931 an expedition led by bushman Bob Buck found Lasseter's body at Winter's Glen, and his diary at Hull's Creek, wherein it describes how after his camels bolted, he was alone in the desert, encountering a group of nomadic Aboriginals who offered him food and shelter. Blind, exhausted and dying, Lasseter made one last attempt to walk from Hull's Creek to Uluru.

The diary was purchased by Ion Idriess from Lasseter's widow in 1931, and from it he wrote the best-seller Lasseter's Last Ride. Tom Thompson has transcribed the diary with its original mud-maps, including those not in the diary itself and Lasseter's drawings.

First edition, 90 pages, available from ETT Imprint.

LASSETER'S LAST RIDE

An epic in Central Australian Gold Discovery

ION IDRIESS

The 45th edition now out from ETT Imprint, Exile Bay, illustrated with photographs, extracts from Lasseter's Diary and letters.

Morning Post (London):-"Perhaps the greatest of Australia's real life epics."

Daily News (Perth) :-"No grimmer tragedy than Lasseter's Last Ride has been recorded in the annals of our exploratory history .... Yet Idriess manages to keep his reader wavering between laughter and tears."

Otago Daily Times (N.Z.) :-"One almost finds it difficult to believe that the story is modern and true."

Sydney Mail :-"One of the most graphic, most poignant, and most absorbingly interesting tales that the chronicles of Australian exploration - those treasure stores of dramatic adventure - have ever revealed."

The Herald (Melbourne) :-"A true story that for sheer excitement, thrills, and sustained suspense, cannot be surpassed by even the most imaginative novelist."

The Telegraph (Brisbane) :-"This thrilling book reveals in convincing colour, the details of a story that is history and that has all the elements of stark tragedy."

PROSPECTING FOR GOLD

ION IDRIESS

From the Dish to the Hydraulic Plant, and from the Dolly to the Stamper Battery. With chapters on Prospecting for Opal, Tin, and other Minerals; and a chapter on Prospecting for Oil, by Dr W. G. Woolnough, F.G.S., Geologist to the Commonwealth of Australia.

This illustrated book, written by a prospector with a lifetime's experience, will save the new chum gold-seeker much labour and time and disappointment, and will teach the old hand many a payable wrinkle.

Dr W. G. Woolnough (Geologist to the Commonwealth of Australia) :-"Your hints should be invaluable to all, beginners and experienced men alike."

Canadian Mining and Metallurgical Bulletin :-"The volume will arouse the reader's interest at the outset and hold it to the end."

Queensland Government Mining Journal :-"It tersely sums up a lifetime's knowledge gained at first hand acquired by a man well equipped to pass his experience on to others."

Engineering and Mining Journal (New York) :-"This book is replete with good methods, described simply. Lack of space forbids quoting the terse directions."

Rabaul Times (New Guinea) :-"Invaluable. Each bit of advice and information is practical, as it comes from an old-time miner himself."

Now in its 21st edition, 190 pages, available from ETT Imprint.

www.ingramcontent.com/pod-product-compliance
Lightning Source LLC
Chambersburg PA
CBHW021229090426
42740CB00006B/448